INDIVIDUAL
REFERENCE
FILE

Edgar Cayce's Famous "Black Book"

Edgar Cayce's secretary, Gladys Davis, and research assistant, Mae Gimbert St. Clair, compiled 130 subjects from the Cayce readings into this *individual reference file*—one of the most sought-after publications of Edgar Cayce's A.R.E., where it came to be referred to as simply, "the black book."

This new paperback edition of *Edgar Cayce's Famous Black Book* is rich in it's sampling of the Edgar Cayce readings, from the Akashic Records and info on allergies to soul development, telepathy, and the treatment for varicose veins, you can find practical information that you can use at once, including simple remedies and guidelines to enhance your health; spiritual and metaphysical truths to live by; and insights into how to make your life more worthwhile.

Edgar Cayce

INDIVIDUAL REFERENCE FILE

of Extracts from The Edgar Cayce Readings

Referred to as the "black book" in
Edgar Cayce, the Sleeping Prophet, by Jess Stearn

Compiled by
GLADYS DAVIS TURNER
and
MAE GIMBERT ST. CLAIR

Note

None of the extracts in this file are presented as sectarian teachings or as prescription for the treatment of diseases. The intention is rather to show the variety and point of view of psychic information obtained by individuals in the course of Edgar Cayce readings on their personal problems and questions. Application of medical information found in the Cayce readings should be undertaken only with the advice of a physician.

For a list of suppliers and sources of hard-to-get items found in the *Individual Reference File* write to: Membership Services, Edgar Cayce's A.R.E., 215 67th Street, Virginia Beach, VA 23451-2061.

2nd Paperback Printing, June 2018

ISBN 978-0-87604-835-1

Printed in the U.S.A.

CONTENTS

Introduction

The ability of Edgar Cayce to give detailed information on any subject while under self-hypnosis is a startling phenomenon. What is even more astounding is the accuracy and reliability of that information on virtually any topic.

The first edition of *Edgar Cayce's Black Book* was compiled in the 1960s by Edgar Cayce's secretary, Gladys Davis Turner, and an early member of Cayce's office staff, Mae Gimbert St. Clair. Since that time, it has served as an A-to-Z guide of information found in the Cayce readings. Because of its helpfulness on many different topics, it has sometimes been called the Individual Reference File (or *IRF* for short).

Although the vast majority of the Cayce material deals with health and every manner of illness, countless topics were explored by Cayce's psychic talent: dreams, philosophy, intuition, business advice, the Bible, education, childrearing, ancient civilizations, personal spirituality, improving human relationships, and much more. In fact, during Cayce's lifetime, he discussed an amazing 10,000 different subjects, and the Edgar Cayce database of readings (available online to A.R.E. members) consists of a mind-boggling 24 million words!

The Cayce legacy presents a body of information so valuable that Edgar Cayce himself might have hesitated to predict their impact on contemporary society. Who could have known that eventually terms such as meditation, auras, spiritual growth, reincarnation, and holism would become household words to millions? Edgar Cayce's Association for Research and Enlightenment (A.R.E.) has grown from its humble beginnings to an association with Edgar Cayce Centers in countries around the world. Today, the Cayce organizations consist of hundreds of educational activities and outreach programs, children's camps, a publishing company, membership benefits and services, an international network of volunteers, massage and health services, prison and prayer outreach programs, conferences and workshops, internet and online activities, and affiliated schools (Atlantic University at AtlanticUniv.edu; and the Cayce/Reilly School of Massage at CayceReilly.edu).

For decades, the Cayce readings have stood the test of time, research, and extensive study. Further details of Cayce's life and work are explored in such classic books as *There Is a River* (1942), by Thomas Sugrue; *The Sleeping Prophet* (1967), by Jess Stearn; *Many Mansions* (1950), by Gina Cerminara; and *Edgar Cayce: An American Prophet* (2000), by Sidney Kirkpatrick.

Throughout his life, Edgar Cayce claimed no special abilities nor did he consider himself to be some kind of twentieth-century prophet. The readings never offered a set of beliefs that had to be embraced but instead focused on the fact that each person should test in his or her own life the principles presented. Though Cayce himself was a Christian and read the Bible from cover to cover every year of his life, his work was one that stressed the importance of comparative study among belief systems all over the world. The underlying principle of the readings is the oneness of all life, a tolerance for all people, and a compassion and understanding for every major religion in the world.

Today, the Cayce organizations continue the Cayce legacy by creating activities and programs that provide individuals with opportunities for profound personal change—physically, mentally, and spiritually. Further information about Edgar Cayce's A.R.E., as well as activities, materials and services is available at EdgarCayce.org.

INDIVIDUAL
REFERENCE
FILE

Adolescence

3350-1   F.55   11/5/43

Remember, in such a program [physical education for teenage girls] to include first spiritual education, next physical—that of exercise, that of proper dress, proper tone of hair, proper care of hair, proper care of body, proper activities that will bring out the better attributes of each individual. For all may have heads and eyes, feet and arms, and a body, yet all may put them to different usages—but all to the glory of God. For God, the Lord thy God is *one!*

Physical, mental, spiritual education, social activities all should be to one purpose. Not too much of the satisfying of the emotions but that the body as the temple of the living God may be a more beautiful place for thine own worship as well as those that may be directed by the activities of the entity.

5384-1   F.19   7/20/44

. . . begin with children in their early teen-age—eleven, twelve, thirteen years of age, the juniors—and make a social life, make a spiritual background; make each of them find within that which they may do the better . . . analyze such activities by the study of the character of each individual child . . .

. . . study camp life for boys or girls of this particular age. That which is character-forming and let the background of each be . . . of spiritual purposes and not of material selfishness.

281-39   1/12/38

Q-9. How can I best direct boys and girls of the junior age in meditation? . . .

A-9. These are periods in the lives of boys and girls when there [are] the greatest chemical changes taking place within their bodies. This must ever be taken into consideration, if the more will be accomplished with such groups.

There is at this period the first of the doubts arising in each mind, by the very field of their individual activity. This, too, must be taken into consideration.

3

This is the period also when ideals are formed in the mind and heart of each. This, too, must be taken into consideration.

And thus programs prepared in which, at the different sessions, all phases of the experiences and changes that are being wrought are given opportunity for full expression.

Hence the presentation of the life of Jesus, of Peter, of the rest of the Apostles, of the Holy Women, of the teachers; not only as to their great accomplishments but as to their faults, their fancies—that each individual may draw comparisons. For as has so oft been given, let each individual realize that to make the Christ Consciousness a part of self is to realize the activities of the individuals that manifested same in their experience and their lives; that their *lives—as* names, as individuals—are not only as history or historical facts but are *experiences* in the life of each and every individual!

What boy or girl has not experienced that quickness of speech as Peter? that desire to step out and *try* those very things as seen by the Christ-life?

What boy has not seen the experience of where he, too, has denied His presence here or there, for the moment, to be as one of the crowd?

What girl has not seen in the life of Mary, in the life of Elizabeth, in the life of Martha, in the life of Rhoda, those things that have been her own experiences?

Then in the preparation, bring these facts—not as histories or historical facts alone, but as expressions of the consciousness of each of the individuals in seeking their closeness, their oneness with that being presented.

5747-3   7/6/35

So, then, give ye unto men as this: Train ye the child when he is young, and when he is old he will not depart from the Lord. Train *him*, train *her*, train *them* rather in the sacredness of that which has come to them as a privilege, which has come to them as a heritage; from a falling away, to be sure, but through the purifying of the body in thought, in act, in certainty, it may make for a peoples, a state, a nation that may indeed herald the coming of the Lord. For this is the problem, that ye keep the law and present same as holy to those who seek. Who seeks? *Every* child born into the earth, from the age of 2½ to 3 years begins to find there is something that takes place within its *body*, and that it is *different;* not as animals, though the *animal* instinct is there, of the biological urge, that is a law! For that is the source of man's undoing. But ye who set yourselves as examples in the order of society, education, Christian principles, religious thought, religious ideals, hold rather than to anything else to that *love* which is *un*sexed! For He hath given that in the heavenly state, in the higher forces, there is neither marriage nor giving in marriage; for they are as *one!* Yet ye say ye are in the earth, ye are born with the urge! The awakening, then, must come from within; here a little, there a little. Each soul, each body, that is preserved unto Him as a channel of blessings has received and does receive that within itself which makes for the greater abilities for awakening within the hearts, minds, souls and bodies of the young who question "what will I do with the biological urge that arises?" *Purify* same in service to Him, in expressions of love; in expressions of the fruits of the spirit, which are: Gentleness, kindness, brotherly love, long-suffering. *These* are the fruits, and these as the urge of sex are in the nature of the association of ideas, conditions or positions as related to the various conditions about the body. Then set the activity in motion and these become either that which takes hold on hell or that which builds to the kingdom within.

415-1   M.4   10/5/33

Hence, through the 12th, 13th and 15th years of experience the activities of the body mentally will need to be directed and kept in those influences wherein the later experience may be ruled through the influences of Mercury rather than Mars, in the application of the mental abilities of the entity in the present experience. For, with those influences in Mars—and in the Mercurian with those from Saturn having made the changes in the experience and application of the entity as related to the mental abilities, as related to Venus and Jupiter, will make for a hard experience for those that are in the care and keeping, unless directed properly. For, madness or temper, or hard-headedness, unless guided in the correct manner through the formative years, and through those experiences that make for the setting of the entity in its activity in the present experience, will make for a detriment to the better development.

The Venus influence also, we find, makes for a temperament that may be easily influenced by love's experience, whether from the spiritual aspect or from the purely material or carnal influences. Hence the more reason why there should be those precautions in the direction of the entity's abilities from the mental aspects of the body in the present experience.

5747-2   6/28/35

For the more oft are the girls or boys in their teens, in their younger years, misdirected when they are only attempting to give *soul*-expression of that which *moves* them! Those that are ground in their *own* subtle selves to *their* idea, without an ideal, *misconstrue* the individual's or child's intent and purpose.

Akashic Records

5231-1   F.64   6/5/44

As to the experiences in the earth, these have been many and quite varied. Many of these are not well even to be known to self, and thus have they been blotted from the book of thy remembrance, even as He blots them from the book of God's remembrance, if ye love one another, if ye mete to thy fellow man, yea, to thy sisters in all walks of experience, that love of which ye are capable in thine self. For he who hath loved much, to that one may much be given.

1650-1   M.37   7/29/38

Upon time and space is written the thoughts, the deeds, the activities of an entity—as in relationships to its environs, its hereditary influence; as directed—or judgment drawn by or according to what the entity's ideal is.

Hence, as it has been oft called, the record is God's book of remembrance; and each entity, each soul—as the activities of a single day of an entity in the material world—either makes same good or bad or indifferent, depending upon the entity's application of self towards that which is the ideal manner for the use of time, opportunity and the *expression* of that for which each soul enters a material manifestation.

The interpretation then as drawn here is with the desire and hope that, in opening this for the entity, the experience may be one of helpfulness and hopefulness.

Thus, in seeing self as it really is before the *self*, before the

Throne, before the Universal Consciousness, it is the hope that this will bring a better understanding as to what the purposes of an experience are in the material plane; with the daily activities and urges that arise from material circumstance, mental attitudes and the work to be accomplished of whatever nature this may be.

Hence we find from the records, the astrological aspects or sojourns of the entity or soul between its earthly manifestations indicate that which has been a part of the entity's experience.

1549-1   F.55   3/11/38

In giving the interpretations of these records, these are upon the skein of time and space. And O that all would realize, come to the consciousness that what we are—in any given experience, or time—is the combined results of what we have done about the ideals that we have set! . . .

Indeed the life and the experiences about every soul are such that if individuals will but take the lessons, the understandings of nature as it manifests in influences about self, they will see that such are the expression of the individual self's unfoldment.

As an illustration: A bulb is an expression of life, of beauty, in its filling its place in whatever environ it finds self. Man *can* change his environ, by the thinking. The bulb cannot. But man may view the purpose of all nature, he may view the bulb and see himself. If the environ is that which tends to enliven, enrich by creative forces added as constructive influences, then the beauty, the richness of the expression is a growth. But if it is dwarfed by an influence which hinders, it does the best with what it has.

So with man, the retrogression or progress is according to the application. The soul of each individual is a portion then of the Whole, *with* the birthright of Creative Forces to become a co-creator with the Father, a co-laborer with Him. As that birthright is then manifested, growth ensues. If it is made selfish, retardments must be the result.

Alcoholic Beverages

[Psychic information on the use of alcohol agrees with accepted opinion, that alcohol can be medicinal, or that it can be a means of unhealthy indulgence.]

275-21   F.18   8/18/31

Q-3. Are light wines good or bad for me?

A-3. In moderation they are *well* for the body. Just so the activities are not such as to become detrimental to digestion, but *light* wines with the digestive forces are beneficial. An over-amount of same, or activity produced by taking with improper foods—with foods that [wines] do not *co-ordinate* with—is harmful for the system. Whether [individuals] would have it or not, *foods* produce that *within* the system that is that same fermentation that is called wines, or beer, or liquor, or ales, or such ,*for* the digestion to be proper in a body! That man overbalances same, by engorging, or taking too much into the system and making . . . a hog of himself, is to be pitied for the man!

462-6   M.51   8/29/35

Q-4. Any kind of intoxicating drinks?

A-4. *Wine* is good for all, if taken alone or with black or brown bread. Not with meats so much as with just bread. This may be taken between meals, or as a meal; but not too much—and just once a day. Red wine only.

821-1   F.50   2/9/35

Not too much pastry, but natural quantity of sugar, natural quantity of wines would be *helpful* to the body if taken *only* with bread; for this produces an activity that is body, blood and nerve building, but wine taken in excess—of course—is harmful; wine taken with bread alone is body, blood and nerve and brain building.

Q-5. Any particular kind of wines that would be best?

A-5. That which is well-fermented, or grape juices or the like; these are the better, not too much of the sour nor too sweet a wine. Tokay, Port, Sauterne.

303-27   F.55   12/8/41

Q-8. Is it well for me to take eggnog, or any kind of spirits frumenti stimulant?

A-8. Spirits frumenti with the eggnog and milk would be very stimulating in the evening, or afternoon when first attempting to rest. Not too much, not too strong—but this will assimilate well.

5233-1   M.79   6/15/44

Q-1. Have personal vices as tobacco and whiskey any influence on one's health or longevity?

A-1. As just has been indicated, you are suffering from the use of some of these in the present but it is overindulgence. In moderation these are not too bad, but man so seldom will be moderate. Or, as most say, those who even indulge will make themselves pigs, but we naturally are pigs when there is overindulgence. This, of course, makes for conditions which are to be met. For what one sows that must one reap. This is unchangeable law. Know that this law may be turned into law of grace and mercy by the individual, through living and acting in their lives in relationships to others.

935-1   F.Adult   6/14/35

In following these diets, it is well that no *fermented* drink be taken; nor ginger ale, Coca-Cola®, or any of the ferments.

However, red *wine* may be taken; *not* white wines nor rye, corn or cereal drinks of such natures for the body.

2533-6   M.37   8/31/42

Q-4. Is the moderate use of alcohol and tobacco harmful to this body?

A-4. The body must answer that within itself. To be sure, if we would give from the ideal—these are made to extract from you the satisfying of appetites. The body *can* produce all the alcohol necessary, as well as the nicotine. Both are needed in the body. If you get it in the mind and spirit that it may be supplied, or can be supplied from other sources, to satisfy social or other relationships, then the body pays the price! Your ideal is not altogether one, is it?

416-18   M.38   6/2/44

Q-3. Is the moderate use of alcohol injurious to this body and what is moderate for this body?

A-3. Occasionally if you took a drink—once a year, it wouldn't be too bad—but wouldn't be too good either. Not that one becomes a total abstainer, but when in Rome, do as the Romans, but needn't get drunk over it—nor become so that ye seek too much of those things. Light wines will do very well, the rest you'd better cut out, not good for this body.

1467-18   M.39   4/10/44

Q-1. Has the amount of whiskey that has recently been taken by this body been harmful?

A-1. The body knows within itself that it has been harmful. While there are times when whiskey has its place (else there wouldn't be any whiskey), it has its place in people's activity. But for this body, ye know that it is poison. Would you knowingly feed your baby or your boy poison? Would you treat yourself worse than you would treat your neighbor? These are not well for the body. Not that it is to be a total abstinence unless there are the needs for it. And don't make excuses to go out and hunt the snake for him to bite you, or hunt someone to pick a fuss with you, or someone you can go out and have a big time with—for you always feel ashamed and you know it isn't well!

323-1   M. Adult   4/27/33

Abstain from *any* intoxicating drinks of *any* kind! This means even beer, too! Too much of these, with the electrical forces [electrotherapy treatments] (if they are to be taken), will be *detrimental* to the better conditions of the body.

Electricity and alcohol don't work together! It burns tissue, and is not good for *anybody!*

3492-1   M.47   11/16/43

For thy body is the Temple of the Living God. Use it as such . . .

Allergy

3644-1   F.31   2/1/44

Q-2. Am I allergic to dust, and does it cause my colds?

A-2. Who isn't? All of these are just part of the general debilitation—the inability of the circulation, because of these disturbances, to call into play, as it were, sufficient of the leukocytes to destroy dust. Or any sufficiently strong odors are just as harmful to the body as dust.

3268-2   F.53   1/13/44

Q-4. Am I allergic to certain foods?

A-4. If you imagine it, you can be allergic to most anything, if you want to! But these conditions in the present come from strep in the blood.

3556-1   F.20   1/12/44

These are not as faultfindings, but if the body would receive the greater help, it must make some definite decisions in regard to its emotions. (This the body should understand.)

There are physical disturbances. These have come about through the dis-coordinating between the sympathetic and cerebrospinal nervous systems. These cause the disturbance in the glands of the body, and the body in this supersensitive state becomes allergic to many varying conditions. These change according to the administrations made, but these have not all been worked out as yet.

We find that there are better ways than the administration of hypodermics. These are good at times. But why put more poison [into the system] as to set up other conditions that later will be hard to combat, when there has been caused—as it would in this body if kept up—disturbance in the soft tissue in the abdominal as well as lung area.

For in the present, with the allergies, there are irritations to the mucous membranes of the sinus as well as from disorders indicated at times in the mastoids.

These cause the sneezing, when these irritations arise these cause the hot flushes, the temperatures, and the general "let-down" feeling of the body."

The areas where the dis-coordination arises are in the 4th lumbar, 9th dorsal and 3rd cervical. These are the areas where lymph centers, and their connection with cerebrospinal nerve and blood circulation, are disturbing the body.

The glands in the throat, the glands in the facial portion—at the point of the cheek bone, at the point of the chin—these are areas that are sensitive to the disturbing conditions.

These, of course, set up reflex conditions in lungs, heart, liver, kidneys; so that the activities through suggestion, as well as from any dust (as in house cleaning) become as dregs or as drudges for the body, and it becomes irritated to distraction at times. But this is the association more than it is the organic condition. However, it can be just as severe as if the body sticks its nose in the dust barrel or dust can! For, these are disturbances in the sensory system and in the glands of the body.

As we find it would be well for the body to have a change of environment where there can be activity more out of doors, as in the west coast of Florida.

There we would have neuropathic manipulations coordinating the centers in those areas indicated, as well as in the frontal portion of body at breast bone, the sternum or at the pit of the stomach about the umbilical plexus and at the pubic plexus. These areas would be manipulated in the neuropathic manner. These massages we would give about three times a week. Afterwards we would apply the low heat of the diathermy in the area of the 6th dorsal and over the gall duct center—about three minutes in the beginning, gradually increasing. But keep this at a very low voltage.

Do these and we will correct these conditions. But let the change begin primarily in the mental attitude of the body. If the body continues to worry over conditions that have arisen or that may arise, this will prevent any of the applications from helping the body.

Control the emotions! Know what you want to do and go at it, in the relationships to the law of the divine nature, not of personal emotions.

Ready for questions.

Q-1. *What are all the things I am allergic to?*

A-1. It would be a list from here to Egypt! If you would add only those [to the list] that are most aggravating in the present, as indicated, dust! Especially dust that's in the home.

Q-2. *What is causing head troubles—ears, nose, throat, and especially eyes?*

A-2. Read just what has been indicated as to how the various centers in the body are affected by this discoordination of the sympathetic and cerebrospinal nerves, and as to how and why the careful massage should be given to coordinate the centers and set up direct coordination through the electrotherapy. And we will break up or, as it were, have direct connections and not short circuits through the body. But much of this has to do with the emotions.

This doesn't mean to imply that the body is mentally unbalanced, not at all. That's the trouble, it's too high-strung, it's too susceptible to suggestion.

We are through with this reading.

2755-2   M.8   7/10/42

Q-1. Since the asthmatic attacks seem to occur every night be-tween the hours of 3 and 7 A.M., is there something in the room in which he sleeps that brings on these attacks?

A-1. It is not that sometimes called an allergy. It is more of the mental, but comes from the associations in the mind rather than physical things.

Q-2. Is there any particular thing to which he is allergic?

A-2. Mostly to himself and his family!

But, as indicated, it is not *things* that he is allergic to—it's con-ditions!

3172-2   F.21 mos.   5/15/44

Q-3. Is there such a thing as allergy?

A-3. This is rather a fad. To be sure, individuals may become al-lergic to certain conditions because of excess of certain elements in the body. But these are rather exaggerated oft.

274-17   M.43   6/17/42

Q-1. Is this rash an allergic case?

A-1. As indicated, there are certain foods, or properties in foods, to which the body has become allergic—which is those that are not assimilated through the regular digestive system.

Hence the necessity of purifying the alimentary canal through the use of the properties indicated (Glyco-Thymoline®), and the application of same externally.

Of course, keep the liver active. This may be best done through the use of massage, or osteopathy, to stir the liver—from those centers or areas from which radiates the impulse for activity to the organ itself. Those areas from the 4th and 5th dorsal up.

Amnesia

3426-1   M.23   1/3/44

Now as we find, there are definite disturbances that are causing many of those unusual reflex activities to the mental body as well as the organic reactions that become disturbing to the body.

These are produced from an injury to the coccyx end of the spine. This has formed a reflex in the brain center that makes for the disorders, lapses of the activity—almost amnesia, but it is not altogether of that nature—merely the semblance of same at times.

If these pressures to the coccyx are corrected, we find that those conditions will disappear that have occurred in various other portions of the body, in reflexes to the activity of organs.

We find that these should be corrected by a chiropractor or an osteopath who would make the proper adjustments in those areas.

There should not be required more than 6 or 8 adjustments, if done properly. Other portions of the spine should be coordinated with the corrections made in the coccyx end of the spine; especially the 1st, 2nd and 3rd and 4th and 5th cervicals.

After at least 4 or 5 of the corrections have been made (not before), we would begin using for one hour each day the Radio-Active Appliance to equalize distribution of energies and circulation through the body. Use such periods for the deep meditation.

Do that.

Ready for questions.

Q-1. *What caused my landing in the hospital in February, 1941?*

A-1. Read what we have just given.

Q-2. *Was I discharged too soon from the hospital after my accident in the spring of 1942?*

A-2. Not necessarily. Needn't have been in the hospital for this condition which has caused or induced the disturbance.

Q-3. *Does exertion bring on my trouble?*

A-3. Yes, activities—for it brings about greater pressures on the whole cerebrospinal nervous system.

Q-4. *I have been studying ship drafting since August 1943 . . . Will my physical condition prevent me from obtaining work in this line, or holding onto job after I get it?*

A-4. Not unless nothing is done about the physical condition! . . . If nothing is done about it, along the lines suggested, then you won't do much at ship-building or anything else that requires physical or mental activities.

Q-5. *Can you tell me what the Government records show is my trouble and what became of all my papers that were lost? [medical discharge from United States Army]*

A-5. We haven't the Government records—we have the body!

Do these things as we have indicated and in the mental application of self construct that which is spiritually creative. Apply that in the life, in the daily dealings with others.

We are through with this reading.

Angels and Archangels

3189-3   M.79   9/3/43

Like all other entities, he has ever the spirit of the guardian *angel* before the face of the throne of the Father.

These, then, are the activities which ye interpret and read aright in the daily activities; that keep the physical, the mental, and the spiritual forces ever present and active in the relationships the entity bears to its fellow man.

For, as has been said or given of old, "As ye do unto the least of these, thy brethren, ye do it unto me" . . .

Q-1. Do I have any direct guidance from invisible helpers?

A-1. As indicated, ever the guardian angel stands before the throne of God—for each individual. Let not thy good be evil-spoken of nor thy bad be such as to cause continued questioning. Rather let the attitude be in that direction of hopefulness for the things to come.

538-59   F.59   10/19/39

Q-7. What has caused the feeling of having had an experience at some time in Palestine?

A-7. The influences or forces that overshadowed the activities through those experiences; because of the union of purpose in these two individuals just named, in their activity or vision over, or influencing of those activities of individuals, see?

For they became then what might be termed as guardian angels. See, these are the conditions—study this that you may perfectly understand:

The sojourn of a soul-entity other than in materiality often influences or bears weight with individuals within the material plane—as an odor, a scent, an emotion, a wave, a wind upon the activities.

Such are termed or called by some guardian angels, or influences that would promote activities for weal or for woe. [Mother and son in this incarnation; in Palestine, the present mother "overshadowed" the activities of the present son.]

1159-1   F.80   5/5/36

Q-1. Please explain the visions I have had regarding being shown a vein of gold and an oil deposit near Woodward's Chimney Corner, in Lamb's Spring, Texas.

A-1. Be these rather not those that are as in the influences that arise as emblems in thine own experience, that are as gold precious to the very souls of men, rather than material things? While the material things exist, yet to thee and to thine own life they be emblematical experience. For the *angels* of light only use material things for emblems, while the angels of death use these as to lures that may carry men's souls away. For the Master gave, "There is a way that seemeth right to the hearts of men, but the end thereof is death and confusion."

Not that these do not exist, but rather choose thou to make as the angels showed thee that gold in the hearts of men and women that *their* lives may overflow with the real *joy* of living.

What has given thee thy strength? That ye sought the material things or rather that thou be a handmaid of the Lord?

Confuse not thyself but know the Lord will do thee good, if ye will but be guided by His ways.

5749-3   6/17/33

With the bringing into creation the manifested forms, there came that which has been, is, and ever will be, the spirit realm and its attributes—designated as angels and archangels. They are the spiritual manifestations in the spirit world of those attributes that the developing forces accredit to the One Source, that may be seen in material planes through the influences that may aid in development of the mental and spiritual forces through an experience—or in the acquiring of knowledge that may aid in the intercourse one with another . . .

Q-4. Are angels and archangels synonymous with that which we call laws of the universe; if so, explain and give an example.

A-4. They are as the laws of the universe; as is Michael the lord of the Way; *not* the Way but the lord of the Way, hence disputed with the influence of evil as to the way of the spirit of the teacher or director in his entrance through the outer door [Moses].

262-28   9/18/32

Q-12. What is the relationship between Michael the lord of the

Way, and Christ the Way?

A-12. Michael is an archangel that stands before the Throne of the Father. The Christ is the Son, the Way *to* the Father, and one that came into the earth as man, the Son of man, that man might have the access to the Father; hence the Way. Michael is the lord or the guard of the change that comes in every soul that seeks the Way, even as in those periods when His manifestations came in the earth.

2897-4   M.35   8/14/31

[Background: [2897] wanted to be convinced—through this reading—that the sources were as high as, or higher than, those he was already reaching through spiritualistic mediums.]

Q-8. Why is Edgar Cayce surrounded by such wrong vibrations and entities in this great work?

A-8. For there has been the continued battle with those forces as Michael fought *with* over the body of Moses. He that leads, or *would* direct, is continually beset by the forces that *would* undermine. He that endureth to the end shall wear the Crown. He that aideth in upbuilding shall be entitled to that that he *builds* in his experience. He that faltereth, or would hinder, shall be received in the manner as he hinders.

Q-13. Is there anything the Forces would recommend for me to do?

A-13. Present thine self to those Forces that make for a more perfect relationship with the *living* God; *not* that of any individual's dead past! that would seek to climb up by *thine own* hard way; for, as was given, he that climbs up any other way than by the way of the Cross is a thief and a robber! So, make thine approach to that Force as manifests itself *in* the *material* world as the Son *to that* Throne, and be satisfied with none beneath *that* approach! So may the consciousness of the Christ-life come into *thine* possession.

Animals, Prehistoric

364-6   2/17/32

Let it be remembered, or not confused, that the *earth* was peopled by *animals* before peopled by man! First that of a mass, about which there arose the mist, and then the rising of same with light breaking *over* that as it *settled* itself, as a companion of those in the universe, as it began its *natural* (or now natural) rotations, with the varied effects *upon* the various portions of same, as it slowly—and is slowly—receding or gathering closer to the sun, from which it receives its impetus for the awakening of the elements that give life itself . . .

2893-1   M.52   8/13/29

In the [experience] before this we find [the entity] among those peoples and in that land when there were the gathering of the nations to combat the forces of the animal world and kingdom, that made men's and man's life miserable. The entity among those that stood for the use of the elements in the air, the elements in the ocean, the elements in the lands as applied *to* forces to meet and to *combat* those of the animal kingdom. Oft has the entity from this experience been able to *almost* conceive wherein the disappearance of those known as prehistoric animals came about. Write about this!

2749-1   M.50   5/15/26

In the [experience] before this we find [the entity] in the days when the peoples of the nations were gathered as one to defend [themselves] against the fowls of air and beast of field. The entity among those as would be called an envoy . . . and came to that gathering in what would *now*—this period—present, be called lighter than air machines, and the entity remained in that dwelling place, for the kingdoms were set within the bounds of that entity's rule, under the name Duddil . . .

2720-1   F.26   12/17/27

In the one before this we find [the entity] in those days when man was the one pursued, rather than being master over the beasts and the creeping things of earth. The entity among those that went as an envoy . . . to consider the ways and means of unity among the peoples that would rise and possess the land—through that injunction given to subdue the earth. Then in the name Shaiti, as it would be called today.

358-3   M.64   12/7/31

In the one then before this . . . during those periods when there were the gatherings of the many peoples of many lands, in that now known as the Indian land, those peoples that came as counselors from the foreign or visiting lands. The entity was then among those from what is *now* known as American, and came as one to counsel with those peoples that determined the manner of dealing with many of the beasts, or those things that made men afraid in the earth. The entity then in the name Uowi . . . gained and lost; for gaining much in the sense of application of *mechanical* appliances for the use of man . . . the entity used same to self's own destruction to its peoples, in that *portion* of the land *now* known as Utah and New Mexico. Would the entity vision much of that portion . . . lying in the southern portions of that land, and those of the Arizona and New Mexico lands, *much* as a dream would come to the entity.

Archaeology, Personal

415-1   M.4   10/5/33

Before this we find the entity was in that land now known as the Arabian . . . then in the name of Xertelpes . . .

And the entity was among those that became the first of the corps of judges in the city, as it took shape in the walled city . . .

There still may be found those remains of the entity near where Uhjltd was entombed, in the cave outside of the city that has recently been builded and termed Shushtar; this to the south and west of that city, in the cave there.

1297-1   M.42   11/25/36

Before that we find the entity was in the Chaldean land during those periods when there were the preparations for the peoples called the Jewish or Hebraic to return to their own land, for their establishing again of the activities in their home land.

The entity may be said to have been the counselor then to the king, Xerxes . . .

The entity then was the Chaldeans. And there may be found . . . in these excavations—look for same—that rod ye once used in thy divining of the individual purposes during that experience. This will be among those things that will be soon uncovered. It is of ebony and of gold.

404-1   F.41   5/14/31

In the one before this we find in that land now known as the Egyptian . . .

The entity was . . . a sister then to the priest [RaTa], going in banishment with those as were sent into the southern land . . . In the name as As-razh. In those places yet uncovered may much of that as was accomplished by the entity in the period be yet found, even the cakes of unleavened bread buried with those of that period made by the entity *still* be found intact. The entity in the experience was one that supplied those of the cakes of the various characters to the various altars, as well as ministering to the *physical* and *spiritual* needs of those that gathered in the temples—either as a portion of the mental worship, or as favorites to the king, or as favorites to those in power in that experience.

462-1   M.45   7/29/29

In the one before this we find . . . the entity was in that period [time of Ra Ta] when the divisions came after the conquering of the peoples. The entity was of the natives that were subdued by the peoples of the north land, yet broken in body—not broken in spirit, and the spirit of rebellion remained with the entity until the rebellion arose at the time of divisions in that known as church and state. The entity, joining with this rebellion, lost through the submerging of self in that period; yet in the latter days gained much of an understanding that remains well into the innate and deeper self in the present. In the name Arlea, and the *name* may still be found among those who *afterward* rose to power in that land.

2157-1   M.19   3/27/40

Before this the entity was in the Norse land, and among those who were the daring, as the sailors; and the entity was Eric, as called through that experience; journeying to or settling in the land of its present nativity [America] . . .

Q-6. In the Norse land experiences, how often and in what years did I cross the ocean?

A-6. In 1552, 1509 and 1502.

Q-7. What was accomplished in that life, either for my own country or for this country?

A-7. In this country there were the settlements in the northwestern lands; portions even of Montana were reached by the entity—because the entrance then was through the St. Lawrence, through the Lakes . . .

Q-8. Are there any proofs to be found now in this country that might prove it?

A-8. They have just been uncovered by a recent expedition there in Wisconsin!

Q-9. What would I find there that belongs to me personally?

A-9. Among the knives and stones that were found, one of those was Eric's!

2454-3   F.43   7/15/42

Before this the entity was in the earth when there were those journeyings from the east to the west—*gold!* In '49 did the entity, with its associates and companions, journey to the western lands.

Hardships were experienced on the way, yet the entity was among those that did attain, and saw, experienced, was associated in those acts with those that were comparable in their relationships to such conditions; rowdy, drink, spending . . .

The name then was Etta Tetlow. Records of these may be found in some of the questioned places in portions of California, even in the present.

1246-2   F.52   8/9/36

Before this we find the entity was . . . in Salem, in Providence Town or a portion of Salem, when through those experiences of the peoples . . . there had come those periods when the daughters and the sons of man saw for themselves visions . . .

The name then was Beatrice Allgood, and there may be found among the archives of old, yet some records of the entity there. In the churchyard there may yet be seen that resting place.

3063-1   M.56   6/26/43

Before this the entity was in the land of the present sojourn, not of the nativity, during those periods of the American Revolution.

The entity came with the leaders of his own land, and was closely associated with Rochambeau; being a non-commissioned officer, as would now be termed. And, through the abilities to observe and to take note, the entity rose to a position of trust, especially in those periods of activity about Yorktown, and the entity was sent upon many a mission . . . The name then was Rhoul Elsnheuser . . .

Q-1. In my previous incarnation did I die a violent death?

A-1. Go down to Williamsburg and look and see! You'll find it wasn't very pleasant. But you shouldn't cry over spilt milk.

Each day is an opportunity—make it such—to the glory of God, and it'll be to the honor of self.

5242—1   M.20   6/3/44

The entity then was among those who first gave those instructions in what would be termed flat drawing, and it was of the subject "Lazarus, come forth!" This still may be seen in some of the caves where the earlier portions of the Christians worshipped, in those early periods when all portions of the country were under the stresses by those in authority in Rome and in other places [which were] stressing the suppression of the tenets or truths of that day.

Asthma

3906-1   M.12   3/20/44

[Background: Male, age 12; Mother's letter, 12/2/43:"Our son has been ill with asthma since he was three years of age. He is now past twelve and after a year of comparative freedom from attack he has suffered a relapse of great severity, culminating in the present attack which is now in its sixth week." Mother's letter, 3/5/44:"We have tried many cures but none of them have given more than temporary relief."]

Here we have truly a pathological condition but a psychological as well as the physiological, and it extends to karmic reactions also. For one doesn't press the life out of others without at times seeming to have same pressed out of self.

If these disturbances are corrected pathologically in the early developing years, so that those pressures apparent in the areas from the 9th dorsal to the 1st cervical are corrected, we may allay oft those bronchial-asthmatic reactions that take the life and breath from the body.

The administration of other things outside are palliatives and will only bring about or create conditions that will not change.

Of course the hypodermics that may be given for such will relieve but will only produce stricture that would make for greater and greater disturbance as the body grows older.

It may be corrected osteopathically, it may require even six years—and a week's treatment out of each month during the whole six years, but it would be worth it for the body; provided the spiritual attitude of those responsible for the body, as well as the body, is set in that way of knowing the sources of forgiveness. For who can forgive sins save those against whom they are committed? And when one sins, the sin is against the giver of life, God.

5682-1   F.Child   5/26/31

[Background: Female, child; Mother's letter, 5/22/31: "The asthma has bothered her only two and one half years."]

For the asthmatic condition, have those properties made into an inhalant, as this: To 4 ounces of pure grain alcohol (not 85%, but pure *grain* alcohol . . . 190 proof), add:

Eucalyptol, or Oil of same.................................. 20 minims
Benzosol .... 10 minims
Oil of Turp, or Rectified Oil of Turp .... 5 minims
Tolu in solution...................................... 40 minims
Benzoin, Tincture of.. 5 minims

Keep in a container at least twice the size, or an 8 ounce bottle with a glass cork. Shake solution together and inhale deep into the lungs and bronchi two or three times each day.

304-3   M.69   4/2/25

The inhalant should be kept up, but we would renew the properties as taken and give them in this manner and form at the present time:

To 4 ounces of grain alcohol, we would add:

Eucalyptus Oil...................................... 15 minims
Benzosol .... 5 minims
Balsam of White Pine or White Pine Oil............ 10 minims

This is to be inhaled into the bronchials or mouth and into the system three to four times each day or when necessary to prevent the tickling sensation or the spasmodic condition occurring at times in the bronchials.

1867-1   F.8   4/22/39

In those periods of gestation, and presentation at birth, there were those portions of the system hindered in the cerebrospinal portion; especially through the lumbar, the sacral, and in the 9th dorsal center there were hindrances in the segments assuming their normal positions.

These, through the supplying of the nerve energies to portions of the system, produced a condition where the spasmodic reactions as in the bronchi and lung cause the asthmatic reaction.

This has hindered a perfect circulation, producing at times such a cutting off of the clarification through the oxidization of the blood flow through the lungs and the bronchi as to hinder normal development; producing in those areas such a weakening to the blood stream itself as to reduce the quantity of the blood cells that should carry even to the afflicted portions the abundant supply sufficient for the carrying on of the normal activity.

This calls for, or produces in the liver and the areas in the digestive system a strain upon the pancreas, the spleen *and* the activity of the lacteal action of assimilation.

All of these arise from hindrances in the areas where subluxations in the cerebrospinal system cause deflection of the conditions, or the impulses for activity.

Rarely, then, have the lower lobes of the lungs themselves been expanded sufficiently to carry the full flow even of the *quantity* of blood through the body for its purification; thus again causing congestion through those areas in the hepatic circulation, both upper and lower, as to produce the spasmodic reaction in the bronchi and larynx and at times the whole of the respiratory system—when there is an unbalancing or an excess acidity.

At times when inflammation from cold or congestion has extended to the soft tissue of the palate, as well as to the antrum and portions of the nasal passages—this then causes excess acid.

And with the dripping, or the exhuming of the inflammation becoming a part of the gastric flow, it upsets and produces the cycle of indigestion—or the lack of proper digestion owing to excess quantities of such fluids through the alimentary canal.

All of these have been and are a portion of the conditions as we find with this developing body . . .

. . . these conditions may be *entirely* eliminated. It will require patience, persistence, care and those precautions as to the diet, as to the activities, as to those properties in the system as will work with that portion of the assimilating system as well as the activity of the organs of the body to produce not only sufficient but rather a bit of excess, so that there may be resistances builded—increasing the quantity as well as quality of the blood supply—but keeping the proper balance between the hormones or the activity of the leuko-cyte and the red blood and the lymph activity through the system.

Those corrective measures that have been made thus far, osteo-pathically, are assisting—but there needs to be, as we find, rather the *specific* centers given more consideration and not so much of a *general* treatment; more of those through the lumbar, the sacral and to the 9th dorsal need attention; coordinating rather than those from the cervical to the 6th and 7th dorsal center *with* the corrections in the lumbar, sacral, and coccyx area.

[The osteopathic treatments] should be given rather in a series; having periods when they are given, and periods when there is rest from same . . . about six to ten treatments and then a rest of three to four weeks without any, then begin again, and these continued in such a way or manner through the whole of the period from the present [April] until September or October.

. . . Calcios™ [given] about once each day, the quantity that would be spread (as butter) upon a whole wheat wafer . . .

Then also we would add the vitamins as may be best found in the compound known as Codiron; this carrying the correct propor-tions of the cod liver oil, iron, and the vitamins A, B-1—and D and G. These are in the correct proportions for this body to take; one of such pellets *with* the morning meal and one with the evening meal . . . for the present.

Then the daily activities: keep in the open air—sea, sand and pines. These should be a regular routine . . . when weather permits at all, because the assimilation of the pine oils, especially during the early spring and summer season, will add materially to the activities through the respiratory system, as the other applications are made.

Understand—these are to be *all* or none. For one is dependent upon the other.

Keep the eliminations near normal. Watch the activities of the kidneys as well as the alimentary canal, that there are not conges-

tions or disturbances to the organs through these periods of corrective measures for this body . . .

*Q-2. When the asthmatic attacks come, what should be done to
relieve same?*

A-2. Take Calcidin—this dissolved in a little water—one to five
grains in an ounce to two ounces of water—this kept warm and a
little bit sipped every fifteen to twenty minutes—will allay as well
as relieve disturbances.

But if these corrections are made *as indicated,* the attacks
should not come.

It is understood, to be sure, that the impulses to the bronchi are
received from the upper dorsal and through the cervical areas of
the cerebrospinal system; but these are *secondary! If* those lesions
in the coccyx, sacral and to the 9th dorsal are removed, then those
applications for the adjustments through the upper portions will
become almost the *normal* adjustments in themselves! . . . Keep
where there is sea, sand and pine! Virginia Beach would be better
[than Norfolk]. There is no better place, if the body will be kept on
the sands and in the pines occasionally, as has been indicated! . . .

*Q-5. Should we plan to spend the winter in Florida, or two
weeks?*

A-5. If the conditions are carried out as we have indicated consistently, persistently, prayerfully—there needs be no consideration
of the kind other than that which would be for the general benefit
of the body . . .

Q-7. Does the doctor in Canada really cure asthma?

A-7. About one in ten, yes—where there are the needs for the
corrections upon those portions of the body producing pressures,
he relieves. Where these have become those conditions that are
constitutional, and are dependent upon organs' activity, no.

2040-2   M.50   10/17/41

While the present environ [Florida] is very well so far as the temperature is concerned, we find that it is not so good as to altitude.

Portions of California would be better, near the edge of mountains, closer to Los Angeles—or the coastal area there. These will
be *natural* helpful conditions.

Attitudes and Emotions

2096-1   F.22   2/17/31

In the mental attitudes of the physical forces of [2096] we find—while the body is sympathetic in its nature, tendency even towards that as may be termed an *affectionate* nature—these have been as of combative forces within the body, and the body has turned more to those conditions that make the body more hardboiled—if we choose to call it such. These *do not satisfy,* and they create an element of discontent.

Find that and spend that affection on something worthwhile; not dogs or cats, or fish or pigs, but something that is animated with a building force within self that will see the expression and give that affection the body has long sought for in self.

Make self interested in something that will make in the lives of some individual, or individuals, that that makes life more worthwhile; for would we have contentment in self we must create the atmosphere in another, and that we give out that we receive; for, as has been given, sow as ye may but ye reap that ye sow.

God is not mocked, and man nor woman can fool themselves into making themselves believe that there is *not* that which repays many, many times for that effort in *whatever* thing given out; for that given out will return to the one spending self.

If we would have life, give it. If we would have love, make ourselves lovely. If we would have beauty within our lives, make our lives beautiful. If we would have beauty in body or mind, or soul, create that atmosphere and that which brings about life itself will bring those forces; for the *spirit* is willing, the flesh is contrary—as well as weak.

In the *spirit* is strength. Give that strength an opportunity of manifesting itself in thine life! as it is manifested in the lives of those whom the entity contacts, for the kind word turneth away wrath, even as the haughty look or the unkind word stirreth up and maketh for troubles in the lives of many.

Make thine life *beautiful,* and it becomes more worthwhile.

1523-4   F.29   1/28/38

. . . the emotions [come] from sojourns in the earth and the innate influences from the sojourns in the environs about the earth during the interims between earthly incarnations.

1599-1   F.54   5/29/38

And those influences in the emotions, unless they are governed by an ideal, often may become as a stumbling stone.

906-2   F.54   5/1/36

Keep the mental attitude in the constructive forces that make for knowing that the body is not only good but good for something. And apply self in those ways and manners that are known to the mental body, and we will find the physical forces, the mental reactions, continually helpful.

4083-1   M.55   4/12/44

Q-1. What are the reasons that the entity so often has felt that he has been unable to make full use of his mental and emotional powers?

A-1. Lack of finding its own ideal, or the setting of thine own self as that which must be gratified . . .

Q-6. Is there some emotional reason for the entity's frequent "clearing" of his throat?

A-6. Read that indicated to thee as to how there is need for the perfect unison between Father, Son and Holy Spirit. There must be perfect unison between body, mind and soul, if the physical would be in accord.

As ye know, there must be perfect accord between the central nervous system, the sympathetic nervous system and the sensory nervous system if there would be perfect accord.

It's a wonder you don't vomit more often than you do!

3637-1   F.35   1/5/44

. . . the entity may play upon the emotions of others or it may use them for stepping-stones or stumbling blocks. It may use opportunities to raise others to the point of anxiety or to the point where they would spend their souls for the entity; using them either as buildings or as serpents or scorpions . . . It may love very deeply, either for the universal consciousness or for the gratifying only of self or the physical emotions.

Again the entity may express each of the emotions in their counterpart—as patience, long-suffering, brotherly love, kindness, gentleness. It can also look on and hate like the dickens! It can look on and smile and love to the extent of being willing to give all for the cause or purpose.

These are abilities latent and manifested in this entity. Use them, not abuse them . . . Use them to the glory of thy ideal, and let that ideal be set in that way of the Cross.

As has been indicated well by others, indicate in thine own life in this experience—for you've shown all phases of it in others: let others do as they may, but as for me, I will serve the living God . . .

In mercy, in justice, in love then, deal thy abilities to thy associates and thy fellow man . . .

As to the abilities of the entity in the present—who would tell a rose to be beautiful? Who would tell a sunset to be beautiful? Who would tell this entity, other than to be true to that thou knowest in thine heart? For the Lord hath given thee much—in body, in mind, in purpose. Use them all to the glory of God.

Anger

2-14   M.49   6/16/30

These should be warnings for *every* human: Madness is certainly poison to the system.

3621-1   F.8   1/7/44

Be angry but sin not. You will learn it only in patience and in self-possession.

1551-2   F.37   3/15/38

One that finds in self often that the little rift, the unkind word grows and is magnified and taken as an individual insult, will become as a separating thing from those with whom there is not only duty, not only obligations because of associations and relations. But do not let *anger* be thy *destructive* principle! Be mad, yes—but sin not!

3645-1   F.36   1/15/44

Poor indeed is he who does not ever show anger, but worse indeed is he who cannot control it in himself. And there most fail.

Though often those who flare up quickly, also forgive quickly—if they remain as little children asking, seeking, living, "Guide thou me, O God, in the steps I take and in the words I say day by day."

1402-2   F.59   11/20/37

. . . while there are what may be called karmic conditions to be worked out, do not let these disturb thee . . .

These then may only be met in the manners as He gave, "If thy brother offend thee and smite thee on the right cheek, turn the other also."

This under the circumstances becomes galling to many. But know that only in the same attitude, the same manner in which He met such rebuffs, such activities, may ye in thy satisfying, in thy bringing peace and harmony, find same in thine experience and thy relationships.

Q-5. What can I do to overcome my anger at her treatment of my friend . . . ?

A-5. These conditions to be sure become such wherein the individual of self, the individual of thy neighbor as thyself, thy friend as thyself would be considered. These must not be taken other than in the manner as just indicated—if peace and harmony would be brought about.

For remember, He is right in that given, "The soft answer turneth away wrath," and in that a gentleness, a kindness meted to those that have been and are in error but heapeth coals upon the mind, the heart, of those who have erred.

Then only in *loving* indifference may the conditions be met.

What, ye say, is loving indifference?

Acting as if it had not been, save disregarding as if [the conditions] were *not*.

Not animosity; for this only breeds strife. Not anger; for this only will produce mentally and physically the disturbances that become as physical reactions that prevent meeting every phase of the experience; whether in the good, the hope, the help ye mete to others, or in keeping self . . . unspotted from the *cares* of the world.

1537-1   M.38   2/18/38

. . . oft there has been allowed anger and madness to control in the experience . . . When ye *should* have been just at times ye have allowed others to overstep because—as thine excuse, or thy justification—ye didn't want a fuss; and yet ye have made a fuss or a racket and been the very cause of much of turmoil in the lives of many!

Why? Gratifying thine own self, without the thought of that "I must meet this in my associations with others day by day!"

Criticism

5098-1   F.55   5/11/44

The entity is one who cannot stand criticism from others and in this attempt to shield self, oft becomes rather sarcastic to others, which causes animosities, or the lack of the closer friendships . . .

Begin with this consciousness and say this, repeat it oft and know it to be true in thine experience, and it will become much easier to apply the seeds and sow the seeds of truth and harmony and of love: *"Lo, I am with you always, even unto the end of the world."* Know this is spoken by Him, who overcame the world and is able through this overcoming the world, to keep all the promises He has made to you, *to you!* as an individual, and behold He stands constantly at the door of your consciousness, at the heart, if ye will open and by just saying, mentioning the name, Jesus, the Christ, my Brother, my Lord, my Savior.

2936-2   F.35   4/8/43

Learn the lesson well of the spiritual truth: Criticize not unless ye wish to be criticized. For, with what measure ye mete it is measured to thee again. It may not be in the same way, but ye cannot even *think* bad of another without it affecting thee in a manner of a destructive nature. Think *well* of others, and if ye cannot speak well of them don't speak! but don't think it either! Try to see self in the other's place. And this will bring the basic spiritual forces that must be the prompting influence in the experience of each soul, if it would grow in grace, in knowledge, in understanding; not only of its relationship to God, its relationship to its fellow man, but its relationship in the home and in the social life.

For, know—the Lord thy God is One. And all that ye may know of good must first be within self. All ye may know of God must be manifested through thyself. To hear of Him is not to know. To apply and live and be *is* to know!

3138-1   F.69   7/17/43

First there must be in the spiritual and mental self, the renouncing of any condemnation of others. Never an attitude of blaming others, but knowing within self that the state in which you find yourself is where the Lord would have you work in His vineyard. The very fact that you have life itself, even, is the opportunity for being a witness-bearing child to the King of kings.

Speak kindly, speak gently. Be patient. Be not faultfinding, be not condemning of others, nor of anything that may have come to be your lot. Be not a gossiper of activities that would bring any condemnation on others.

This in itself will change the whole outlook on the body's [physical] condition. Let your prayer be continuously:

Lord, use me, such as I am, in Thy kingdom.

And mean it, and *do* it. When you see, when you speak with others, let them know that you walk closely with Him; not by bragging, but by gentleness and by the wonderfulness of His love and His grace even to you. Let it be known to others.

3054-4   F.50   2/16/44

We would magnify the virtues, we would minimize the faults, and yet a criticism if sincerely given is often more effective or helpful than too much praise when not wholly justified in the experience of the entity.

Hate

1537-1   M.38   2/18/38

As to the associations with others—if ye would have friends, show thyself friendly. This does not mean becoming the butt of others' fun, nor of thy using others in the same manner. But if ye would have love, love others; do good to them, even that despitefully use you, even to those that misrepresent you. Not because it is ennobling, but because it is *right* in *thy* sight!

Do not belittle, do not hate, for hate *creates* . . . and brings turmoils and strifes.

Show thyself to be a son of the living Father, holy and acceptable unto Him; not ashamed, but keeping thy face towards the light and the shadows fall far behind.

4021-1   M.45   8/25/44

To be sure, attitudes oft influence the physical conditions of the body. No one can hate his neighbor and not have stomach or liver trouble. No one can be jealous and allow the anger of same and not have upset digestion or heart disorder. Neither of these [disorders] is present here, and yet those attitudes have much to do with the accumulations which have become gradually . . . tendencies towards neuritic arthritic reactions. Stiffness at times is indicated in the locomotories; a nausea, or upsetting of the digestive system; headaches seem to arise from a disturbance between liver and the kidneys themselves, though usually the setting up of better eliminations causes these to be eased . . .

Then [regarding] the attitudes of the body: Know that there is within self all healing that may be accomplished for the body. For, all healing must come from the Divine. For who healeth thy diseases? The source of the Universal supply.

As the attitude, then, of self, how well do ye wish to be? How well are ye willing to cooperate, coordinate with the Divine influences which may work in and through thee by stimulating the centers which have been latent with nature's activities. For, all of these forces must come from the one source, and the applications are merely to stimulate the atoms of the body. For each cell is as a representative of a universe in itself. Then what would ye do with thy abilities? As ye give to others, not hating them, to know more of the Universal Forces, so may ye have the more, for, God is love.

Do that, and ye will bring bettered conditions for yourself. Work where you are. As was given to those who were called, "The ground upon which ye stand is holy." Begin where you are.

1196-11   M.60   10/18/38

It is true that the body feels it has not been given the consideration it should have been given, from many angles; but to hold animosities makes for the creating . . . of poisons . . . not easily eliminated—especially with an already overtaxed condition . . . of the digestive system.

And here we find that hate and animosity and anxiety may be the poison that causes *much* of the disturbance.

Live more in keeping with that as thou hast professed, that He is able to keep that committed unto Him against any experience. Did He justify Himself before His accusers? Did He attempt to even meet the words that were spoken condemning Him? ...

Do as indicated ... But don't do just part and say "I've done all!" Do it all or do none! and doing it means leaving off animosity, as well as [doing] the physical application!

Humility

1402-1   F.58   7/4/37

And hence, as has been indicated, by those indications seen through the experience of the entity in the present sojourn, there have been periods when—with the high temper, with the strong will—those conditions have been created where these have become disconcerting, discouraging, disappointing to the entity.

So, it is to learn, then, that which is as a portion of life ... the lesson of patience—*patience!*

Hence the more oft there is the humbling of the spirit that there may be the better hold, a better understanding gained ...

And in the application, study self. Be humble, but not timid; be positive, but not in that determination of rule or ruin. But rather in that as was given—mercy, justice, patience, love, long-suffering, brotherly kindness, and forgetting those things that easily beset one in grudges or hatreds or hard feelings ...

Do not let things *rule*, but give them—as to self, as to others—their proper sphere, their proper place, in the experience of others ...

Q-4. What are my present errors in conducting my personal life and my work?

A-4. As has been indicated, a little more patient, a little more tolerant, a little more humble. But, as has been indicated, not a tolerance that becomes timid—this would make rebellion in self. Not a patience that is not positive. Not an humbleness that becomes morbid or lacking in beauty. For as orderliness is a part of thy being, so let consistency—as persistency—be a part of thy being.

290-1   F.51   3/3/33

Q-1. What would cause my husband to take a different attitude toward life, as a whole?

A-1. There must be a reawakening to the necessity of the regenerating influence within self.

To reach the first approach, do not condemn. Do not pamper, nor agree; but rather in that *humbleness* of spirit *show*, in the love, the condemnations are not as condemning but as working with, working toward the renewing of the spirit within that makes for cooperative influences in the life of those that have obligations one for another. Or, it comes to this:

He that gives the kind word, even when coals of fire are heaped upon the soul, shall be recompensed in saving not only self and the growth of self's own soul, but many another . . .

Faint not; and know He is able to bear thee up, lest *thou*—in thine distress—bring even a greater sorrow in thine experience . . .

There are both physical and mental conditions that disturb the body, but as there may be given out by self that of less and less condemnation—not condoning, not apologetically, but rather in the spirit of truth, of love—there may be the better, the greater awakening.

2173-1 F.50 4/19/40

Hold fast to that thou hast purposed in thy heart. Look ever, and oft, within for thy direction. Be satisfied with nothing less than knowing . . . that He is mindful of thee. Then, speak as face to face. For the promise has been, and is, "I stand at the door and knock. If ye will open, I will enter, and I and the Father will abide with thee."

This applies to thee—not as a laudation over others, but humbleness of heart, humbleness in thy speech and thy conversation.

Trust

3374-1 F.35 11/23/43

Before that the entity was in the English land during those periods when there were preparations for the activities when overzealousness oft, as it did in the days of yore, led man to do strange things in the name of his Maker.

The entity then was among those who were left; being left by the companion to look after and to take care of those things under peculiar circumstances. These have made for the entity a stableness in the belief in self, and the questioning of some who make vain promises.

Here you find your relationship with your present companion, and it will be necessary that both of you work out some of those things where ye mistrust each other. Keep them inviolate, for the time to work them out is now—through the trust in that which is the center of thy life's seal [the open book, the Holy Bible].

Let not those things of the nature of gossip hinder thee, for it is best to trust a soul and that questioning than to doubt that soul which if believing would bless thy life with true meaning.

165-26   M.60   11/8/37

. . . because of discouragements and because of failures, and because of heartaches, and because of those things that make men afraid, will ye turn thy back upon the opportunity before thee, now?

Then what is the real problem?

Hold fast to that as ye purpose in thy heart, that there *will* be the opportunity for those that are through their own shortcomings losing, or have lost, sight of their relationships.

Then put on rather the whole armor. Look within self, first. Clear that doubt of thy association, thy connection with that divine source, that *with* which ye may conquer *all;* and *without* which even all the fame, all the fortune of the age would not bring that ye have purposed to do into the experience of even *one* soul . . .

But whom the Lord would exalt, He first brings low that they may know the strength is of the Lord—and not in hosts but the still small voice that beareth witness with thy soul, thy spirit, that ye walk that straight and narrow way that leadeth to understanding. And in saving those of thy own shortcomings, ye find ye have been lifted up.

1599-1   F.54   5/29/38

. . . ye are allowing much of the material things to become the stumbling block to thy spiritual and thy soul development.

. . . there must be in the heart, in the mind, in the soul of every entity that which is its ideal, its God, its trust, its hope!

And they that trust in themselves alone are not wise!

Rather know *who* is the author, then, of thy wisdom. *Who* is the keeper of thy hopes? In *whom* have ye believed?

5108-1   F.30   5/15/44

Let that faith, that trust, which has sustained thee in the present, keep thee from fear of any kind . . . Trust in the Lord . . .

602-7   F.49   1/18/42

Fill the place better *where ye are*, and the Lord will open the way! Is this not in keeping with His life, His teachings? These are worthy of acceptation. These are worthy of being trusted, of being lived.

Worry

1523-5   F.29   5/23/38

Q-10. What causes the circles under the eyes?

A-10. Nervous condition, and worry!

Q-11. Any spiritual advice for the body?

A-11. Just that which has been indicated for the body; study to show thyself approved unto thy *own* good conscience—that which does not decry nor bespeak condemnation. For as ye would not be condemned, then condemn not.

And as ye keep this attitude towards self, towards others, let the spiritual reactions for a *constructive* experience be thine own.

1005-17   M.28   3/21/37

To worry or to become cross and antagonistic creates poisons that are already in excess. Smile even though it takes the hide off, even when you are cross—this will be very much better [than worry].

2502-1   F.42   2/26/30

One that is at times easily worried about material things. One that at times worries as respecting the application others make of their abilities.

In the matter of worry, this—in its last analysis—is that of fear. Fear is an enemy to the mental development of an entity, changing or wavering the abilities of an entity in many directions.

2981-1   M.33   4/27/43

Q-5. How can I keep from worrying . . . ?

A-5. Why worry, when ye may pray? Know that the power of

thyself is very limited. The power of Creative Force is unlimited.

900-345   M.32   10/9/27

One thing—remember this: Do not burden self with that as is unncessary to be met until the time arises, for *worry* killeth. Labor strengthens—for through the efforts of the self *little* may be done, yet through that the body and the consciousness is able to direct *much* will be accomplished. As the necessary conditions arise, that as is best will be given thee.

357-13   F.40   6/11/42

As concerning thy fellow man, He gave, "As ye would that others do to you, do ye even so to them," take no thought, worry not, be not overanxious about the body. For He knoweth what ye have need of. In the place thou art, in the consciousness in which ye find yourself, is that which is *today*, *now*, needed for thy greater, thy better, thy more wonderful unfoldment.

But today *hear* His voice, "Come unto me, all that are weak or that are heavy-laden, and I will give you rest from those worries, peace from those anxieties." For the Lord loveth those who put their trust *wholly* in Him . . .

Q-9. *Please give an affirmation that will help me.*

A-9. . . . as ye pray, in the morning, in the evening:

Here, Lord, am I. Use Thou me, this day, this evening, as Thou seest I may serve others the better; that I may so live, O God, to the glory of Thy name, Thy Son Jesus the Christ, and to the honor of mine own self in Thy name.

Automatic Writing

262-24   7/24/32

Q-14. *Could I develop automatic handwriting?*

A-14. Anyone could.

262-25   8/7/32

Q-12. *You told me that anyone could do automatic writing. Will you please tell me how I may develop it?*

A-12. By practice. Sit alone with pencil and paper, and let that guide that may be sought—or may come in—direct. It will come.

Anyone may; but is it the better may oft be the question. This may only be the better when surrounding self with those influences that may bring those of the *constructive* forces alone.

1602-1   F.40   5/30/38

Q-8. Are the inspirational writings I receive to be relied upon as coming from a worthy and high source or should I not cultivate this form of guidance and information?

A-8. We would *not* from here counsel *anyone* to be guided by influences from without. For the *kingdom* is from within!

If these come as inspirational writings from within, and not as guidance from others—that is different!

1297-1   M.42   11/25/36

Q-2. To further my work in possible radio reception of cosmic messages, should I attempt to train myself in automatic hand-writing, or use a medium?

A-2. As has been indicated, rather than *automatic* writing *or* a medium, turn to the voice within! If this then finds expression in that which may be given to the self in hand, by writing, it is well; but not that the hand be guided by an influence outside of itself. For the universe, God, is within. Thou art His. Thy communion with the cosmic forces of nature, thy communion with thy Creator, is thy birthright! Be satisfied with nothing less than walking with Him!

5259-1   F.46   6/8/44

As indicated, do not listen to voices or rappings outside of self; do *not* use incense or music or automatic writing, for too many may desire to use this entity.

3054-4   F.50   2/16/44

And it is this influence which the companion of that period so often would impress upon the entity's consciousness, when the entity enters into deep meditation or when the entity attempts to write—that is, automatic writing. This influence is not always for good, for it is impelling upon the entity.

317-4   M.42   4/21/33

Q-1. Is my automatic writing inspired and how can I develop it to the best advantage?

A-1. As we have indicated, this is rather the harking of the mental development of self through the experience when the entity was the scribe to those of many lands, and many positions, and many tongues, that sought counsel. In developing same, depend and call upon rather that of the *universal*—than the independent—influence.

Exercise self ever rather with:

Let Thy hand, O God, guide: through the ways Thou seest are needed for those that seek to know Thy way through any effort of mine.

5124-1   F.55   5/18/44

But begin to study all of psychic phenomena, though don't begin with automatic writing. For this would soon lead to such channels as to be more detrimental than beneficial.

But begin to read the Scripture, searching for those portions of same that give the warning, as well as the instruction as to how one would seek to be an individual who may give a great deal to mankind. This undertaken, the entity may set itself to be of a great help to others through any phase of psychic forces it would choose to demonstrate.

Know that it is not too far afield, but do gain thy understanding from beginning with this: Take Exodus 19:5. To be sure, it is interpreted by many here that the Creative Forces or God are speaking to a peculiar people. You were one of them. Why not, then, today? Although through the years your name has been changed, the soul is the same. Hence this is, as it were, spoken to thee.

Then take the 30th of Deuteronomy, where there is the admonition as to the source, that it's not from somewhere else, but it is within thine own self. For that influence of the Creative Force is so near, yea closer even than thy own hand!

Then analyze that, reading in connection with same all of the story of Ruth as to her sincerity. And if it needs to be, those companionships may be drawn from thine own activities, and the fear of what may be in the future will fade as the mists before the morning sun.

For in the study of these, not merely read to know them, but get the meaning of universal love, not attempting to make it personal but universal. For God is love and, as ye go about to manifest same in thy conversation, ye may find the true meaning of love.

Study also astrological subjects, not as termed by some, but rather in the light of that which may be gained through a study of His word. For as it was given from the beginning, those planets, the stars, are given for signs, for seasons, for years, that man may indeed (in his contemplation of the universe) find his closer relationships.

For man is made a co-creator with the Godhead. Not that man is good or bad according to the position of the stars, but the position of the stars brings what an individual entity has done about God's plan into the earth activities during those individual periods when man has the opportunity to enter or come into material manifestations.

In the study, forsake not, of course, the true way and light. As is given from the beginning: God said, "Let there be light" and there was light, and that light became, and is, the light of the world. For it is true that light, that knowledge, the understanding of that Jesus who became the Christ, is indeed thy Elder Brother and yet Creator, Maker of the universe; and thus are ye a part of same and a directing influence.

Then, as ye practice His principles ye become aware of same. And these are first: "Thou shalt love the Lord thy God with all thy heart, thy mind, thy soul, and thy neighbor as thyself."

Study then, also the 14th, 15th, 16th, and 17th of John as it speaks to thee, and as to how ye may apply thyself in the intuition, in the walks with divine influences.

And it is with what spirit ye entertain that ye measure that kind of helpfulness to thy Maker.

Do what thou doest intuitionally, or as the spirit moves thee.

Balanced Life

3352-1   M.45   11/5/43

We find that these arose as a result of what might be called occupational disturbances; not enough in the sun, not enough of hard work. Plenty of brain work, but the body is supposed to coordinate the spiritual, mental and physical. He who does not give recreation a place in his life, and the proper tone to each phase—well, he just fools self and will some day—as in this body in the present—be paying the price. There must be a certain amount of recreation.

There must be certain amounts of rest. These are physical, mental and spiritual necessities. Didn't God make man to sleep at least a third of his life? Then consider! This is what the Master meant when He said, "Consider the lilies of the field, how they grow." Do they grow all the while, bloom all the while, or look mighty messy and dirty at times? It is well for people, individuals, as this entity, to get their hands dirty in the dirt at times, and not be the white-collared man all the while! These are natural sources. From whence was man made? Don't be afraid to get a little dirt on you once in a while. You know you must eat a certain amount of dirt, else you'll never get well balanced. For this is that from which all conditions arise. For of dust man is made, and to dust he returns. Because he doesn't look dirty once in a while is no sign he isn't dirty in mind, if not in body, if not in spirit. For these are one, ever one . . .

But take time to add something to your mind mentally and spiritually. And take time to play a while with others. There are children growing. Have you added anything constructive to any child's life? You'll not be in heaven if you're not leaning on the arm of someone you have helped. You have little hope of getting there unless you do help someone else.

Do that and live a normal life, and you'll live a heap longer. Be worth a heap more than the position you occupy. For it is not what you do but what you really are that counts. This shines through—what you really are—much more than what you say.

440-2   M.23   12/13/33

Q-5. *How can I develop the ability to work long hours? And what are the best hours for work?*

A-5. What are the best hours for work? When the lesser number of people are *thinking* about work; for *any* individual! Hence, by raising the resistances [to illness] in the body, the body will be able to control the hours of labor physically and the hours of labor mentally. Remember that which has been given, that all work and no play will make just as dull boy as all play and no work—and will make one eventually *just* as worthless, to self and to that it would desire to accomplish!

Best that *every* individual . . . budget its time. Set so much time for study, so much time for relaxation, so much time for labor mentally, so much time for activity of the physical body, so much time for reading, so much time for social activities. And while this does not mean to become merely a body of rote, it does mean that each of these changes and each of these activities make for the creating of a better balance—that not only facilitates the individual's activities but gives the ability to *concentrate* when desiring on *whatever* the activity may be!

Baldness

4056-1   M.26   4/2/44

[Background: Male, age 26; Mr. [4056]'s letter, 2/11/44: "Is there any chance of restoring my hair . . . ? I am the only one of six brothers who is going bald . . . "]

As we find, there is a lack of activity of the glands in the thyroid areas. This causes a weakness in the activities to nails and hair over the body.

We would take small doses of Atomidine®* to purify in the thyroid activity. Take one drop each morning for five days in succession. Then leave off for five days.

During that period give the scalp a thorough massage with crude oil; using the electrically driven vibrator® with the suction applicator. This should be done very thoroughly, not hurriedly and should require at least thirty to forty minutes for the massage with the crude oil and then the application of white vaseline and then the electrically driven vibrator® using the suction cup applicator.

Then begin the first of the next week with the Atomidine®, one drop each morning for five days.

Then during the next five days (now the middle of the week) give another crude oil shampoo® following with the white vaseline and the vibrator® treatment.

Leave these off then for two weeks.

Then have another complete series, but between each two series allow two weeks to elapse.

Atomidine®. Molecular iodine is found in solution or tincture form. Through independent research aided by readings of Edgar Cayce a new form of iodine in atomic form called Atomidine® was developed. Originally claims for its internal use were made by the manufacturer but today it is recommended only for external use as an antiseptic.

Warning: Under no conditions should Atomidine® be taken internally unless prescribed by a doctor.

Doing these, we will find that in six or eight months it will begin to stimulate the activities for the growth of hair over the scalp and on body.

Do use the diets that carry iodine in their natural forms. Use only kelp salt or deep sea salt. Plenty of sea foods. These are preferable for the body.

Not too much sweets. The egg yolk but not the white of egg should be taken.

Doing these we will bring better conditions for the body.

3904-1   F.21   3/20/44

[Background: Female, age 21; Miss [3904]'s letter, 12/16/43: "I have very weak hair and a decided tendency to baldness."]

As we find, there are conditions causing disturbances with this body. These are because of improper coordination of the activities of the inner and outer glandular force as related to the thyroid. This allows for deficiencies in certain chemical forces, especially as related to the epidermis, or the activities in the toes and the fingers and the hair. These are distressing disturbances to the body.

There is that which has caused much of the disturbance—a long-standing subluxation existent in the 3rd and 4th lumbar centers, which prevents the perfect circulation through the glands of the thyroid area.

We would make corrections osteopathically in that specific area, coordinating the 3rd cervical and the lumbar axis with same.

We would also begin taking Atomidine® internally as a purifier for the glands and to stimulate better thyroid activity. This may change the heart's regularity for the time but if it is properly administered and the osteopathic corrections are made properly, we will find changes wrought in the activities in the epidermis and as associated or related to the hair.

For the scalp we would prepare a close-fitting cap—oil cap—to be used once a week or left on overnight, when the scalp would be massaged with pure hog lard. Not that which has been mixed with vegetable matter, but with the pure pork or hog lard. Massage this in at night. Sleep with it in the hair and scalp, using the cap as protection. In the morning have a thorough shampoo with Olive Oil shampoo®, massaging the scalp afterward with white vaseline cut with a little alcohol solution—just sufficient to cleanse same; about a drop of grain alcohol to an ounce of water—just enough to change the activity of same. [Or just enough to rinse most of the vaseline out of the hair.]

Do eat more of sea foods, more carrots, and—while certain times will have to be chosen for such—do eat onions and garlic.

4086-1   F.32   4/12/44

[Background: Female, age 32; Mrs. [4086]'s letter, April, '44: "I am losing my hair at an alarming pace. Apparently it is inherited from my mother and several doctors told me that there is nothing they can do to help me. Otherwise I am well and have a baby of half a year. A few years ago I took some electrical treatments to stimulate the scalp but I do not think that has actually helped my condition. Lately, since I have had my baby I have lost some more hair . . . "]

As we find, general conditions in a manner are very good, yet there are disturbances that cause a great deal of anxiety to the body. These, however, are more in the purely physical, than that having to do with the body as an entity. For these are rather the activities in the reflexes in the sensory and sympathetic nervous system, and arise from the body attempting to improve in a selfish manner upon what nature had intended for the body to be.

Thus there has been an upsetting of the glandular system by the activities in the body that destroy the effect of these glands, producing such elements in the thyroid glands, especially; thus destroying the oils that were a portion of the activity in the sympathetic nervous system as related to the epidermis.

These may later, unless corrections are made, cause splotches where there will be discolorations in the skin until these may become rather patches over portions of the body, especially the upper portion of the limbs, the hands and on the arms. Yet, as we find, if there will be a change of attitude mentally—much change may come physically—the body needn't laugh at this, for it will find that one day the conditions will be rather serious unless there are measures taken to correct the mental, and not merely the physical or pathological conditions.

For, as it has experienced, these have had little to do with changing of the activities in the gland force of the body.

We would first begin with the taking internally once a day for at least four days out of each week—and have it the same four days each week—one grain of Calcidine as prepared by the Abbott Company, Chicago. This take say Mondays, Tuesdays, Wednesdays and Thursdays. Leave off until the next week and repeat for a period of at least six weeks.

After this has clarified the respiratory and perspiratory system by the increasing of the activity through the respiratory and the lung and throat area and the iodine has acted upon the system, begin by massaging the scalp about once every twelve days with pure hog lard—yes this is an aversion to the body—but these properties will be needed in the physical self. Massage this thoroughly into the . . . scalp, then cleanse with soft tepid water and with Fitch's Dandruff Remover Shampoo. This will purify scalp but let the grease that is rubbed into scalp remain for at least twenty minutes before it is washed out. Then add a small quantity of white, massaging thoroughly into the scalp.

In the diet eat the soup from the peelings of Irish potatoes. Add more often the raw vegetables such as lettuce, celery, watercress, radishes, onions, mustard greens and all of those that may be prepared as salads and the like. Carrots will make better conditions in combination with these for the sparkle of the eye and for the general vision.

Have the full evacuation of alimentary canal at least once a day and do at least once a month purify the colon by the use of high enemas. These may be taken by self, provided the colon tube is used. Use about a half a gallon of water, putting at least a heaping teaspoonful of salt and a heaping teaspoonful of soda in same, dissolved thoroughly. Have the water body temperature and have the thermometer at least ninety or above.

Do these, be very careful with the general eliminations.

Keep away from all of those things such as hard drinks, carbonated water or the like and we will gain better health and have better superficial circulation.

Ready for questions.

Q-1. Did childbirth cause this condition to become worse?

A-1. It only aggravated, it is not the source of condition but too much of drying out of the scalp, as has been indicated, to improve upon nature. Be natural: You'll be much more attractive.

We are through with this reading.

1710-7   M.27   3/12/42

Q-2. Why doesn't the growth of hair show improvement?

A-2. This is the natural consequence of conditions that have been in the scalp. The activity of the body shows that the glands do produce same, but getting it on the head is different! That would require more of the use of the vacuum treatment *and* the stimulating of the scalp to better activity.

The gland force is improved, and *does* grow hair—but not on the head so much.

Bible Characters

1541-11   F.62   7/31/41

For, the entity was among those of the group called the holy women or those that saw, that knew many of the associations with the disciples, the apostles, and the helpful, direct influence of the Master Himself.

For, the entity then was the mother of Peter's wife, once healed by the Master Himself.

Those periods brought to the entity the closer associations through the latter periods of the activity. For, being healed as it were, physically, by the Master Himself, the entity's sojourn in the earth was long and varied, and would make a book in itself.

The entity's ability to write in the present should be manifested, especially in the stories as concerning the life of the Master as might be read by children. For, these the entity would be able to do; as it brought through those experiences the channel through which the early church attracted others; as many lived and drew upon those truths as illustrated by the entity.

During that experience the entity had *two* activities; the growing of plants, especially adaptable for the healing of the body, and flowers; and also the ministering to the sick. Not as a nurse, rather as a comforter. For the entity at periods acted in the capacity as a hired mourner, as was the custom of that period.

The name then was Esdrela.

1710-11   M.28   4/8/43

[Background: Biographical sketch of their experience as Deborah and Barak in Palestine, the period of the Judges.] Yes, we have the records as indicated through these channels, as well as that which is a part of the record of the Judges of Israel.

As indicated there, they each had their definite activities; Deborah as the elder in the experience, and the prophetess—thus raised to a power or authority as a judge in Israel; to whom the people of the various groups, of that particular portion of Israel, went for the settling of their problems pertaining to their relationships one to another.

With the periods in which the peoples of the adjoining countries made war upon Israel, or that part of same, the people then appealed to the entity Deborah—in the capacity as spokesman, for the spiritual and mental welfare of the peoples, to select one or to act herself in the capacity as the leader in the defense of the lands.

Then did the entity Deborah appoint or call Barak to become the leader in the armed forces against the powers of Sisera. These are the outstanding portions as presented to Holy Writ.

As to the activities—these, as may be interpreted from same, were close in their associations, in their respect one for the other as to their abilities in given activities respecting the defense of the principles as well as the lands of the peoples.

Deborah, as given, was much older in years in the experience, and a prophetess—being a mother and the wife of one of the elders in that particular portion of Israel.

Those activities together, then, were as related to the mental, the spiritual and the material welfare of the peoples as a whole.

As to the activities of Barak in those periods—there was something like some twelve years' variation in the ages. Barak was also a family man, of the same tribe—though not of the same household as Deborah. Their activities, then, brought only the respect one for the other in their associations, their dealings and relationships with others.

In paralleling, or in the application of the lessons as may be drawn from those experiences in the material plane—these in the present make for more than the purely material attraction one for the other. For, the mental and the spiritual become not a part of the heart or soul of each, but of their relationships as dependencies one upon the other that are to be taken into consideration . . .

Beware that there is not the attempt on the part of either to dictate to the other, but rather in a singleness of purpose may they, together, manifest their own experiences that consciousness that was manifested by those promptings through that experience.

5030-1   F.50   4/16/44

Before that the entity was the Holy Land when there was the entrance of the children of promise; among the Canaanites who made overtures for consideration by those people who were under direction of Joshua in the experience.

The entity came to know those people, yea was even wedded to a Canaanite whose sister was one familiar with spirits, that brought fear to the entity; then in the name Leah.

Thus this has brought, combined with the knowledge that it companioned with those outside of its own peoples—the consciousness of a fear of things dealing with people connected with varied characters of groups or principles.

5373-1   F.48   7/2/44

Before that we find the entity was in the Holy Land and when there were the foregatherings at Bethsaida. Then the entity knew the Master. For it was one of the entity's children who was among those first blessed by the Master, when it became necessary to rebuke the disciples for their attempting to rebuke the peoples. Thus, as is indicated in the symbol, the Cross, as well as Holy Writ. For as the Master gave Himself, "Search the Scriptures, for in them ye think ye find eternal life and they are they that speak of me."

3659-1   F.10   2/15/44

For, before that the entity was in the Palestine land as a companion of Miriam, who aided in directing spiritual precepts, yea in the tenets of law that Miriam's mother and brethren gave to those peoples.

The days at Sinai brought misery, brought strength, brought power. And entity is still afraid of thunder and lightning, yet such has its attraction. The Lord is in the storm, for He is the Lord the storm also.

The name then was Shushan. The entity was among the daughters of Aaron, and thus one of the household and understanding the priesthood.

5056-1   M.22   5/6/44

Before that we find the entity was in the activities in the Temple of Solomon in Jerusalem when there was the choosing by David of those who were to be prepared for the service of music in the Temple which was yet to be built.

David chose young men and they were given the physical as well as the mental and spiritual training through the activities in the preparations in the school as had been undertaken or begun by Elijah Carmel.

Thus the entity in the name Apsha was among those who were in the Temple service when the activities were begun through those periods of Solomon's reign. Those were the periods when there was the great amount of what today would be called notoriety or during those periods when the Queen of Sheba visited Solomon the entity was chosen as the one to make music for Solomon to make love by, to the Queen.

5241-1   F.19   6/16/44

Before that we find the entity was in the Egyptian land when there were the activities in the preparations for the exit from Egypt to the favored land, the people through whom was chosen the hope of the world.

The entity was then the close friend of Joshua. Yes, one of those to whom Joshua was engaged, as would be called in the present, and of the daughters of Levi, not the same as Moses and Aaron but rather of Korah. There we find the entity beautiful, lovely, beloved of Joshua and yet weak in body, because of conditions under which the entity had in a portion of its experience labored, and thus weak-lunged, passing away during the period of the journey to the Holy Land. But to have been beloved of Joshua was sufficient to have builded, into the personality, that individuality of the entity, that which still makes the entity beloved of all who know the entity best, loved by all its companions, its associates, just as in those experiences with the great leader who was to carry the children of promise to the Holy Land. The name then was Abigal.

4087-1   M.6   4/15/44

For the entity was the prophet who warned Jereboam. Read it! You will see why he is not to listen at all of those who may counsel him as to the manner in which he is to use the abilities that have been and are a portion of the entity's experience; but to trust in Him who is the way . . .

. . . the entity was the prophet of Judah who was sent to Jereboam to warn him, and who brought about the withering of the hand, and also the healing of same; yet turned aside when faced with that in which the mind said "A more excellent way."

There are no shortcuts. What God hath commanded is true. For the law of the Lord is perfect and it converteth the soul . . .

For in the experience before this the entity attempted to buy same from Peter. Hence that tendency, that realization that the misuse of same [psychic ability] may bring destructive forces into the experience.

In that experience the entity being warned, as he asked, "Pray that I may be forgiven for the thought that such might be purchased," he was forgiven.

Bible Study and Interpretation

1599-1   F.54   5/29/38

Knowledge is well, and understanding is good; but to use these in a manner in which self—the own ego—is to be exalted, makes for confusion to those who would seek to know their place in the activities of the realm of opportunity that is given in the present . . . And they that trust in themselves alone are not wise! . . . If these are to be used for self-aggrandizement, self-indulgences, do they not become rather as He gave of old? "Ye shall come and say, Did we not in thy name heal the sick? Did we not in thy name cast out demons?" and He will say, "Depart from me, I never knew you!" Why? *Why?* Because the desire, the purpose is that self may be exalted, rather than the humbleness of the heart before Him. For he that would be the greatest must be the servant of all. *These* be those things that ye must choose within thine own experience. For there is ever, as given of old, set before thee each day good and evil, life and death—choose thou!

2828-5   M41   1/10/44

[Background: TB of the spine]

This, as it may be given, is not intended other than that the entity in its seeking should indeed interpret the law of the Lord. For what is stated in His word isn't fooling. It means what it says. The law of the Lord is perfect. It converteth the soul. If the soul be perfect in its purpose and ideal—whatever the state may be, it will call on the Lord. It will rely on the Lord. It will use every measure to comply with His will and purpose. His purpose was for man to subdue, to conquer, to use, to apply the earth in its every use for man.

When it was given "Whosoever sheddeth man's blood, by man shall his blood be shed." That is, in this case, the blood of his will, of his purpose, of his physical desire to carry on in his own ways of activity and by those conditions in the body itself being thwarted. The entity thwarted others and is meeting it in self. That is karma. In the blood of the Christ as was shed, karma is met and then it becomes the law, not of cause and effect, but of being justified by faith in Him. Then, may we use, may we apply those things of the material earth *and* the spiritual combination to become again sons of God. Not sons of Belial or of the devil!

In conditions here, then, the type of lamp is helpful, but is not preventing at times conditions making inroads upon the body-forces. Do get the ultraviolet light; the hand lamp may do, the stand lamp is better. *Do* apply all in the manner as has been indicated. Not just a makeshift. If it is the best the body can do—then he must take the consequences. But there are lamps still to be obtained from the manufacturers of those, in various places.

The information will not do it for you. Did the Lord prevent Abel from being slain? Did He prevent Cain from slaying? Did He not say, "It is in thine own self to do"? So it is with individuals who may be warned or directed. It is within yourself to do or not to do . . .

Q-3. *Anything that might warn of approaching attacks?*

A-3. Has it not been illustrated for thee? If the good man of the house knew when the thief was coming, he would be prepared. To be prepared would be to have the sword of the spirit, the purpose of the mind; and the conditions will not be broken up.

2537-1   F.33   7/17/41

Truth and life emanate only from one source. Man—the offspring of the Creator—may diffuse, disseminate or alter same as to cause half a truth to appear a living truth.

But analyze all. Know the author of what ye believe, and let that author be that living truth which fadeth not—who is able to keep *every* purpose, every hope, every desire against *any* disturbance that may arise in thy experience—mentally, spiritually, materially.

For, as ye find—thy body, thy mind and thy soul are each in their sphere of awareness *one.* Hence the ideal must be one.

Thus He that came into the earth as an example, as a way, is an ideal—is *the* ideal. They that climb up some other way become robbers of that peace, that harmony which may be theirs—by *being* at-one with that He manifested in the earth.

949-5   M.22   1/26/37

Let these be the thoughts and activities: Nothing better may be followed than that as has been given by Moses, Joshua, David, the prophets, and Jesus. In these we will find that which may produce and is the beauty of nature, the love in man's experience for his fellow man; the applications not only for the hope of the material world, the beauties of the hereafter, but the continuation of Life in its experiences—may all be had by those studies as in the 30th chapter or last of Deuteronomy; especially the 4th, 5th, 7th of Joshua and the last of same; the 1st and 2nd Psalm, the 24th, the 91st, the 23rd, the 150th—all of these proclaim that as may be man's experience; and are constructive in creating songs or vibrations for beauty in nature or in the dealings of man to man.

1213-1   F.Adult   7/24/36

Q-4. How may I get hold of myself, in order to forget myself?

A-4. As has been given, as the strength and the vitality are gained, and the aptitude and attitude by the use of those applications, we will find quite a different outlook. Use those texts or chapters as indicated as if the writer, as if the Father was *speaking direct* to the *entity,* to *self!* Read them with that understanding, that interpretation. And ye will find that the attitude towards individuals, towards conditions, will have a much greater meaning; bringing into the experience harmony and an activity worthwhile.

987-4   F.49   11/2/37

Q-3. If possible, what can I do to finish my earth's experience in this life?

A-3. It is ever possible. Studying to show forth the Lord's death till He come again!

What meaneth this? Just living those that are the fruits of the spirit; namely: peace, harmony, long-suffering, brotherly love, patience. *These*, if ye show them forth in thy life, in thy dealings with thy fellow man, grow to be what? *Truth!* In Truth ye are *free*, from what? *Earthly* toil, *earthly* cares!

These then are not just axioms, not just sayings, but *living* truths! Ye *are* happy in His *love! Hold* fast to that!

Q-4. What is holding back my spiritual development?

A-4. Nothing holding back—as has just been given—but *self.* For know, as has been given of old, "Though I take the wings of the morning in thought and fly unto the uttermost parts of the earth, Thou art there! Though I fly into the heavenly hosts, Thou art there! Though I make my bed in hell, Thou art there!"

And as He has promised, "When ye cry unto me, I *will HEAR*—and answer speedily."

Nothing prevents—only self. Keep self and the shadow away. Turn thy face to the light and the shadows fall behind.

843-9   M.55   10/19/38

Q-2. For what purpose did I make my present appearance and how can I more successfully carry out that purpose?

A-2. To make thy paths straight!

Remember as has just been indicated, the good lives on. And how oft was that injunction by he that was the forerunner, as well as the early teachings of the Master, "Make thy paths straight!"—that is, to undo those things ye have *bound* in thyself and in the experiences of others, that one may be free indeed in the love and the service of the Master.

3189-2   M.79   9/3/43

Q-1. What would be a wise course for me to pursue in regard to my various business interests, in view of my life expectancy?

A-1. It might be said to thee as to the rich young ruler; keep the faith, keep the tenets; but follow closely in the way of the Lord. Not as to disposing of all, no—but the using of same to the glory and for the honor of God.

69-5 F.61 7/24/42

Q-5. Please advise how I can realize my desire for healing to come without physical remedies. Is it possible for me to demonstrate this?

A-5. Anyone may demonstrate that which is really desired, if the entity is willing to pay the price of same!

As we have indicated so oft—when there are disturbances in the physical that are of a physical nature, these need to be tended to or treated, or application made, through physical means. There is as much of God in the physical as there is in the spiritual or mental, for it should be one! But it was as necessary, when the Master demonstrated, to use that needed in the bodies of individuals as curative forces as it was in the mental. To some He gave, "Thy sins be forgiven thee." To others He applied clay. To others, they were dipped in water. To others, they must show themselves to the priest—offering that as had been the mental and the material law.

3384-1 M.32 12/2/43

Read and study carefully the 30th of Deuteronomy, also the 14th, 15th, 16th and 17th of John. Know, as ye read that these words are applicable to yourself indeed. Not that you attempt to hypnotize yourself, but rather knowing deep within the soul-self that all the forces or powers of creative energies that give life itself are within yourself; that you can trust wholly in the Creator, the divine within. Make those choices that ye must in every activity of body, mind, soul, trust wholly in Him—that ye must let thy will be one with Him, without reservation, *without* reservation.

Birthmarks

573-1 F.Adult 6/6/34

Q-6. What caused the birthmark on my baby's arm? How may this be removed?

A-6. By massaging it with an equal mixture of Olive Oil and Castor Oil it will be prevented from increasing. Marks on many bodies, as on this one, are for a purpose—and if a life reading would be given it would be seen that it [the child] has a purpose to perform in the affairs of those in its own surroundings and in many others. A mark!

This would be well for Miss [Esther] Wynne to follow:

Take individuals everywhere, where there has been or is a mark in the body, and analyze their activity and associations among individuals; for their lives and their associations are different from the ordinary ken. Many will be found to have almost caused or averted tragedies (as called in the earth) in the lives of individuals. This is given her [Miss Wynne], for many are close about her.

585-6   F.43   10/11/39

Q-10. Was I marked by RaTa in the Egyptian period? If so, where and what is the meaning of it?

A-10. In the face and the mouth; that there be not too much talk.

1100-26   F.43   6/12/39

Q-1. Was I given a mark by Ra Ta? If so, where is it, and what is the meaning of it?

A-1. The upper portion of the lip, or between the nasal passages and the corner of the lip—which exists there at times—especially a feeling of twitching there: the messenger, the speaker to those that need counsel and advice.

Q-2. Was my present husband, [470], also given a mark?

A-2. Given a mark rather in the latter portion of the entity's experience, as there came a closer activity *after* the return of the Priest into the Egyptian land. This, as we find, was in the palm of the hand: a doer, an armor bearer, a messenger; a carrier of activities—as is indicated in the palm of the right hand.

1165-1   F.10 days   5/10/36

Now, in reference especially to those conditions that are indicated by the mark on the forehead and the cheek or side of head:

... much might be given as respecting same—as to the pathological effects, as to the influences that arise from the psychological effects and the psychopathic effects that had to do with those things which manifest in this way and manner.

Rather would we approach same from that which we have indicated through these sources heretofore, as to how each individual in its manifestations in the earth bears within its physical expression the marks of that which has been or may be termed as an expression of a development in the soul and spiritual forces.

This is being sought, however, more from the material experience or expression; and that is being sought that may remove or may cause or may effect a change in the personal appearances that are to be a portion of the experience of the body—if it is to carry on in this experience.

These then, we would give: From the pathological changes, these are from pigments that are active in the texture and in the conditions in the physical forces of the body.

To apply injections, or to apply that which would change these in any *material* way and manner would be to effect an effacement of that which would make for a full expression of that to be met by the body and those about same—in that which would make for the real, greater development.

Be rather mindful of those conditions-physical that are arising with the body in its ability for assimilation, for those conditions that will make for the regular body-development as to its digestion and assimilation.

As for body activities in making for a helpful experience, we would massage the body—not so much over the area itself but *along* the sides of same and over those areas from which this portion of the body receives its impulse for circulation to the superficial portions of the body—with Camphorated Oil.

And we would massage the whole portion of the body from the lower lumbar area to the head with Olive Oil *and* wine.

These will make for a change sufficient to assist the effacement, that is the most helpful in the experience.

But it is more of an activity upon the part of those that are in the material sense the expression of that manifested in this body, [1165].

For the individual experiences of the body—if it is to carry on— are to be such that these will be lost sight of in that [which] may be builded from the spiritual forces. And in its expression in meeting those things that to most minds, or to the material-minded, become as an effacement—or as a marring of the influences that bear upon its own personality.

Then, aid in giving the expression more and more of that individuality that is shown here. And we will find this will bring to all a real blessing that may make for a greater and greater understanding of the relationship of individuals to Creative Forces and the manifestations of same in a material world.

In the applications, these we would do each evening as it is prepared for its evening rest.

The equal portions of wine—red wine—and the Olive Oil; stirred together in such a way and manner as to make for an absorption to those portions of the body from the lower lumbar area to the base of the brain.

And the face, the head, those portions of the neck, even to the vagus centers or those about the upper portions of the thorax, or extending even to the breastbone, massaged very gently with the Camphorated Oil.

These, as we find, offer the better opportunities for the expressions in the present.

As conditions change, or when it has reached those periods of its full expression—or at nine months—then we would give those changes; if there remains within the innate desire of those that seek in the present for those periods when there begins then the developing of the *individuality*, rather than the personality of this soul expressing and manifesting itself as [1165] . . .

Q-1. Should the Camphorated Oil be massaged just around the edges of the mark?

A-1. Just around the edges as indicated, rather than over the place; for with the massage and the proper assimilations and digestions that will make for the building of blood forces and the pigments in portions of the body, this will aid in the effacement of the disturbance; or it becomes less and less perceptible—save at periods.

But most, hold to the spiritual expression and not the physical.

Blood Poisoning

[Because of their brevity, three complete readings are presented on the subject of blood poisoning.]

670-2   M.19   1/1/35

Yes. Now as we find, the conditions in this body are somewhat serious. Those activities in the system from the preventative [injection] produce temperature and make for a great deal of discomfort; and [they] do not insure, in the present conditions, the prevention of infectious forces from disorders or disturbance.

We would add in the present, about the affected parts—not over the portions where the injury has been made, but about same—turpentine with salt. Saturate the salt with turpentine; not as a saturated solution, but *dampen* [salt] with same and apply—*not on* the affected parts, but about them!

Also we would keep [using] the heart stimulant, especially if there should be any further indication of the . . . affectation's spreading. In these particular conditions the strychnine would be better, but it should carry with same an eliminant, or an eliminant [should be] taken soon afterwards . . .

Ready for questions.

Q-1. Is there danger of lockjaw?

A-1. Always *danger* from any infections; but as indicated, use these applications in the present.

Q-2. Describe just what the condition is, if it isn't lockjaw.

A-2. Infection!

Q-3. From what does the infection come?

A-3. The injury! [Mule bite]

Q-4. Any other advice?

A-4. This we would do in the present.

Q-5. How long should the salt and turpentine packs be kept on at a time?

A-5. Until they get cold! Not *on* affected parts, but *about* same—between there and the body, see?

We are through for the present.

670-3   M.19   1/2/35

[Same case, continued the next day.]

As we find, there are considerable improvements in the general condition of the body. The lack of fever or temperature indicates the assimilation of those precautionary measures [or substances] that have been taken, and their activity with the general reactions in the system. The lack of discoloration in portions of the arm indicates an improvement also.

It would be more helpful, we find, to let the salt and turpentine extend the whole length of the member that is afflicted, thus drawing from the body more of the poisons, by this application. Use rather the heavy salt, not crystals but the heavy salt, and the spirits of turpentine. Apply for periods of two, three, four times each day; they will be found to be most helpful. Allow to remain for a sufficient period to produce the perspiration that comes with this drawing [of] circulation; which [perspiration] should be bathed off with an anti-septic—weak solution, very weak—and then kept warm, of course. Unless it is heated too hot, it should not make terrific burning; more of a drawing sensation, see?

As an eliminant we would give Castor Oil, followed in forty-eight hours afterwards with broken doses of Fletcher's Castoria.

Only give the heart stimulant (strychnine) under the advice of a physician, as to dosage and as to the frequency of same.

As to the matter of diet, we would keep the more alkaline foods; such as orange and lemon juices combined, grapefruit juice, pine-apple juice and the like—with whole wheat toast. Broths of any character, whether combining the meat stock or vegetable—or these combined. Not too large quantities of sweets. But keep a wholesome, well-balanced diet.

2015-9   F.2½   7/16/42

Yes. As we find, this acute condition arises from a bite, but not of any very *severe* type—though this might become so.

There should have been first (and this will now materially aid) this application over the bite and swelling.

Moisten salt or make it wet with turpentine, and put on as a poul-tice, not binding. Change this about every hour or so until most of the swelling is gone. Then keep the body quiet.

Start eliminations with a good emit, as Castoria®, Syrup of Figs—the Milk of Bismuth® may be added with same to purify the system. But Milk of Magnesia® would be very well to keep down the temperatures.

Bathing the body, of course, with the weaker solution of the salt and turpentine will be helpful—along the spine, but this [solution should be] very weak. Apply the poultice over the bite and the ankle and foot.

Do not give heavy foods; only those that are almost predigested, when foods are given. And give plenty of water. These as we find are the better [treatments] under the present conditions.

Ready for questions.

Q-1. Is the temperature from the bite?

A-1. It is from the whole combination of fright as well as a bite.

Q-2. Was this bite from a spider?

A-2. From a bug, not a spider. Do this, as we find, but do it right away. We are through with this reading.

Burns

2015-6   F.1   10/11/40

[Background: The following complete reading indicates the pattern of treatments suggested for burns.]

While these [burns] appear very serious in the present, because of the blister or the water, we do not find the injury to the eyes, but rather to the lids.

As we find, we would cleanse and use[then] the tannic acid; followed with the [use of] Unguentine® and the Sweet Oil (camphorated) to prevent or remove scars, as the tissue heals.

Be very mindful that eliminations are kept above the normal. Use *both* the Podophyllum and the Calomel as a base for eliminants, at various times; not together; but under the direction of the physician. While these would not be used, under most circumstances, for a child, these would be the better in this case—because of the poisons from [having] so much area covered with the burn, and the shock to the system, as well as the kind of poisons to be eliminated and the need for the excess lymph.

Ready for questions.

Q-1. Apply tannic acid?

A-1. Tannic acid; the light, to be sure. This is understood by the physician. Cleanse it first, then apply the tannic acid.

Q-2. How should it be cleansed?

A-2. Would you ask how to tell a doctor to cleanse a thing!

Q-3. Are they using the tannic acid in the way suggested here?

A-3. Not using it as yet, but these are a part of the bandages.

Q-4. Then after the tannic acid apply the Unguentine®?

A-4. As it heals; not, of course, while the tannic acid is being used, but as it heals. See, this cuts away air, produces dead skin, and leaves a scar. Then the oils from the Unguentine®, and the Sweet Oil and Camphorated Oil are to take away scar tissue, see? These are to follow within ten days to two weeks, see?

Q-5. The eyes themselves are not injured?

A-5. As indicated, the lids; though there will be, of course, some inflammation [of the eyes]. But keep down the excesses of poisons by increasing the eliminations, to remove these poisons that are as natural accumulations from such an area burned.

Q-6. Any suggestions for relieving the pain?

A-6. As just given, this will relieve the pain when it cuts off the air! We are through for the present.

Bursitis

340-47   F.55   3/14/43

As we find, there are the acute conditions of neuritis; and a combination of disturbances arising from pressures in the colon. Though the disturbance is in the bursa of the arm and shoulder, the source of this arises from a colon distress.

With the excruciating pain, we would take, to be sure, some palliative. Aspirin with Soda-Mint is preferable, or a hypnotic of some character—which should be administered by a physician if this is taken, though the Aspirin may be taken with impunity by self up to twenty grains.

Begin applying saturated solution of Epsom Salts in packs over the affected area of arm and shoulder.

Also begin immediately with an eliminant; preferably the mineral salts, such as Eno®, Sal Hepatica or Rochelle Salts or Citrocarbonate®.

Then, when these have acted, *do* have a good colonic. This will remove the pressure and alleviate the distresses.

After this particular spell is alleviated, do be mindful to take the Eno Salts® regularly for some time; five days at the time, leaving off about an equal period and then taking again; a teaspoonful of mornings before any meal is taken.

Be mindful that not too much roughage at any time is taken in the diet through the period of these treatments, nor too much of raw foods.

357-11   F.36   11/25/38

Q-1. What is the cause of soreness in right shoulder and cure for same?

A-1. Lack of proper eliminations. Tendencies for the cord[?] where fats are taken to be irritated. Hence no fried foods, nor great quantities of fats.

3901-1   F.20   3/26/44
Q-2. Pain in right shoulder?
A-2. This is only reflex from the poisons.

1086-1   M.Adult   12/23/35
Q-3. What should I do for relief of pains in the shoulders?
A-3. As we find, if the sources of these toxic forces are relieved, then the adjustments or equalization made, these will disappear.

When these are acute, the use of an eliminant—and hot Epsom Salts Packs—will relieve same.

Manipulations or adjustments should be rather in periods; three-week periods, two, three times a week. Then a rest period of two to three weeks, and then again.

Do these.

1688-11   F.33   1/27/44
Q-3. What is cause of constant soreness in right arm (shoulder and upper arm mostly)? Also right leg?
A-3. As just indicated, pressures from lack of poisons being eliminated. Do as indicated, if we would bring better conditions for the body.

Business Advice

1634-1   M.50   7/11/38
In giving advice or counsel regarding the dealings and relationships with others, we would give the entity these as a premise—on and from which reasoning may be drawn:

Know, in thy forming of policies and attitudes towards others, that there are immutable laws; and that what ye would give out—if ye would have any semblance of success, or a growth within thy own experience—must be constructive in its nature.

Also know that what ye sow, in mental, material and physical relationships, will be measured back to thee again.

This should be the basis of thy policies, of thy attitudes, of thy dealings with others.

Then, that as ye would prepare for distribution among thy fellow men must in itself have a place in bringing greater hope and help in the experience of the users of such.

There must be, naturally then, the same consideration given those who would act in the capacity as the distributors of such products.

Know that there are very, very few individuals who do not by nature respond to constructive thought, constructive application.

Then, have that policy to do unto others as ye would have others do to you. *Expect* that! *Live* that in thy dealings! and ye will find that He who is the Giver of all good and perfect gifts will bring to thy experience not only harmony and peace but greater opportunities, with material, social and financial success . . .

Q-2. Does this distributor intend to drop my contract if I do not grant his demands?

A-2. There has been the consideration of such, but if there is not animosity nor hate nor dislike nor distrust allowed to enter in, but the same consideration for each of these as ye would have them give to thee—then ye may expect proper consideration in return. Talk it over! Be honest with self, be honest with them—and they will be honest with thee! . . .

Q-5. Have you any further advice for me concerning proper handling of this matter?

A-5. If there will be a careful analysis—of self, self's purpose—as in relationships to those to whom benefits are supposed to, or are to accrue; and then all of these taken into consideration in the same way and manner as indicated, we will find the better conditions coming into thy experience. Remember, ye *are* indeed thy brother's keeper.

239-1   M.61   7/22/29

But well here may it be given this body, as long as there is held the consciousness of money and money power alone in the forefront of the body's endeavors, these will only be ordinary in returns from same. Have, set, make for self a goal to which the body would work to accomplish a definite thing in this experience, and not be just mediocre in the ideas, or most of all the ideas of that that is attempting to be accomplished other than just making money. Money takes wings easily. The body *mentally*, [239], has *abilities*—many abilities—many abilities, in that the body may accomplish—may accomplish in most any direction that it desires, but fear so often takes hold, loss of confidence in others so often pushed forward, that the hindrances are ever apparent . . .

Q-24. Please advise the body as to how he may best gain control of himself and utilize his abilities to best advantage.

A-24. Depend more upon the intuitive forces from within and not harken so much to that of outside influences—but learn to listen to that still small voice from within, remembering as the lesson as was given, not in the storm, the lightning, nor in any of the loud noises as are made to attract man, but rather in the still small voice from within does the impelling influence come to life in an individual that gives for that which must be the basis of human endeavor; for without the ability to constantly hold before self the ideal as is attempted to be accomplished, man becomes as one adrift, pulled hither and yon by the various calls and cries of those who would give of this world's pleasure in fame, fortune, or whatnot. Let these be the outcome of a life spent in listening to the divine from within, and not the purpose of the life.

290-1   F.51   3/3/33

Q-9. Will my business continue to be a success?

A-9. As known or viewed from the very activities of self, if there are to be continued the torments within self, the indecisions within self, the expectancy that disorders or disruptions will arise, these create those very influences in the contacts, in the groups, in the relations that are necessary in the activities. But, if there is shown faith, hope, understanding, cooperation in the activities, it will continue not only to be as the present—but an increased success; for there is the spirit of valuation and protection, for those very ideals that self would build within self.

Q-10. Is there any advice to me in regard to my business?

A-10. This is very good advice we are giving, as respecting how the attitude shall be! If it is felt, if it is created first within self, then it may be given out. Should fear become the basis of the condition, then there is created fear in the minds and in the experiences of many whom the body contacts in the business associations. The very *nature* of the association creates such!

238-2   F.43   2/13/30

Q-2. In the association of Mr. Lynch with [238] and her husband [240], what do the forces feel to be the matter and what procedure would the forces suggest?

A-2. This becomes rather of the personal or individual nature, for in the supervision there comes those of combative influences—for the *soul* of [238] has grown beyond that of Lynch and to be led by one that is beneath is but to bring those developments that are often contrariwise to the understanding of each, and builds for each that which brings and *breeds* discontent. Being content, is a happy position. Being *satisfied,* is being lost.

239-1   M.61   7/22/29

Treat those individuals with whom he would deal in the manner he would like to be dealt with under the same circumstances and conditions, and unless this *is done* don't expect remuneration for the work given out!

Castor Oil Packs

5186-1   F.44   5/30/44

[Background: Gall stones]

Have at least three to four thicknesses of old flannel saturated thoroughly with Castor Oil, then apply electric heating pad. Let this get just about as warm as the body can well stand, cover with oilcloth to prevent soiling of linen. Keep this on every afternoon or evening for an hour. Then sponge off with soda water. Do this for at least seven days without breaking. One hour each day, same hour each day. After and during these periods, take small doses of Olive Oil, two, three times each day. These should not be so severe as to cause strain, but be careful after about the third or fourth day to observe the stool, and there should be indications of the gall ducts being emptied, and should be gravel, and there should be some stones. This can be eliminated. If there are none indicated, rest one day, then repeat for another seven days, and we will find changes come about, unless there is undue exercise . . .

Q-1. Should packs extend clear across abdomen or just what area?

A-1. Over the gall duct area, and extend to the caecum down the right side, and across the abdomen.

2451-1   F.66   2/13/41

[Background: Distension in ascending colon; prolapsus in transverse and descending colon; skin rash.]

First we would begin with the use of hot Castor Oil Packs for about an hour each day for at least three days a week. These would be applied especially across the abdomen in the caecum or in the right area of the body.

Following each three-day period of using the Packs, we would take pure Olive Oil internally; not too great a quantity in the beginning, but as much as the body may assimilate.

Then following same—say the next evening—have a colonic irrigation, using a colon tube for same. To each quart of water used (body-temperature) put a heaping teaspoonful of table salt and a level teaspoon of baking soda, dissolving same thoroughly in the water before it is used. In the last or rinse water we would put an antiseptic, such as Glyco-Thymoline®—tablespoonful to a quart of water, body temperature.

After each meal, for four days each week—and leaving off entirely on the other days, we would take about a quarter to half a teaspoonful of *Alcaroid*. First dissolve this in a little water, then fill the glass; then drink another full glass of water afterward.

Then, after the third or fourth series of the cleansings of the system (not before), we would begin to use the electrically driven vibrator®. This would be applied especially upon the areas between the shoulders and down to the caecum—that is, the sacral area along the spinal system. Use the Sponge Applicator for such. Do this about once or twice each week, after it is begun, for twenty to thirty minutes.

1523-9   F.32   1/21/40

[Background: Pyrene poison]

As we find, the acute conditions arise from the effects of a poison—*pyrene*. From this activity the acute indigestion as produced through the alimentary canal has caused an expansion of, and a blocking in, the colon areas.

As we find in the present, we would apply hot Castor Oil Packs continuously for two and a half to three hours. Then have an enema, gently given . . . the oil alone given first, see? Olive Oil would be the better for this; about half a pint; so that there may be the relaxing. And then give the enema with body temperature water, using a heaping teaspoonful of salt and a level teaspoonful of baking soda to the quart and a half of water. Give this gently at first, but eventually—that is, after the period when there has been the ability for a movement—use the colon tube. Then we would take internally—after the Oil Packs and the enema—a tablespoonful of Olive Oil.

1523-15　F.33　4/28/42

Q-7. Please explain the following experience: When taking a Castor Oil Pack, as I dozed, I began to feel paralyzed, unable to move, speak, or hardly breathe. At first I fought against it; as I relaxed I began to feel as though I was moving into space and the feeling that I had great power concentrated in my eyes. Suddenly I was at my parents' home, talking with my father, knowing I had the power to influence him to do what I felt was best for him to do, yet knowing I should not. A large police dog which sat beside him, came toward me as if hypnotized. The dog kept coming towards me, even when my father and I both commanded it to stop. Then the scene changed and I was back in my home. I saw scraps of bacon in the skillet multiplying and growing and recognized the growth as manna known to the children of Israel; which I could pick up in my left hand, but vanished when I touched it with my forefinger and thumb of my right hand. Felt elated that I could describe manna to the study group.

A-7. This was an interbetween emotion, or—as indicated—a partial psychic experience. Consider that which takes place from the use of the oil pack and its influence upon the body, and something of the emotion experienced may be partially understood.

Oil is that which constitutes, in a form, the nature of activity between the functionings of the organs of the system as related to activity. Much in the same manner as [oil would act] upon an inanimate object it acts as a limbering agent, or allowing movement, motion, as may be had by the attempt to move a hinge, a wrench, a center, or that movement of an inanimate machinery motion. This is the same effect had upon that which is now animated by spirit. This movement, then, was the reflection of the abilities of the spirit of *animate* activity as controlled through the emotions of mind, or the activity of mind between spirit *and* matter. This was a vision, see?

Q-8. Should I allow this to happen, or fight against it?

A-8. Depends on whether you know what you want to do with it or not! This is where individuals not able to control are apt to allow other forces to control them.

Read the description and understand what's taking place. If there is the desire that the spirit of truth, the Master, direct—then there may be gained an understanding of the relationships between spirit and matter. If there is the desire that the masterfulness of self be experienced, or domination for self—as experienced over not only the lower kingdom [the dog symbol in above question] but of the higher kingdom [father symbol in above question] as well—or if there is the desire for self-indulgence, or for mental exploration into the unknown, you'll find it—but it may make self unknown to the better interests of self. Hence it must be used properly, correctly. Pray about it.

Catarrh, Nasal

3480-2 M.49 8/28/44

Changes in the environments would be well, yet these are not the primary causes. We would find, if there would be the leaving off of some of the diets which have become obnoxious, then the purifying of the alimentary canal, the setting up of better drainages from the head and the soft tissue in ear, nose, throat and stimulating the eliminations, it will be the better manner in which to control these disturbances . . .

Q-1. Can anything be done to relieve the nasal catarrh?

A-1. Do these which have been indicated.

[Reading 3480-1 gave colonics, change of altitude (from Montana to West Coast), and the following diet suggestions: " . . . keep away from red meats of any kind. Fish, fowl and lamb may be taken but not ever fried; in fact, no fried foods . . . There should never be taken those food values only for weight or that will pack. Hence leafy vegetables—not too much of these, except the broths of these; but plenty of raw vegetables; especially watercress, grated or scraped carrots, and cooked beets, should be often taken."]

Use the inhalant which may be outlined for the body in this: Prepare a large-mouth bottle. Put two vents into the opening of the bottle in which solution is put. Leave a two ounce space, at least, above solution in container. Add the following ingredients in the order named:

Pure Grain Alcohol...4 ounces

Oil of Eucalyptus.. 20 drops

Rectified Oil of Turp.. 5 drops
Tincture of Benzoin... 15 drops
Oil of Pine Needles.. 10 drops
Tolu in Solution .... 5 drops
Shake the solution, then removing the cork from vents, inhale deep-ly into the nasal passages—not too much in the beginning, just once or twice. Then inhale into the throat.

But do set up better eliminations with colonic irrigations.

Q-2. Have the colonics been sufficient and frequent enough to clear up all mucus?

A-2. We would not imply such if these had been correctly given. Do have them sufficient to remove the mucous which causes the disturbance. This should be observed in the periods of giving co-lonic irrigation.

Q-3. Am I getting enough valuable food elements?

A-3. Enough valuable food elements if they are kept balanced properly. Do have more of the B-1 and E. These may be supplement-ed in the activities in Zyrone and in wheat germ oil.

Child Care

1788-5   M.4 mos.   4/3/39

Q-2. How may he be broken from sucking his thumb?

A-2. Give him a pacifier or let him keep it as it is. Better a pacifier than the thumb, though, because this might eventually cause some deformity with the [practice of] same, see?

Q-3. Does sucking a pacifier cause any abnormal conditions?

A-3. Some hold that it causes adenoids. No. It does not cause other than a period when the will [of the child] must act with the habits of the body.

1788-7   M.1   12/20/39

Q-5. Should anything be done to prevent [continued] thumb sucking, since the roof of his mouth is being pushed out of shape?

A-5. This is not a harmful condition as yet; but this—too—can best be controlled by suggestion in the manner indicated. Howev-er, this must not be done as mere rote, or as something just to be gotten through with—but by very positively giving the very gentle suggestion as he sinks to sleep; not after he has gone to sleep for a long time, but as he is losing consciousness and there is the ability to control or suggest to the greater subconscious self, see?

3172-2   F.21 mos.   5/15/44

Q-8. How can one avoid the enlarging of adenoids and tonsils?

A-8. By massage. Stimulating the centers through which the circulation goes to the various portions of the adenoids or tonsils being affected, by too little or too much.

475-1   F.1   6/12/34

Q-2. What should be done to correct the nail-biting habit?

A-2. . . . this is the effect of nervousness, from the gnawing that has been . . . existent for some time in the system, see? And with those corrections [suggested in the reading], and with the tendency for the body to watch or be careful with self, this may be eliminated from the habits of the body. For, if we take away the cause the habit is more easily changed. For, we correct habits by forming others! That's everybody!

1788-7   M.1   12/20/39

Q-4. How can he be helped to learn to urinate regularly, or to keep his pants dry?

A-4. This is a natural consequence, and needs only to be considered as the growth and development comes about, by suggestion. The greater [effectiveness of] suggestion in controlling anything of this nature may be made by the parents as the body goes to sleep.

308-2   F.10   8/29/34

Q-5. Will following this treatment prevent bed-wetting?

A-5. This may be accomplished best by making the suggestion in this direction as the body is almost asleep, by the one who makes the application of the massage and rubs. *Positive* suggestion! Not that she *won't* do, but that she *will* do this or that, see? [Suggest] that when the desire is for the activity, the body will arouse and attend to same!

1208-6   M.3 mos.   10/3/36

There should be those precautions taken as respecting cold and congestion. As is indicated, there is a little in the system at present.

It would be well that mornings and evenings there be more [clothing] about the chest and back. Occasionally the camphorated oil rubs, especially of evenings, would be well for the body . . . Keep the rubs for the body, as it will assist in strengthening the spine and aid the development of the structural portions of the body. The massaging across the chest, around the ribs, also aids in the circulation for more and better blood. Colds should be worked off with Castoria, which sweetens the stomach and makes for the better digestion . . .

Q-8. *Is there any immediate danger of rickets?*

A-8. This is foolish! If there was, we would have given it! We have given those things for the keeping of the body in its nominal, normal development. Oil rubs and camphorated oil rubs will *do more* for the correction of the properties that make for the structural development than all the fish foods that you can ever give! . . .

Those activities of cod liver oil work upon the glands, and *not* upon structural portions! Keep the proper balance [of foods], keeping from the system any sugar other than that which may be assimilated—or [avoiding] any *cane* sugar; and this will make for better assimilation through the glandular forces. Remember, everything assimilated in a developing body is produced *by* the glands. And this *assimilates* same from the foods that are given.

161-1   M.11   5/21130

Q-4. *Should he be circumcised?*

A-4. *All* boys should be.

1958-4   F4   9/8/43

Q-1. *Is there a glandular condition resulting from whooping cough?*

A-1. The glands need to be cleared. Give the body one drop of Atomidine® in water before the morning meal for two days in succession each week, for four or five weeks. Just two days a week, but let those days be together, you see . . .

Q-4. *What causes the body to bite her fingernails? What will correct this?*

A-4. Lack of calcium in the body. Give the body *Calcios*™ about twice a week, and this will clear up. (Eat a whole wheat cracker thinly spread with Calcios™, about twice a week, preferably at the noon meal—say Tuesdays and Friday.)

Q-5. Does the body have worms?

A-5. If it didn't it would be in a bad fix! but these are not abnormal or out of the ordinary for the general conditions of the developing body in the present . . .

Q-13. Is the body too young to take pre-school age lessons on the piano? What age is best to begin this training?

A-13. Not if it will take them! There has to be the inclination from the body, desiring or wanting such, before it would be worth anything! You can't just make the body take it and be worth very much. If there is the desire, from the time they can know that they would like it, it is time to begin . . .

Q-17. Regarding the training: Will it break the will to give the body a switching after trying to reason with no result, or should she be ignored and left alone after trying to reason? What form of punishment will be most effective with this body, when reason fails?

A-17. Switching will be the most effective.

Q-18. And will not break the will?

A-18. You won't break the will of this body much! She may do some switching herself later, but then if it is controlled properly, it will be the better way.

Q-19. Any other advice regarding this body?

A-19. Do increase the spiritual attributes and purposes for the body and for its environs.

1208-8   M.13 mos.   8/12/37

Soon there should be considerations for some changes in the diet, but during this period of the warm weather and the forming of the teeth it is not well that those things be attempted that would tend to upset or to cause such a mighty change in the activities of the body.

We find that of a morning crisp bacon, well mashed, taken at the time the yolk of egg is given, would be most satisfying as well as agreeing with the digestive forces of the body. It is well to keep the Lime Water with the milk. We would *not* make any change in the formula, at least during this present month. There may be more and more of the vegetable foods given the body as prepared in the Gerber® manner. These should *not* be made to take the *place* of the milk but should add the properties to produce weight; that is, weight for the digestive system, producing more dilation for the stomach.

For under the present growth, the milk is absorbed and digested very soon. Hence these may be given—that is, the vegetables and the combinations—a little more often.

Do not overfeed; this is worse than underfeeding.

In the case of the mental and the spiritual atmosphere of the body—watch the developments, the tendencies. Be positive but not severe with the mental forces and influences of the body; this is much preferable to that of severity. Do not break the will, but rather guide same in the constructive suggestions as to the activities of the body in every way and manner.

These kept, as we find, we will have a developing body, mentally and physically near to normal . . .

Q-1. *What can be done to keep him from catching cold so easily?*

A-1. Keep the acidity of the system below normal. Make the tests of same with litmus paper from the kidney effusion—or the urine . . .

Q-3. *Should the Gerber® vegetables be given at noon and at the evening meal also?*

A-3. As indicated. These are to supply that which is to fill in, you see; while the real food values are more from the milk, the egg, oatmeal and the like, that should be altered during the day.

Q-4. *Should more than one kind of vegetable be given at a meal?*

A-4. The one kind at a feeding is preferable. There may be given more than one kind in a day, but not at one feeding during this month especially. Remember those conditions of the body-development. There is the necessity for calcium and lime, that is obtained more preferably through the milk and through the Lime Water for the system; for the formation not only of bone, but the activity for the thyroids to produce activities for the growth of the skin, the hair, the nails, the teeth—all must be kept not overactive but nominal.

Q-5. *Is there further information that can be given the parents that will be helpful in training him during the next few years?*

A-5. These that have been given are the manners; positive but not making for such severeness as to break the will. Rather by precept *and example;* for remember, the example is well, as is the precept; but the example is much more effective to the body . . .

Q-7. *Please give us any other helpful information regarding the rearing of the child.*

A-7. This should be given as the development comes. For during these periods, or until after the 18th month, the precautions are most for the *physical* being. *Then* from the 18th month we may find more for the mental. And do not forget the spiritual atmosphere for the developing entity.

Clairvoyant Examples

3477-1   What a peculiar street!

3526-1   [for a woman in Canada] Kind of snowy!

568-5   [for a man working in the Norfolk Navy Yard] (It's a busy place!—have to wait until he comes back here—this is his place.) Yes, we have the body . . .

3601-1   [for a man in Wyoming] Come back here and sit down!

849-75   [Florida] Pretty rough wind this evening!

3531-1   [for a man in Alaska] Hurry up and get through talking!

3471-1   [Chicago, Illinois] Cregier Avenue—yes, where the trees are.

3599-1   [reading for an individual who lived in the country, which included the direction of one and a half miles northeast] . . . yes, it's one and five-eighths.

3063-3   [for an individual in his New York City office] Yes, we have the body here. This we have had before. The body is just leaving, going down in the elevator now.

2983-2   Jacksonville—looks like rain.

1171-1   Yes, we have the body here. And the body is experiencing one of the little attacks it has with the nerves . . .

3322-1   [Buell Cottage, New Smyrna Beach, Fla.] Yes—up here on the right.

5188-1   [Guadalcanal, 6/3/44, 10:30-11:30 A.M. EWT] Yes, yes, what a combination of colors!

5078-1   [for a child of 10] Yes, we find the mother praying.

168-1   *Q-3. Mr. Cayce, is this body [for whom the reading is being given] in bed?*
          A-3. No, she is sitting in a large chair, talking to a man.

745-1   [woman's address . . . France, reading taken 3:40 to 4:10 P.M. EST] Yes, it's nine-thirty.

3331-1   [woman, in a church in Tucson, Ariz.] Not alone, but accompanied by many besides those visible to the physical eye.

1887-1   Yes—something wrong about the address here, but we have the body—for she is praying . . .

795-1 [child, age 3; mother's questions] *Q-2. Is a life reading advised . . . ?*
A-2. A little bit later. May not need it! But don't put that in the reading!

1311-1 [for a man whose address was given as 418 N. Cedar Street] Yes. That's where he was yesterday; he's at 419 now.

632-2 Yes, we have the body . . . Some odors about this we don't like—iodoform—flesh—

4888-1 *Q-6. Where is the body at the present time . . .. ?*
A-6. He is here at this address, you see, right at present. Just came in.
Q-7. Where did you first locate him?
A-7. At the street here, Union.

4029-1 Yes, we have had this room before but not this person.

3408-1 [1048 Sierra St., Reno, Nevada] Nevada—still cold! Sierra Street—that's under the hill!

4637-1 Yes, we have the body here. Smells much like a drug store.

3235-1 [12 miles from Memphis, Tenn., 9/23/43] Yes yes, we have the body here—peculiar odor here in the air right now, from the pollen—from the flooded waters.

2068-1 [child, first physical reading on 12/22/39, Okla.] Yes—mesquite trees. Yes. [second physical reading given 5/11/40; the parents did not understand the significance of the reference to mesquite trees, and asked the following question] *Q-4. Did the mentioning of "mesquite trees" in the first reading have any special significance?*
A-4. Only that these existed in those points through which there was the passing when the location was made. It had nothing to do with the body, save the associations of the environs or surroundings.

[The preceding are side comments Edgar Cayce made at the beginning of physical readings, when he reached the location of the individual sought. The following are side comments Edgar Cayce made at the beginning of *life* readings, usually just before saying, "Yes, we have the records . . . "]

3374-1 Yes—what a beautiful record!

5125-1 [F.30, born in Bokhoma, Okla.] A new vibration! Very

good. Quite an interesting fact about people born here. One out of ten thousand would ever commit suicide. Something in the soil; get it between your toes and you'll never commit suicide.

5118-1   A fourth-dimensional mind!

5112-2   [F.51, missionary in Belgian Congo for 15 years] Yes, yes, we have the records here—what funny little bungalows—of that entity now known as or called [5112]. There is the tendency here to tell the entity the difference between what life has been and what the rest of the life is to be. For there's quite a difference, and we do not find it the best for the entity to return to this region of the peculiar looking huts . . .

5106-1   [Date of reading, 5/12/44; F.44, born in Krumbach Schwaben, Germany] Krumbach Schwaben isn't much of it there now!

2061-1   [EC in undertone] You know, she should do something about this antrum trouble! [After saying this, EC coughed.]

5366-1   [F. born 10/31/90, Bellefontaine, Ohio] My, some very interesting characters have been born near Bellefontaine!

1120-1   [M. 29] There was some discussion here about the naming of the body—but [the name is] rather well chosen . . .

5733-1   [M. b. 11/23/89, Winterthur, Switzerland] Winterthur—isn't it pretty! Nice, beautiful stream—that's a good place to fish!

5400-1   [M. b. 2/25/06, Sylvester, Texas] Sylvester, Texas—quaint place! February 25, 1906—not too nice a day either, is it?

3054-4   [F. 50, b. 12/26/93, in Harper, Kansas] Before that the entity was in the English land during the early settlings . . . in those environs from the latter portion of the reign of the Judean King in Palestine.

The entity was among those who grew up in that changed environ . . . when those from the Norse land the hardier, sturdier people from that land now being overrun (and there is a right good battle there today) [2/16/44] brought changes in the activities.

Co-Creators with God

1549-1   F.55   3/11/38
And O that all would realize . . . that what we are—in any given
experience or time—is the combined results of what we have done
about the ideals that we have set! . . .

The soul of each individual is a portion then of the Whole, *with*
the birthright of Creative Forces to become a co-creator with the
Father, a co-laborer with Him. As that birthright is then manifested,
growth ensues. If it is made selfish, retardments must be the result
. . .

We find, as given from the beginning, each may attain to that
whereunto it has set and does set itself, according to the consciousness indwelling of the Creative Forces within.

For He has promised to meet and to be with those who call, and
who do His biddings, and keep His commandments.

And if He comes and abides with thee, what would be the limita-
tions? There are none, from the spiritual angle. And it is spirit—in
self in the Creative Forces—that will and does direct.

622-6   M.85   2/6/41
As is understood, that which is mental arises from those abilities
innate and manifested in life's expression itself—as in the fact that
every phase of life is the image of the Creator, or has the ability
within itself to *create* itself; thus the ability to make its own environment, if the activity for such is in keeping with the pattern *of* the
ideal the entity has chosen.

Thus it becomes each soul—in its realization, in its awareness,
in its seeking—to know the Author of its ideal, spiritually, mentally, materially. The spiritual is the life, the mental is the builder, the
material is the result of that builded through the purposes held by
the individual entity.

Then the entity finds himself as a co-creator with the divine that
is manifested in self. Thus, if the choice leads the entity into the
exalting of self, it becomes as naught in the end. If the choice is that
self is to be used in whatever manner—as in the talents, the attributes, the associations with its fellow men—to *glorify* the Creative
Force, then the body, the mind, finds that peace, that harmony, *that
purpose* for which it chose to enter a material experience.

Then, to the entity, it might be easily said, "Go *thou* and put that principle into thy daily practice."

3003-1   F.61   5/16/43
. . . as a corpuscle in the body of God, ye are free-willed—and thus a co-creator with God . . . An individual entity's experience must be finished before the entity may either be blotted out or come into full brotherhood with the greater abilities, or the greater applications of self in the creating or finishing of that begun . . .

Each appearance [in the earth] is as an opportunity. An opportunity is to the grace of God. The very fact of being aware of thyself is assurance of the fact that the Father-God is mindful of thee—now, *today* . . .

For, each soul enters with a mission. And even as Jesus, the great missionary, we all have a mission to perform. Are we working with Him [continually], or just now and then? . . .

For He faileth not. For He is ever the same, yesterday, today, tomorrow.

Color

5319-1   F.55   7/7/44
The [vitamin] B-1 should be rich in the foods which are taken. We would find this from all foods which are yellow in color, not as greens that would turn yellow, but as the yellow variety of squash, carrots, wax beans, peaches, all of these . . .

281-29   10/26/36
. . . consider the effect of the color itself upon thine own body as ye attempt to apply same by either concentration, dedication or meditating upon these. For as has been given, color is but vibration. Vibration is movement. Movement is activity of a positive and negative force. Is the activity of self as in relationship to these then positive?

3637-1   F.35   1/5/44
. . . color itself is vibration, just as much vibration as—or even more than—music.

428-4   F.48   2/20/31

. . . we will find . . . that colors influence the entity a great deal more even than musical forces in its tone—or color in music. Drabs, or certain greens, have an effect that is almost that to bring *illness* in the physical body; while the purples or violets, or shades of tan, bring an exultant influence that would make for the bringing of building influences in the entity.

288-38   F.29   9/19/34

Q-13. What are my best colors, or does it really make any difference?

A-13. Each body, each activity, each soul-entity vibrates better to this, that or the other color. As with this, certain colors of green and blue are those to which the body vibrates the better . . .

Colors are naturally the spiritualization of tone or sound . . .

3395-2   F.63   1/15/44

The entity came from the land of Saad or of the Indian land. Thus we find that dress, certain colors and tones have much of a "feel" in the experience of the entity. And if the entity will wear white, mauve and shades of purple, it will ever be as a helpful vibration to the entity. For what is builded from any experience in the earth is as a habit in the present, having that same character of influence upon an individual's ability towards things and conditions; not having power within themselves, but as that which has been builded by the entity.

1406-1   F.14   7/13/37

Colors—these become as means in which the entity may, for itself, determine much. But know as to what colors mean. For the entity is not only able and capable to receive the vibrations of individuals about the entity as to their colors, but as to their vibrations. And these then make for a sensitiveness that is often disturbing to the entity.

This may be developed or it may be passed over. But those that are as symbols or signs or conditions that may be used constructively, use same; do not abuse same. For that which is good, to be sure, may be used to one's own undoing.

Know that when there is felt, seen or experienced those vibrations of low, leaden or dark red, these are as dangers: not only for self but self's associations with individuals. This is not always to the entity, neither will it be found to be, compatible. For there will be oft, as has been in the experience, those individuals that mentally or materially the entity likes and likes the associations, yet there are resentments.

Then study those influences. And know when such arise in the experience that warnings are ahead, and govern the associations and the activities accordingly.

When there is felt that glow of orange, and the violet hues with the orange, know that these bespeak of sentimentality in the experience and are not always good; yet these in their proper relationships should be a portion of the experiences . . . in which one may know what such vibrations and such colors mean—that the individuals may be trusted.

When these reach those stages as to where there is felt the lighter red, and those that turn to shades of green with the influences that make for shadings into white, then these trust, these hold to; for such individuals, such associations, may bring in the experience of the entity that which will make for spiritual enlightenment, a mental understanding, and the influences that would bring helpful influences in every experience.

Hence the opal that is called the change, with the moonstone, should be stones about the body or entity oft. Wear the fire opal as a locket about the neck. This would be well. Not upon the hands nor upon the wrists, but about the neck.

Wear the others, as of the pearl with moonstone or the like, as rings or amulets or anklets; but never those upon the neck or in the ears—rather upon the extremities; for they will make for the bringing out—in the experiences of those the entity meets—of those very colors and vibrations that have been indicated to which the entity is so sensitive . . .

These then may be summed up or put in another manner: To thine own self be true and thou wilt not be false to anyone . . .

For being a "sensitive" and capable of the interpretations of the emotions of others is not easy, yet it must not be abused; else there may come those experiences in which there may rise many misunderstandings—and gossip is never kind! . . .

Know that that which has not its foundation in spiritual way *must* eventually fade . . .

It would be impossible for the entity to go even among a group of a thousand and not all be conscious that the entity had entered. Why?

As the colors, as the vibrations are a portion of the entity, they also radiate from the entity. Hence many, many, *many* are influenced by the entity . . .

Hence of that one to whom much has been given is much expected.

Hold fast to that which is good. For the way is before thee, and many look to thee—even as in all thine experiences in the earth—for directions.

987-4   F.49   11/2/37

Q-6. What is the meaning of the white lightning I have seen?

A-6. That awakening that is coming. More and more as the white light comes to thee, more and more will there be the awakening. For as the lights are in the colors: In the green, healing; in the blue, trust; in the purple, strength; in the white, the light of the throne of mercy itself. Ye may never see these save ye have withheld judgment or shown mercy.

4501-1   F.22   2/19/27

. . . for, as is seen, the body mentally—and the body in its nerve reaction—would respond as quickly to color forces as it would to medicinal properties . . .

Common Cold

902-1   2/17/41

Mrs. Cayce: You will have before you the human ailment known as the common cold. You will give information, advice and guidance as to how people may so conduct themselves as to avoid the common cold, or—having contracted a cold—to cure it. You will then answer the questions, as I ask them.

Mr. Cayce: Yes.

As we find, much has been written in many places respecting such, and much has been given through these channels respecting the various stages and the cure—or helpful applications.

For, it is a universal consciousness to the human body. Thus it is almost as individual as all who may contract or even come in contact with such.

Each body, as so oft considered, is a law unto itself. Thus what would be beneficial in one for prevention might be harmful to another; just as what might have beneficial effects upon one might prove as naught to another.

The cold is both contagious and infectious. It is a germ that attacks the mucous membranes of nasal passages or throat. Often it is preceded by the feeling of flushiness or cold sensations, and by spasmodic reactions in the mucous membranes of the nasal passages.

Then, precautionary or preventative measures respecting the common cold would depend upon how this may be fully judged in the human body, or as to what precautionary measures have been taken and as to what conditions exist already in the individual body.

First: A body is more susceptible to cold with an excess of acidity *or* alkalinity, but *more* susceptible in case of excess acidity. For, an alkalizing effect is destructive to the cold germ.

When there has been at any time an extra depletion of the vital energies of the body, it produces the tendency for an excess acidity—and it may be throughout any portion of the body.

At such periods, if a body comes in contact with one sneezing or suffering with cold, it is more easily contracted.

Thus precautions are to be taken at such periods especially.

To be sure, this leaves many questions that might be asked:

Does draft cause a cold? Does unusual change in dress? Does change in temperature? Does getting the clothes or the feet damp? etc.

All of these, to be sure, *affect* the *circulation;* by the depletion of the body-balance, the body-temperature or body-equilibrium. Then at such times if the body is tired, worn, overacid or overalkaline, it is more susceptible to cold—even by the very changes produced through the sudden unbalancing of circulation, as from a warm room overheated. Naturally when overheated there is less oxygen, which weakens the circulation in the life-giving forces that are destructive to *any* germ or contagion or such.

Then if there is that activity in which the body becomes more conscious of such conditions, this of itself *uses* energies oft that produces *psychologically* a susceptibility!

Consequently, as we find, this is one of the most erratic conditions that may be considered as an ill to the human body.

Much at times may also depend upon the body becoming immune to sudden changes by the use of clothing to equalize the pressures over the body. One that is oft in the open and dresses according to the general conditions, or the temperatures, will be *less* susceptible than one who often wraps up or bundles up too much—*unless*— *unless* there are other physical defects, or such conditions in the system as to have reduced the vitality locally or as a general condition through the system.

So much, then, as to the susceptibility of an individual or body to colds.

Then, precautions should be taken when it is known that such tendencies exist; that is, weakness, tiredness, exhaustion, or conditions arising from accidents as of draft, dampness of clothes, wet feet or the like, or contact with those suffering with a cold.

As is known, all vital forces are activities of the glandular system; and these are stimulated by specific glandular activity attributed to the functioning of certain portions of the system.

Then, when exposed to such—under the conditions as indicated, or the many other phases of such that make up the experience of an individual, these would be the preventative measures:

The use of an *abundant* supply of vitamins is beneficial, of *all* characters; A, B, B-1, D, E, G and K.

Vitamins are not as easily overcrowded in the system as most other boosters for a general activity. For, these are those elements that may be *stored*—as it were—in their proper relationships one to another, to be called into use when needed or necessary.

This does not mean that it may not be overdone as a preventative, or in cases where infection already exists. For, that which may be helpful may also be harmful—if misapplied—whether by the conscious activity in a body or by an unconscious activity in the assimilating forces of a system. If this were not true, there would never be an unbalancing of *any* portion of the functioning system; neither would there be the lack of coordination or cooperation with the various organs in their attempt to work together.

It is true that the functioning system (assimilating, distributing and eliminating system) attempts to create that necessary for a balance. Yet it can only use that it has at hand. Thus, with a deficiency of any structural building, blood building or tissue building influence, it may cause weakness by drawing on that necessary to supply the needed conditions for the system's balance.

For instance, if there is a bone fracture the body of itself creates that element to knit this fracture or broken area. Yet it does not supply or build as much of such element during the periods when the fracture does not exist. Hence when it exists, unless there is an abundant supply of that needed—by or from that assimilated—other portions of the body will suffer.

Know that the body must function as a unit. For, one may get one's feet wet and yet have cold in the head! One may get the head wet and still have cold in the head! The same is true in any such relationships. For, the circulation carries the body forces in same, in the corpuscles, the elements or vitamins needed for assimilation in every organ. For, each organ has within itself that ability to take from that assimilated that necessary to build itself. One wouldn't want a kidney built in a lung; neither would one want a heart even in the head (yet it is necessary to function mentally that way often!).

These are conditions to be considered in preventing as well as in correcting colds. Hence it may be said that the adding of vitamins to the system is a precautionary measure—at all seasons when the body is the most adaptable or susceptible to the contraction of cold, either by contact or by exposure or from unsettled conditions.

The diet also should be considered—in that there is not an excess of acids or sweets, or even an excess of alkalinity, that may produce such a drawing upon some portion of the system (in attempting to prepare the assimilating system for such activity in the body) as to weaken any organ or any activity or any functioning as to produce greater susceptibility.

Hence there should be kept a normal, well-balanced diet that has proven to be right for the individual body—if precautionary measures are to be taken through such periods.

Also there should be precautions as to the proper clothing, as to drafts, as to dampness of feet, as to being in too hot or too cold a room, as to getting too tired or exhausted in any way or manner.

Precautions in all these directions to keep a near normal balance are measures best to be taken towards preventing the contracting of cold.

When once the cold has attacked the body, there are certain

measures that should always be taken.

First, as has so often been indicated, *rest!* Do not attempt to go on, but *rest!* For, there is the indication of an exhaustion somewhere, else the body would not have been susceptible. Then, too, the inflammation of the mucous membranes tends to weaken the body, so that there is the greater susceptibility to the weakened portions of the body throughout the special influence of the lymph and emunctory activity—such as the head, throat, lungs, intestinal system. Then, if there has been an injury in any structural portions of the body, causing a weakness in those directions, there becomes the susceptibility there for the harmful effects from such.

Then, find or determine next where the weakness lies. Is it from lack of eliminations (which causes many ailments)?

Hence quantities of water, as well as an alkalizer, as well as a booster to assimilating forces, are beneficial things towards producing a balance so that the cold and its consequences may be the more readily or easily eliminated or eradicated.

Do not neglect to take the precautions first. Then if there is the contraction, determine the weakened factor; knowing that what will aid that portion of the body to more easily attain an equilibrium will prove to be the most beneficial.

Many things in many ways are beneficial to those who have contracted cold—dependent, to be sure, upon the general constitution of the body, the amount of vitamins stored in the system, and so on. Also the response depends greatly on whether or not there is the opportunity given for rest, and the not eating too much, so that the body may be aroused to gain its equilibrium.

Hence it is necessary that there be given the booster for those portions of the body needing the stimulation; and those elements that produce more of vital energies are the more helpful influences.

Ready for questions.

Q-1. What diet is recommended once the cold has been contracted?

A-1. This depends upon what is the condition. It may be one cause or another that has weakened the system. More generally, the liquid diet is best—or that the more easily assimilated that carries the greater strengthening ability to all portions of the body. Not heavy or solid foods then. Little of meats, unless given at the period of recuperation when those the more easily assimilated would be the better—such as fish, fowl or lamb—never fried, however.

Q-2. Is the absence of meat in the diet an important factor in avoiding colds?

A-2. Not necessarily. It depends upon the combinations, rather than any one element that may be singled out as producing destructive forces. If rare meats are taken, or those that have the life in same, in such measures as to set up a weakening of some portion of the digestive forces, in the attempt of the body to assimilate, it may produce a condition of susceptibility. In that case meats should be avoided by that particular body, or in such quantities at least.

Complexion

2072-6 F.31 1/30/42

Q-5. What soap, manner of cleansing, creams and makeup would be least harmful and most helpful in correcting and beautifying the skin?

A-5. Pure Castile soap is the better as a cleanser. As a cleansing cream or the like, the Genuine Black and White products are nearer to normal.

404-8 F.49 7/2/40

Q-8. Give a good skin freshener.

A-8. To one half pint of Olive Oil add one ounce of Rose Water, a few drops of Glycerine and one ounce of a 10% solution of Alcohol, and shake these well together. This is a skin invigorator.

1968-7 F.31 7/28/42

For making or keeping a good complexion—this for the skin, the hands, arms, and body as well—we would prepare a compound to use as a massage (by self) at least once or twice each week. To six ounces of peanut oil, add: olive oil, two ounces; rose water, two ounces; lanolin, dissolved, one tablespoonful. This would be used after a tepid bath, in which the body has remained for at least fifteen to twenty minutes; giving the body then [during the bath] a thorough rub with any good soap—to stimulate the body-forces. As we find, Sweetheart or any good Castile soap, or Ivory®, may be used for such.

Afterwards, massage [with] this solution, after shaking it well. Of course, this [amount] will be sufficient for many times. Shake well and pour some in an open saucer or the like; dipping fingers in same. Begin with the face, neck, shoulders, arms; and then the whole body would be massaged thoroughly with the solution; especially in [the area of] the limbs—in the areas that would come across the hips, across the body, across the diaphragm. This will not only keep a stimulating [effect] with the other treatments indicated [hydrothera-py, massage and osteopathy] taken occasionally, and give the body a good base for the stimulating of the superficial circulation, but [the solution] will aid in keeping the body beautiful; that is, as to [being free from] any blemish of any nature . . .

Q-2. Should I continue the mud packs?

A-2. These are well occasionally; not too often . . . But once a month, for the very pleasure of it, we would have the mud pack.

1947-4   F.32   10/11/39

Q-16. How can people avoid aging in appearance?

A-16. The *mind!*

Q-17. How can sagging facial muscles be avoided? How cor-rected?

A-17. By massage, and the use of those creams as indicated [Black and White Genuine], over the chin and throat, around the eyes and such conditions [of sagging]. Occasionally, the use also of the Boncilla or mud packs would be very good.

1968-3   F.29   3/14/40

Also about twice a month . . . we would have the mud packs; face and neck, across the shoulders and upper portions about the neck; especially extending over the area of the thyroids—as an astringent and as a stimulation for a better circulation throughout the system.

1709-5   F.20   3/22/40

Q-3. Is the mud pack I'm using the proper sort?

A-3. As we find, the Boncilla would be more preferable than this, that is more of the nature of chalk in same.

2072-9   F.32   7/22/42

Q-9. Is there not a treatment or method that might be used by the entity for the removal of blackheads from the face?

A-9. The general building up of the body-forces and the establishing first of correct coordination of eliminations. These [blackheads] will gradually be removed. There might be used bleaches or cleansing creams, but these would eventually give more trouble than the blackheads are causing in the present. Get to the basic conditions of these, as is now being accomplished through the use of the fumes [fume baths], the rubs, and now the violet ray® [hand machine, bulb applicator].

5223-1   F.55   6/13/44

Q-3. For freckles?

A-3. You'd better try to keep your freckles and not try to get rid of them. Genuine Black and White for skin is preferable for such, but these [freckles] are in the pigment of the skin, and unless you wish to upset something else, don't attempt to bleach more [freckles out] than you would have from the regular conditions. These are partially liver conditions but don't be touchy about freckles, they're good for you!

1947-4   F.32   10/11/39

Q-14. Would you give me a formula for destroying superfluous hair, but which does not injure the skin in any way?

A-14. There's no such animal! This may best be done by [proper] diet *and* the applications to the skin for keeping the pores open *and* the body-actions better—such as the Black and White Creams (the *Genuine* Black and White preparations, made in Chicago—*not* Plough's).

2582-4   F.35   4/23/44

Q-9. Since diet has not caused hair on lips to diminish, is there anything which will prevent this that can be used externally? Will cutting or bleaching increase growth?

A-9. Do not shave off, do not attempt to bleach or dye, but use this mixture: Cocoa Butter, 3 drams; Calomel, 2 grains; Epsom Salts, 20 grains. Mix these thoroughly, as with [mortar] and pestle. Massage this ointment gently in the areas where there are the disturbances from superfluous hair, and after leaving on for 15 to 20 minutes, rub off. This, used as an ointment will remove hair without injury to the body. To be sure, mercury is in the Calomel, and this is a poison, but with this combination and in this quantity there is not sufficient for a body to absorb enough to become detrimental to the body-forces. After this is used, as the base for a better skin condition use the Genuine Black and White cream.

920-2   F.48   5/17/35

Q-2. How can one permanently remove superfluous hair?

A-2. This, as we find, arises from *a general* condition that is from the activity of the diet—and from this activity of the glands that *makes* for the *growth* of same in or upon the body . . . *For this body*, then, we find it would be well to use the Atomic Iodine, or Atomidine®; one to two drops in half a glass of water before the morning meals and at night just before retiring, in periods of four to five days [taken for four to five days]—then leave off for a week, then take again . . .

The diets would consist often of the seafoods; once or twice a week, you see. Only the potato peeling, or the very small potato used with the peeling is preferable to the pulp of same. All those vegetables that make for the carrying of iron and silicon; [such] as squash, cucumbers, radishes, the oyster plant, or such natures, should be a portion of the diet quite often—if there would be kept the proper balance as related to those activities of the glands that make for the growth of the hair. For if these [foods] are kept with the *normal* activities, we will find these will not only produce the *proper* growth of the hair but will cause its normal or natural color [to stay] . . . Naturally, though, this is a long-drawn-out method and [to be effective] must be a persistent and consistent thing upon the part of the users of same.

Coughs and Hiccoughs

Coughs

274-11   M.37   2/21/36

To the white only of one egg (not a cold storage egg, but a fresh egg), beaten very thoroughly, add: Juice of one lemon, added *very* slowly and stirred. Teaspoonful of strained honey, added drop by drop and beaten into same. Glycerine, two minims (not more than the two drops). This [mixture] may be taken a teaspoonful about twice a day, until the condition is cleared.

243-29   F.58   3/10/38

As a cough medicine, an expectorant, and for a healing through the whole system, prepare: Put 2 ounces of strained pure honey in 2 ounces of water and let come to a boil. Skim off the refuse, then add 1 ounce of Grain Alcohol. To this as the carrier, then, add—in the order named:

Syrup of Wild Cherry Bark .... 1 ounce
Syrup of Horehound .... ½ ounce
Syrup of Rhubarb .... ½ ounce
Elixir of Wild Ginger .... ½ ounce

Shake well the solution before the dose is taken, which would be about a teaspoonful—and this may be taken as close together as every hour. It will allay the cough, *heal* those disturbing forces through the bronchi and larynx, and make for better conditions through the eliminations.

303-25   F.55   9/4/41

In making applications for the body in the present, we would make this as an aid for the cold and for assistance in expectoration; this to be taken about three to four times a day, or at night when there is the tendency for spasms of coughing.

Dissolve 1 ounce of Rock Candy, as a syrup, in a pint of good Rye Whiskey. Then add, in the order named:

Syrup of Horehound .... ½ ounce
Glycerine .... 10 drops
Elixir of Lactated Pepsin .... 10 drops

Shake these well together before the dose is taken.

2600-1   F.62   10/8/41

For the cough, for the activities to the *general* bodily forces, we would have at least three to five osteopathic corrections; these specifically in the dorsal and the cervical areas . . .

Prepare an inhalant in this manner: To 4 ounces of Pure Grain Alcohol, add—in the order named: (and in an 8 ounce bottle)

Oil of Eucalyptus .... 20 minims
Compound Tincture of Benzoin .... 15 minims
Rectified Oil of Turp .... 5 minims

Balsam of Tolu in Solution.......................................20 minims

Shake the solution together, inhale through the nostril and through the mouth, two or three times through each, and two or three times a day. This will aid in purifying, in clarifying the membranes in the nasal passages and in the throat.

1745-5   M.48   7/23/41

Q-2. What causes the severe headaches and cough?

A-2. The cough is caused by the pressure upon the bronchi, by this [the poisons] backing up of impulse. The headaches arise from the congestion in the liver.

Do these things as we have indicated.[Osteopathy, Castor Oil Packs]

3079-2   M.55   10/17/43

Q-5. What causes the small cough even without any cold?

A-5. This is rather a reflex condition. Nothing to be alarmed at. If there will be the use of Minit-Rub™ around the throat, at the trachea, we find that this would be allayed. Put this on every night or two for several nights and it will allay the condition.

3632-1   M.67   1/29/44

Q-1. What is the cause of the cough and what treatment will relieve it?

A-1. This is an effect of the deterioration and a drooping or dropping of the palate. Tie up a piece of hair in the center of the head. Keep it tied up, like a wig. Tie this tighter each day.

Every three days make it a little bit tighter, a little bit tighter, it'll soon stop the cough and raise the palate.

Hiccoughs

2752-3   F.2   1/17/44

Q-4. What causes hiccoughs when she laughs? Please advise corrective measures.

A-4. Do this massaging as indicated, over the liver and gall duct area. You see, a hiccough is the convulsion in the diaphragm where the esophagus enters the upper portion of the stomach. And as this rash [discussed earlier in the reading] is caused from incoordination of the eliminations, you will kill two birds with one little pebble.

50-1   M.Adult   6/25/23
It is rather a serious condition . . . in this body. The body has grown rather weak. His coughing spells and hiccough spells are bad for him. Not very much to be done for this body for a cure. May be some things done to bring relief. May be some extension made to the life of the body . . .

Q-3. What causes him to cough and hiccough so much?

A-3. Condition of the eliminated elements in [the] liver and hepatic circulation. These are choked. The application [suggested] will localize the condition, then we will be able to operate successfully. As it [poison] is distributed over the system, the blood is not capable of taking care of it.

1839-1   M.39   3/7/39
Q-1. What should be done to relieve hiccoughs which he has had for six days?

A-1. Let this be done by suggestion, through such as Kuhn.

Creation

5246-1   F.26   5/27/44
Know there is the physical body and its attributes, its hopes, its desires, physical, just as that of animated matter, animated spirit.

Then there is the mind, the physical mind and its associations; the spiritual mind and its hopes and desires.

Then there is the soul body also. Thus as you find in self, body, mind, soul, in its three-dimensional manner, it is as the spiritual three-dimensional concept of the Godhead; Father, Son, Holy Spirit.

These, then, in self are a shadow of the spirit of the Creative Force. Thus as the Father is as the body, the mind is as the Son, the soul is as the Holy Spirit. For [the soul] is eternal. It has ever been and ever will be, and it is the soul made in the image of the Creator, not merely the physical or mental being . . .

For, as is given in the beginning: God moved and said, "Let there be light," and there was light, not the light of the sun but rather that of which, through which, in which every soul had, has, and ever has its being. For in truth ye live and move and have thy being in Him.

3508-1   F.45   12/13/43

In analyzing self, the entity finds itself body, mind and soul, that answers in the three-dimensional plane to the Godhead—Father, Son, Holy Spirit.

God moved, the spirit came into activity. In the moving it brought light and then chaos.

In this light came creation of that which in the earth came to be matter; in the spheres about the earth, space and time; and in patience it has evolved through those activities until there are the heavens and all the constellations, the stars, the universe as it is known—or sought to be known by individual soul-entities in the material plane.

Then came into the earth materiality, through the spirit pushing itself into matter. Spirit was individualized, and then became what we recognize in one another as individual entities.

Spirit that uses matter, that uses every influence in the earth's environ for the glory of the Creative Forces, partakes of and is a part of the universal consciousness.

As the entity, an individual, then applies, it becomes aware—through patience, through time, through space—of its relationship to the Godhead—Father, Son, Holy Spirit.

3491-1   M.32   11/17/43

Then, from whence comes creation? Whence comes the abilities for self-production? In the beginning was given all things in nature, all things that are in man's body. There was found within same the ability to reproduce its own kind. Then, when this ability becomes lacking—as it does in deterioration through age in human experience—it is because there is set up those consciousnesses in the cycle or atoms of the body itself, as of tiredness, weakness, the desire for rest . . .

Then in this body, as we find here, the closer study of creation, the closer study of God's relationship to man, the closer study of what the creating of vibrations in body may mean, will bring—What is promised?—through suffering a more excellent, a more perfect way . . .

Do study creation, man's relationship to God. What is light, that came into the earth, as described in the 3rd verse of Genesis I? Find that light in self. It isn't the light of the noon day sun, nor the moon, but rather of the Son of man.

Cremation

1472-2   F.57   11/13/37

Q-1. Does death instantly end all feeling in the physical body? If not, how long can it feel?

A-1. This would be such a problem; dependent upon the character of which unconsciousness is produced to the physical reaction—or the manner in which the consciousness has been trained.

Death—as commonly spoken of—is only passing through God's other door. That there is continued consciousness is evidenced, ever, by the associations of influences, the abilities of entities to project or to make those impressions upon the consciousness of sensitives or the like.

As to how long—many an individual has remained in that called death for what ye call *years* without realizing it was dead!

The feelings, the desires for what ye call appetites are changed, or not aware at all. The ability to communicate is that which usually disturbs or worries others.

Then, as to say how long—that depends upon the entity.

For as has been given, the psychic forces of an entity are *constantly* active—whether the soul-entity is aware of same or not. Hence as has been the experience of many, these become as individual as individualities or personalities are themselves.

Q-2. If cremated, would the body feel it?

A-2.What body? The physical body is not the consciousness. The consciousness of the physical body is a separate thing. There is the mental body, the physical body, the spiritual body.

As has so oft been given, what is the builder? *Mind!* Can you burn or cremate a mind? Can you destroy the physical body? Yes, easily.

To be absent (what is absent?) from the body is to be present with the Lord, or the universal consciousness, or the ideal. Absent from what? What absent? Physical consciousness, yes.

As to how long it requires to lose physical consciousness depends upon how great are the *appetites* and desires of a physical body!

275-29   F.19   12/21/32

Q-11. How long should one wait before burial?

A-11. Depending upon that which causes the separation from the body, and dependent upon the manner in which the disposition is to be made of [the] body.

Q-12. How should a body be prepared for burial?

A-12.This depends upon the development or that builded in the consciousness of the individual, as to what is necessary for the loosening of the elementals from the physical body. As has been noted, this may best be studied by the manner in which the various religious forces or cults dispose of such bodies in India; for, as has been given, "Here we may know their belief, or what they think they believe by the manner in which disposition is made of the body."

That that would be *ideal* is that it may be hermetically sealed, or by fire, or by the separation of the atmosphere from the body.

Q-13. What is the best disposition of a body, for the sake of all?

A-13. By fire!

Cycles

3684-1   M.56   2/21/44

As we find, there are disturbances with this body—physical, mental, spiritual. For while a very material-minded individual might say that "bad luck" had come to the body, we find that nothing happens by chance.

For each soul is as precious in the sight of the Creative Forces or God as another—just as a mother doesn't have her love changed for another, no matter how many children there may be—unless she's a foolish mother.

For God is not a respecter of persons. And when an individual, as this, through conditions brought about physically, has sudden collapses by the breaking of cells as to cause paralysis to portions of the body, while it is pathological, it is also psychological, it is partly karma.

Then, if there will be a release of the physical conditions that are at present useless, there must be a change of attitude towards spiritual and mental things. For mind is the builder . . .

Just because there has been the breaking of cellular force in the brain, so that reflexes are not possible in the body at present, does not indicate that these conditions need necessarily to remain so.

For the body renews itself, every atom, in seven years.

How have ye lived for the last seven? And then the seven before? What would ye do with thy mind and thy body if they were wholly restored to normalcy in this experience? Would these be put to the use of gratifying thine own appetites as at first? Will these be used for the magnifying of the appreciation of the love to the infinite?

For who healeth all thy diseases? If ye think it is the doctor or the surgeon, who is thy doctor? Is his life different from your own? Life itself, comes from the Infinite. There ye must begin if ye would have healing for this body, not merely by saying, "Yes, I believe Jesus was the Son of God—yes, I believe He died that I might have an advocate with the Father."

Yes, this also—but what are ye doing about it? Are ye living like that? Do ye treat thy brother, thy neighbor, thy friend, thy foe, as though this were true? For no matter what ye say, the manner in which ye treat thy fellow man is the answer to what ye really believe. For the manner in which ye treat thy neighbor is the manner in which ye are treating thy Maker. And be not deceived, God is not mocked; whatsoever a man soweth that must he also reap.

Then, kick not against the pricks, because ye are meeting thine own self.

When ye have righted thy mind to the correct thinking as to the Creative Forces and what they may bring to thee, study Exodus 19:5. Know that it means you—*you*! Then pattern thy life in that manner.

Turn then to John 14, 15, 16, 17 and know that it is to thee He speaks, not merely those who were physically present. For the earth is the Lord's and the fullness thereof, and without Him . . . Jesus, as ye call Him, the Light—as He is in the mind and soul of individual entities—without Him, there is no way to the Father. He speaks to thee, "Ask in my name." "Love ye one another" is His last command—pure, simple; not possessive, but love that casteth out fear, that putteth the heart, the mind, the soul at ease and not in doubt and in fear . . .

Don't be weary in well-doing. If it requires years, give years—but give a service and a praise continually to God, if ye would have life. For as He gave, and gives to every individual entity who seeks His face, "I came that ye might have life and have it more abundantly."

But grow first in grace, in knowledge and then apply the mechanical sources for the healing and correcting of the body.

No, climatic conditions will not change the body, unless ye

change in mind. These are very well—but what ye need is a change of mental attitude, and then—do the first things first—and then apply the mechanical applications.

Be consistent, be persistent.

3117-1   F.7   7/28/43

[Background: Injury at birth]

... there may be a great deal of help for this body. This is the bungle of the doctor, not of this soul-entity. Someone must eventually pay, much, for this ...

Those that minister may gain a great deal in spirit, and in understanding, as they minister here to this body, [3117].

True, there are adhesions, and there is the lack of the circulation through portions of the brain. But this is at the beginning of a cycle for body change.

Each atom may be changed within seven years. If there are those interested in contributing to this, *begin*. If you are not interested in doing it for fourteen, don't commence!

3236-1   F.12   9/23/43

[Background: Retarded since birth]

Here we have an abnormality that presents itself from a very poor attendance at the time of the birth of the body ... there can be help. As to just how far-reaching this will be will depend upon how persistently and consistently the applications are made for improvement. Remember, there are gradual changes that take place in a body, and especially in a developing body, a growing body. The whole anatomical structure is changed in each cycle—or every seven years. Unless this suggested treatment is to be continued ... persistently—until the second cycle for this body, don't begin it—just put it away and forget it.

3226-1   F.44   9/20/43

As to the appearances in the earth, these we find quite varied. Not all [appearances] would be given in the present, for—as indicated—different groups come to choose manifestation [in the earth] at varied cycles.

... the entity is entering what might be called the sixth cycle in the present, for there is the using of the entity in the application of those tenets or truths, those inclinations that arise from the urges and the sojourns in the earth.

For, those sojourns are as lessons, as grades, as activity of which, in which and through which the entity may use or abuse within the experiences of self.

3128-1   F.48   8/2/43

. . . each cycle brings a soul-entity to another crossroad, or another urge from one or several of its activities in the material plane.

But these [appearances] are chosen with the purpose to indicate to the entity how and why those urges are a part of the entity's experience as a unit, or as a whole.

For, one enters a material sojourn not by chance, but there is brought into being the continuity of pattern or purpose, and each soul is attracted to those influences that may be visioned from above. Thus *there* the turns in the river of life may be viewed.

To be sure, there are floods in the life; there are dark days and there are days of sunshine. But the soul-entity stayed in a purpose that is creative, even as this entity, may find the haven of peace as is declared in Him.

Deaf-Mutism

3676-1   M.8   2/19/44

Here we have quite a disturbance with this body, [3676]. This is of a karmic nature. It is as much or more for those responsible for the body, as well as for the learning of patience by the body itself.

The auditory forces and all of the organs of the sensory system are involved. These are partly karmic, partly prenatal, and partly what might be called elemental forces; not elemental forces in the nature of earthbound, but elemental in the sense of the spiritual manifestations towards materiality. Thus the treatments here would be best given by the mother; that is, in the present circumstances.

Use the low electrical vibrations from the Wet Cell Appliance® carrying into the system vibratorially the properties of Chloride of Gold to build nerve energy and to coordinate the relations of the cerebrospinal, the sympathetic and the sensory organism. The proportions would be one grain Chloride of Gold Sodium, to each ounce of distilled water and use three ounces of the Solutions for each charge; renewing the Solution every fifteen days.

Every thirty days renew the charge for the Appliance. The small plate would be attached to three different centers alternately. The Appliance would be used for thirty minutes each day; one day attaching the small plate to the 3rd cervical, the next day to the 9th dorsal, and the next day to the 4th lumbar. Be sure to rotate the attachments in this order.

There are the three centers through which there is the activity of the kundalini forces that act as suggestions to the spiritual forces for distribution through the seven centers of the body.

The large plate, through which the Gold Solution® passes vibratorially, would be attached to the lacteal duct and umbilical center, which on this body would be the width of two fingers, the mother's fingers, from the navel center towards the right, and one finger up from that point.

Do keep the attachment plates clean and do remove the connections from the Solution® when not in use and connect at least twenty minutes before it is applied to the body.

Use that period for suggestions to the body. Though there may not be the hearing, there may not be the perfect vision, there may not be the normal taste, the normal voice, we find that the soul, the entity, the subconscious, the unconscious and the superconsciousness will respond—by the continual drum of the suggestion given. Use the mother's own words, but this as the purpose of such a prayer or suggestion:

May this body be so attuned to the Infinite that it may be prepared here and now for the greater service it may render to its fellow man in this experience.

Do that.

We are through with this reading.

Deafness

3679-1   F.56   2/19/44

[Background: Mrs. [3679]'s letter, 9/19/43: " . . . I have suffered for years with almost maddening head noises which interfered with hearing from the very first. Gradually my natural hearing was lost and for the past 13 years I have had to rely entirely upon a hearing aid. I have had the very best of medical care but no benefits have ever been obtained in this. There seemed to be nothing to cure such as inflammation or catarrh. One 'Eye, Ear, Nose and Throat' specialist suggested that it probably was caused by a gradual paralysis of the auditory nerve. He frankly admitted he could do nothing and suggested 'faith' as a possible cure . . . "]

. . . there are many conditions in the physical forces that are very good with this body. Yet there are disturbances, which at times upset the whole physical organism. These are physical expressions reflexing from a subluxation which has long existed in this body. While this has been of a minor nature, there will be found a definite lesion between the 5th and 6th dorsal centers. With this removed, and then measures taken to aid the liver and gall duct to react to the impulses of the circulation and the reflex action from cerebrospinal and sympathetic nerve system to the area from the ganglia at this center, we would find much better conditions for this body.

These, then, are the manners in which we would begin the applications:

First we would begin applying Castor Oil Packs for an hour and a half twice each day, for at least three days in succession each week, over the liver and the gall duct area. Saturate three to four thicknesses of old flannel with the Castor Oil and apply to the liver and gall duct area, extending to the caecum area. Apply it warm and then use an electric pad to retain the heat—just so it is not too uncomfortable. Do this for three days—the same three days each week.

At the end of the three days, begin to take internally small doses of Olive Oil; about a teaspoonful three to four to five times each day. For, if this in the beginning causes belching or regurgitation reduce the quantity and keep on taking it, at least every other hour during the waking state.

The next week have the Castor Oil Packs again, twice each day for three days.

Keep up the Olive Oil until there have been thorough eliminations and until there are indications that there has been a draining of the gall duct area.

Then have at least 8 to 10 osteopathic treatments, with particular reference to the 5th and 6th dorsal centers, coordinating the 3rd cervical, 9th dorsal, and the sacral and lumbar axis . . .

After 8 to 10 osteopathic adjustments have been made, then empty or drain the gall duct osteopathically.

In the matter of the diet—through the period that there is the draining [of the gall duct], we would have particularly semi-solid or semi-liquid foods, preferably. Then a great deal of raw vegetables, prepared in many different ways, oft prepared with gelatin. Not too much meats, and no fats; not even butter during the first two to three series of these treatments. Soups and broths, fish, fowl and lamb, but never any foods fried.

Ready for questions.

Q-1. Has some minor dislocation in the spinal column gradually caused the auditory nerves to become paralyzed?

A-1. This is rather a prolapsus of the Eustachian tube, but with the corrections in the dorsal area, setting up better drainages in the gall duct and liver area, we should find these corrections aiding the disturbances in the ear. It would be well, when the corrections or drainages are set up, that the Eustachian tube also be corrected osteopathically.

Q-2. What causes the very pronounced snap, or cracking noise at the base of the skull whenever the head is turned to either the right or left?

A-2. This comes from the disturbance in the lower dorsal or at the 5th and 6th dorsal, which does not coordinate with the 3rd cervical centers.

Q-3. How can relief be obtained from the almost constant pain from one or two vertebrae located between the shoulder blades?

A-3. By the corrections to set up drainages for the conditions that are causing neuritic reactions in nerves and muscles.

Q-4. Are nerves inflamed or bone infected in nasal region?

A-4. This is a sinus disorder from a catarrhal condition that causes the prolapsus [the Eustachian tubes].

Do these things and we will have better conditions for this body. The head noises will be relieved and drainages will be set up in the liver and gall duct so that areas throughout the body will be improved.

That causing the gradual loss of hearing arises from a liver and gall duct disturbance.

We are through with this reading.

5461-1   M.21   11/1/29

Q-2. What can be done to make body hear, as body is deaf at present?

A-2. The pressure removed from the lower portion of the cervical and upper dorsal region, and the Eustachian tube cleansed, we will find the vibratory forces [from osteopathy and ultraviolet ray) to the system will bring bettered conditions . . . We would *also* cleanse the ear . . . that is, when the Eustachian tubes are massaged (we wouldn't begin these until at least a portion of the pressure in the upper dorsal and cervical is relieved) then begin gradually, see?

Q-3. Should any medicinal properties be taken to cleanse the alimentary canal?

A-3. As has been given, we would take that which *will cleanse* the alimentary canal, after removing those impactions in the colon.

Q-4. How often should the manipulations be given?

A-4. Every day, until those conditions in the whole of the cerebrospinal system are corrected. The corrections should be made at least three times each week.

195-9   M.41   11/7/24

Q-2. If the tonsils are removed, would it assist in restoring the hearing?

A-2. Yes, if removed properly, it would, for with this we would break many of the lesions that hinder the circulation in this portion of the body.

Q-3. What osteopathic treatment should be given for clearing up deafness, and how often should [they] be given?

A-3. When the tonsils have been removed, and the body is kept in shape by the general osteopathic treatments, then the lesions along the Eustachian tubes must be broken, you see, and allow the circulation to renew the condition necessary to equalize the balance in [the] central portion of [the] ear. These must be given at least every other day, until five to seven are given, and then every third day until sixteen in all are given. By the time the seventh to eighth is given, we will see the change in the hearing.

5404-1   M.65   8/26/44

Q-1. May anything be done for hearing?

A-1. This should have been done long since. The head and neck exercise will contribute more to the assisting of this in the present than mechanical applications to the ear. This is the character of exercise: do these of a morning standing, of an evening sitting. Sitting

erect bend the head forward three times at least, then back as far
as it may be bent three times; to the right side three times; then to
the left side three times. Then circle the head and neck to the right
three times, then to the left three times. Be consistent with this
though, not just doing it occasionally. Thus we will make for helpful
forces in the auditory activities with the inhalant as it purifies the
circulation through soft tissue [of the head and neck].

3697-1   F.22   3/16/44
. . . in contemplating or in giving that which would be more beneficial to the body it is necessary to take into consideration more
than just the physical conditions.

For with the particular conditions that are preventing the hearing, we find that there is much more than may appear upon the
surface to be considered.

To what has the body attuned itself as to its hearing? Hearing
is one of the senses of the nervous systems of the body, and the
nervous system of the sensory organism which is as the passage
between mental and spiritual aspirations of an individual entity.

True there are purely pathological conditions, yet these—if
attuned to or centered upon the spiritual things and spiritual desires—may indeed be helped so that, even with the loss of auditory
reaction there may be even greater hearing attuned by the body.

Have you considered the great artist as a pianist who accomplished his greater works when little or no hearing was available
of a physical nature? As to how the inner sense was attuned to the
infinite?

As the sensory forces or nerve centers are the passage of the
finite to the infinite, why not attune the body-forces of self to the
beauties of the infinite and study to show thyself approved unto
God, a workman not ashamed? No, one not hindered even by the
handicap, as might be termed, of imperfect hearing.

True, catarrhal conditions in the nasal passages and the throat,
and the tendency of the body to disregard the existent conditions
when there are periods of cold and congestion having to do with
the organs of generation in the body, have also contributed to the
reckoning to which the body is responding in the present.

Attune self to the divine within, using the abilities of every nature
for the reconstruction of self as well as that about self. For if you

would have hearing, give it and make the listening to something that the entity might accomplish be worthwhile—and ye will hear.

Then use finger surgery, osteopathically; correcting subluxations that exist in the 4th lumbar, upper portion of [the] 9th dorsal, 3rd and 4th dorsal and in the 1st, 2nd and 3rd cervical; preparing the body for finger surgery. Thus there may be gained physically fifty percent of the hearing, which is now existent only about sixty. So we may attain almost to full hearing, or to at least ninety-four percent . . .

Do the first things first. Don't begin with the mechanical treatments. Begin first with self and the correcting of body energies towards creative forces.

Do keep close to music.

Deodorant and Powder

Deodorant

404-8   F.49   7/2/40
Q-11. Should one use a deodorant, especially under the arms, to stop perspiration . . . ?
A-11. The *best* to use—the safest—is soap and water!

2072-6   F.31   1/30/42
Q-6. What deodorant and anti-perspirant would be effective and unharmful for this body?
A-6. The use of pure soaps is preferable to any attempts to deodorize. *Any* [substance] that allays perspiration certainly clogs the activity of the respiratory and perspiratory system. And the activity of the glands closest, of course, [to the area] under the arms and between the thighs or limbs, is that which causes such conditions. Then, the more often there is the use of the bath or the soap and water, the better it is.
Q-7. What ingredients in such preparations are harmful?
A-7. Anything that closes the pores of the skin to prevent perspiration.

585-11   F.47   6/14/43
Q-6. Is it harmful to use Odorono®, or any depilatory, for excess perspiration under arms?

A-6. This is not the best, but where these are not carrying any form of lead, they are not harmful to the body.

Q-7. What is the best to use?

A-7. Any that is minus these ingredients.

Powder: The distinctive element in the body powders recommended is usually Balsam of Peru.

5403-1   M.38   8/26/44

Following this treatment each day there should be a thorough massage of the body with Peanut Oil. Begin at the 1st cervical, massage downward, more along the nerves outside of the central nervous system, or the sympathetic, down to the end of the spine; then through the hips, across the sacrum to the limbs, the feet and toes. This do thoroughly. If there is used a good talcum after the body is cleansed off from the oil, this will not irritate the skin.

2752-1   F.6 weeks   5/20/42

After the bath, do dust with the powder that carries Balsam in same. This is healing. But don't tend to dry up [the skin] too much.

322-5   M.60   10/28/34

Then dust over this the stearate of Zinc with the Balsam, which we find is made—or combined—by Johnson and Johnson®. Or we may obtain this combination in the older concern, Eimer and Amend—that has had same combined heretofore, see?

2743-1   F.42   5/5/42

After this has been taken for about a week, and [after] using a powder the base of which is stearate of Zinc with Balsam, we find that the rash will be improved.

Diet

Acclimatization

2-14   M.49   6/16/30

In the noon, there may be those of the vegetables that are fresh, and as are *especially* grown in the vicinity where the body resides.

Shipped vegetables are never very good.

3542-1   F.50   1/7/44

Do not have large quantities of any fruits, vegetables, meats, that are not grown in or come to the area where the body is at the time it partakes of such foods. This will be found to be a good rule to be followed by all. This prepares the system to acclimate itself to any given territory.

4047-1   M.36   4/1/44

Q-1. Is the climate of Austin, Texas, satisfactory, and should I remain here?

A-1. The climatic conditions here are not the basis of the trouble. The body can adjust itself. As we have indicated, bodies can usually adjust themselves to climatic conditions if they adhere to the diet and activities, or all characters of foods that are produced in the area where they reside. This will more quickly adjust a body to any particular area or climate than any other thing.

Q-2. Is a diet composed mainly of fruits, vegetables, eggs, and milk the best diet for me?

A-2. As indicated, use more of the products of the soil that are grown in the immediate vicinity. These are better for the body than any specific set of fruits, vegetables, grasses, or whatnot. We would add more of the original sources of proteins . . .

Q-4. Are daily heavy chocolate malted milks detrimental?

A-4. Chocolate that is prepared in the present [4/1/44] is not best for *any* diet. This too, the chocolate, is not produced in the vicinity of Austin. Those foods that may be taken from the vicinity, or food values of that nature, are the better. Take plenty of milk—you will find some of that around Austin.

2981-4   M.34   12/1/43

Q-10. In keeping with the foregoing advice, exactly what city or place is the best place for me to live, in order for me to express myself more fully?

A-10. Where you are—wherever you are! For as has been indicated from the beginning, the place whereon thou standest is holy ground.

2094-2   M.70   5/3/40

As we have oft indicated, where an individual is allergic to certain influences, vegetables, activities, or any form of foods carrying the various calories, proteins and vitamins—it will be found that these will vary in various sections. But adjust self to those that are grown the more in the section in which the individual resides at the time—this is the preferable way, when practical.

Apples

3180-3   F.20   12/21/43

An almond a day is much more in accord with keeping the doctor away, especially certain types of doctors, than apples. For the apple was the fall, not [the] almond—for the almond blossomed when everything else died. Remember this is life!

416-9   M.30   7/30/36

Q-3. What foods should I avoid?

A-3. Rather is it the combination of foods that make for disturbance with most physical bodies, as it would with this . . .

. . . do not combine . . . the reacting acid fruits with starches, other than *whole wheat bread!* that is, citrus fruits, oranges, apples, grapefruit, limes or lemons or even tomato juices. And do not have cereals (which contain the greater quantity of starch than most) at the same meal with the citrus fruits.

341-32   M.24   4/20/31

Do not eat too many apples while this [treatment outlined] is being taken, or until the digestive system has adjusted itself. No bananas. No candies.

623-1   F.Adult   1/6/33

Mornings—citrus fruit or stewed fruits (as figs, apples, peaches, or the like), but do not serve the stewed fruits with the citrus fruit juices; neither serve the citrus fruits with a dry cereal. When cereals are taken there may be added buckwheat cakes, rice cakes or coddled egg, and a cereal drink. It would be well for these to be altered or changed.

5097-1   F.28   5/10/44

Have raw vegetables also, but not a great deal of melons of any kind, though cantaloupes may be taken, if grown in the neighborhood where the body resides; if shipped don't eat it. The fruits that may be taken: plums, pears, and apples. Do not take raw apples, but roast apples aplenty.

820-2   M.25   2/10/35

No raw apples; or if raw apples are taken, take them and *nothing else*—three days of raw apples only, and then Olive Oil, and we will cleanse *all* toxic forces from any system! Raw apples are not well unless they are of the Jenneting variety. *[Jenneting, an obsolete word: a variety of early apple, so named for being ripe about St. John's Day, June 24th.]* Apples cooked, apples roasted, are good. No bananas, unless you are in the territory where they are grown and ripened there. Do not use large quantities of potatoes, though the peelings of same may be taken at all times—they are strengthening, carrying those influences and forces that are active with the glands of the system. But beware of those things indicated; as for the rest, keep a well-balanced diet.

Names of other varieties of apples suggested in the readings [see 294-182, A-3]: Black Arkansas, Sheep Nose, Delicious, Oregon Red, Jonathan, and Arkansas Russet.

*Artichoke, Jerusalem**

1963-2   M.60s   1/10/41

Q-2. What can he do to protect himself against it [diabetes]?

A-2. . . . And twice each week take the Jerusalem artichoke, about the size of a hen egg; first raw—say on Tuesdays—and the next time cooked, say on Thursdays, but cooked in its own juices (as in Patapar Paper®). Only eat one each time . . . When cooked, season it to make it palatable, but do not eat the skin—save the juices and mash with the pulp when it is to be eaten. Eat it with the meal, of course; whether it is taken raw or cooked. Do not take it between meals, but at the regular meal . . .

*See also "Kidneys."

Do not take injections of insulin. If more insulin is necessary than is obtained from eating the amount of artichoke indicated, then increase the number of days during the week of taking the artichoke, see?

2472-1   M.67   3/26/41

A very positive reaction may be had that will relieve a great deal of this tension, if there will be eaten each day—with the meal—a Jerusalem artichoke; one day cooked, the next day raw; one not larger than about the size of a hen egg. Preferably keep these fresh, not by being put in the refrigerator but by keeping them in the ground; by necessity protecting them from animals—dogs, hogs, pigs or the like; for these will scratch 'em up—as would cats also!

There is needed that booster, or the effect of insulin as may be derived from the artichoke, for the system . . .

As to the matter of diet (other than artichoke)—refrain from those foods that tend towards creating sugar; as excess of starches or sweets.

A little honey may be taken occasionally.

Yellow corn meal is very good for the body, in whatever way it may be prepared; whether made into spoon bread, egg bread, cakes or the like.

The Wheat Germ Oil would be beneficial, taken in moderation; that is, one to two drops a day; but *not* white flour or wheaten flour so much. Rather use the rye bread and the corn bread.

The meats should be rather fish and fowl—though no fried foods.

Use the leafy vegetables rather than any of those of the pod variety . . .

If sweetening is desired for [coffee] use either honey or saccharin.

480-39   F.25   7/12/37

And *especially* artichoke, preferably the Jerusalem artichoke; this not with vinegar, to be sure, but this should be taken—a little of it—for *every* evening meal! This carries those properties that are as of an insulin reaction, that will produce a cleansing for the kidneys as well as producing the tendency for the reduction of the excess sugar [diabetes] that is indicated in the inflammation noted in blood tests in the present.

Do not give the injections of insulin, but those properties as indicated that may act with same . . .

1523-7   F.30   4/5/39

Occasionally—once a week or oftener—the Jerusalem artichoke should be a part of the diet. This will tend to correct those inclinations for the incoordination between the activities of the pancreas as related to the kidneys and bladder. These, as we find, even in this form, will make for better corrections.

Beef juice

5374-1   F.60   7/21/44

Beef juice should be taken regularly as medicine, a teaspoonful four times a day at least, but when taken it should be sipped, not just taken as a gulp.

1343-2   F.Adult   3/1/37

Take a pound to a pound and a half preferably of the round steak. No fat, no portions other than that which is of the muscle or tendon or strength; no fatty or skin portions. Dice this into half inch cubes, as it were, or practically so. Put same in a glass jar without water in same. Put the jar then into a boiler or container with the water coming about half or three-fourths toward the top of the jar, you see. Preferably put a cloth in the container to prevent the jar from cracking. Do not seal the jar tight, but cover the top. Let this boil (the water, with the jar in same) for three to four hours. Then strain off the juice, and the refuse may be pressed somewhat. It will be found that the meat or flesh itself will be worthless. Place the juice in a cool place, but do not keep too long; never longer than three days, see? Hence the quantity made up at the time depends upon how much or how often the body will take this. It should be taken two to three times a day, but not more than a tablespoonful at the time—and this sipped very slowly. Of course, this is to be seasoned to suit the taste of the body.

Well, too, that whole wheat or Ry-Krisp crackers be taken with same to make it more palatable.

1100-10   F.41   12/29/36

As we find, we would use small quantities at a time—but take almost as medicine—of the beef juices . . . This is easily assimilated, gives strength and vitality, and is needed with the vital forces of the body in the present. Take at least a tablespoonful during a day, or two tablespoonsful. But not as spoonsful; rather sips of same. This, sipped in this manner, will work towards producing the gastric flow through the intestinal system; first in the salivary reactions to the very nature of the properties themselves, second with the gastric flow from the upper portion of the stomach or through the cardiac reaction at the end of the esophagus that produces the first of the lacteals' reaction to the gastric flows in the stomach or digestive forces themselves; thirdly, making for an activity through the pylorus and the duodenum that becomes stimulating to the activity of the flows without producing the tendencies for accumulation of gases.

2535-1   F.61   7/15/41

Also once a day it will be most beneficial to take beef juice as a tonic; not so much the beef itself but beef juice; followed with red wine. Do not mix these, but take both about the same time. Take about a teaspoonful of the beef juice, but spend about five minutes in sipping that much. Then take an ounce of the red wine, with a whole wheat cracker.

1424-2   M.50   8/30/37

Q-5. What quantity of beef juice to be taken daily?

A-5. At least two tablespoonsful, but no fat in same. A tablespoonful is almost equal to a pound of meat or two pounds of meat a day; and that's right smart for a man that isn't active!

Beverages: Carbonated water

1523-17   F.36   12/29/43

Any cereal drink may be taken, but keep away from carbonated drinks.

5545-2   M.41   2/24/30

No slop, or those of soft drinks of *any* kind, should be taken . . .

243-24   F.56   7/11/36

Keep away from Coca-Cola®, the soft drinks that carry carbonated water. If limeade or lemonade is taken without the carbonated water, very well.

1710-6   M.26   7/30/41

The effect of the anaesthesia [hernia operation] is to produce periods or mornings when there are headaches, a bit of dizziness, an upset at times of the digestive forces . . .

Hence for this body, it is well to take occasionally—a couple of times each day—carbonated water. This does not mean merely soft drinks, but drink carbonated water—half plain and half carbonated water, at the fount. This is well to counteract the effects of general conditions which exist through the lymph in the general blood supply, especially through these periods of hot days or hot weather.

Beverages: Coffee

303-2   F.45   8/5/32

Coffee, taken properly, is a food; that is, *without* cream or milk.

1568-2   M.51   4/20/38

Q-2. Will coffee hurt the body?

A-2. Coffee without cream or milk is not so harmful.

Preferably the Washington Coffee®, because of its *manner* of brewing.

404-6   F.46   1/15/36

Q-8. Is coffee good? If so, how often?

A-8. Coffee taken properly is a food value.

To many [types of physical] conditions, as with this body, the caffeine in same is hard upon the digestion; especially where there is the tendency for a plethora condition in the lower end of the stomach.

Hence the use of coffee or the chicory in the food values that arise from the *combinations* of coffee with breads or meats or sweets is helpful.

But for this body, it is *preferable* that the tannin be mostly removed. Then it can be taken two to three times day, but *without* milk or cream.

4436-2   F.Adult   5/9/24
   Q-2. Is coffee harmful to this body?
   A-2. With meats, yes. Without meats, no.

294-86   M.49   11/22/26
   . . . coffee is as of those properties as stimulants to the nerve system. The dross from same is caffeine, as is not digestible in the system, and must necessarily then be eliminated. When such are allowed to remain in the colon, there is thrown off from same poisons. Eliminated as it is in this system, coffee is a food value, and is preferable to many stimulants that might be taken . . .

243-22   F.56   3/31/36
   Q-1. Does it hurt me to use sugar in my coffee?
   A-1. Sugar is not near so harmful as cream. May use sugar in moderation.

Beverages: Milk

1208-2   M.5 days   6/26/36
   Q-2. Any suggestions for the mother's diet, regarding the milk for the baby?
   A-2. Plenty of calciums, plenty of the irons, plenty of those food values that are included in such [a diet] that a balance may be kept proper for the body. Plenty of proteins but not too *much* of proteins that arise from too great quantities of fat.

1208-3   M.1 mo.   7/26/36
   We would change [the milk in] the diets to the Carnation Milk®, making the formula sufficiently strong, yet weak even for the age of the body . . .
   And *do not* use other *than* the Carnation Milk®! Do not *change* from one [brand] to another.

2752-1   F.6 weeks   5/20/42
   As we find, it would be better to use the milk that we have so oft

indicated for such conditions [of infancy], the Carnation Milk®. For this particular body, however, make with the pectin rather than with the Karo®, but the formula should be weak.

2752-3   F.2   1/17/44
. . . and raw milk [is best]—provided it is from cows that don't eat certain characters of food. If they eat dry food, it is well, if they eat certain types of weeds or grass grown this time of year, it won't be so good for the body.

404-6   F.46   1/15/36
Q-9. Is buttermilk good?
A-9. This depends upon the manner in which it is made. This would tend to produce gas if it is the ordinary kind. But that *made* by the use of the Bulgarian tablets is good, in moderation; not too much.

560-2   F.48   5/26/34
. . . plenty of milk—the Bulgarian [buttermilk] the better, or the fresh milk that is warm with the animal heat which carries more of the phosphorus and more of those activities that are less constipating, or acting more with the lacteals and the ducts of the liver, the kidneys and the bowels themselves.

Beverages: Tea

303-2   F.45   8/5/32
Q-20. Is [the use of] tea and coffee harmful to the body?
A-20. Tea is more harmful than coffee. Any nerve reaction is more susceptible to the character of tea that is usually found in this country, though in some manners in which it is produced it would be well.

1622-1   F.68   6/24/38
Q-4. Are tea and coffee harmful?
A-4. For this [particular] body tea is preferable to coffee, but [tea] in excess is hard upon the digestion.To be sure, it should never be taken with milk.

462-14   M.57   1/6/42
Q-3. What about tea?

A-3. Tea might be taken when the body is resting—but this is rather a pick-up for the body and does not last as long with the body even as coffee, and coffee is more of a food than tea.

5097-1   F.28   5/10/44

If coffee is taken, do not take milk in same. If tea is taken, do not take milk in same. This is hard on the digestion and especially for conditions as exist here.

Beverages: Vegetable Juice

243-33   F.60   4/29/40

At least once each day take an ounce of raw carrot juice. Use a juicer to extract the juice from fresh raw carrots.

Have plenty of vegetables.

1968-3   F.29   3/14/40

Once or twice a week take vegetable juices that would be prepared by using a vegetable juicer, but only using the vegetables for same that would combine well. They may be combined or taken separately; the juices from such as lettuce, celery, beets, spinach, mustard, carrots, radishes, and a tiny bit of leek or onion—not more than one very small onion, if it is desired that this be mixed with same. All these may be combined or used according to the taste of the body.

Beverages: Water

1131-2   M.Adult   10/29/32

Q-10. How much water should the body drink daily?
A-10. Six to eight tumblers or glasses full.

574-1   F.Adult   6/6/34

Q-12. How much water should I drink daily?
A-12. From six to eight tumblers full.

311-4   M.28   4/11/31

Well to drink *always plenty* of water, before meals and after meals—for, as has oft been given, when any food value *enters* the stomach, *immediately* the stomach becomes a storehouse, or a medicine chest that may create all the elements necessary for proper digestion within the system. If this [stomach] *first* is acted upon by aqua pura, the reactions are more near normal. Well, then, each morning upon first arising to take a half to three-quarters of a glass of *warm* water; not so hot that it is objectionable, not so tepid that it makes for sickening—but this will clarify the system of poisons. This [is] well especially for this body. Occasionally a pinch of salt should be added to this draught of water.

1861-18   M.38   4/17/44

Q-9.We have been using our hot water, cooled, for drinking, to avoid the chemicals put into it to purify it. Is this well?

A-9. If the water has come to a boil, it is well. If it hasn't, you've just changed the chemicals into that which may be active! Boil the water, then put it on ice or [put] ice in it.

2273-1   M.55   6/8/40

. . . and above all, drink plenty of water every day, that there may be a flushing of the kidneys, so that the uric acid and the poisons that have been as accumulations may be removed.

Menu

1523-17   F.35   12/29/43

These would be given in an outline—not [as] the only foods, but [as] an outline.

Mornings: Whole grain cereals or citrus fruit juices, though not at the same meal. When using orange juice, combine lime with it. When using grapefruit, combine lemon with it—just a little. Egg, preferably only the yolk, or rice or buckwheat cakes, or toast, or just any one of these would be well of mornings.

Noons: A raw salad, including tomatoes, radishes, carrots, celery, lettuce, watercress—any or all of these, with a soup or vegetable broth, or sea foods, or the like.

Evenings: Fruits, [such] as cooked apples; potatoes, tomatoes, fish, fowl, lamb, and occasionally beef, but not too often. Keep these as the main part of a well-balanced diet.

3224-2 F.6 12/27/43

Q-7. Would appreciate outline of an ideal daily diet at this [child's] age and for the near future.

A-7. *Mornings:* Whole grain cereals or citrus fruits, but these never taken at the same meal; rather alternate these, using one on one day and the other the next, and so on. Any form of rice cakes or the like, the yolk of eggs and the like.

Noons: Some fresh raw vegetable salad, including many different types. Soups with brown bread, or broths or such.

Evenings: A fairly well-coordinated vegetable diet, with three [vegetables] above the ground to one below the ground. Sea food, fowl or lamb; not other types of meats. Gelatin may be prepared with any of the vegetables (as in the salads for the noon meal) or with the milk and cream dishes. These would be well for the body.

3823-3 F.59 5/3/35

Mornings: (This is not all that is to be taken, but [is given] as an outline.) Citrus fruit juices; when orange juice is taken add lime or lemon juice to same; four parts orange juice to one part lime or lemon. When other citrus fruits are taken, as pineapple or grapefruit, they may be taken as they are from the fresh fruit. A little salt added to same is preferable to make for the activity of same. Yes, and we mean for this body, too—*salt*—sodium chloride, see? Whole wheat bread, toasted, browned, with butter. Coddled egg, only the yolk of same. A small piece of very crisp bacon, if so desired. Any or all of these may be taken. But when cereals are taken, *do not* have citrus fruits at the same meal! This has been disregarded at times! Such a combination produces just what we are trying to prevent in the system! When cereals are used, have either cracked wheat or whole wheat, or a combination of barley and wheat—as in Maltex®, if these are desired; or Puffed Wheat®, or Puffed Rice®, or Puffed Corn®—any of these. And these [cereals] may be taken with certain characters of fresh fruits; as berries of any nature, even strawberries if so desired (no, they won't cause any of the rash if they are taken *properly!*) or peaches. The sugar used should only be saccharin or honey. A cereal drink may be had if so desired.

Noons: Only raw fresh vegetables. *All* of these may be combined, but grate them—don't eat them so[hurriedly] that they would make for that [unbalanced] combination which often comes with not [having] the proper mastication. Each time you take a mouthful, even if it's water, it should be chewed at least four to twenty times; whether it's water, or bread, or a carrot, onion, cabbage, or what! Each should be chewed so that there is the [necessary] mastication, and [so] that there is the opportunity for the flow of the gastric forces from the salivary glands [to be] well mixed with same. Then we will find that these [foods] will make for bettered conditions [in the body].

Evenings: Vegetables that are cooked in their *own* juices, not combined with others—each cooked alone, then combined together afterward if so desired by the body, see? These may include any of the leafy vegetables or any of the bulbular vegetables, but cook them in their *own* juices! There may be taken the meats, if so desired by the body, or there may be added the proteins that come from the combination of other vegetables or combination of vegetable forces in the forms of [a] certain character of pulse or of grains. Any of these may be taken.

275-24   F.18   12/8/31

In the matter of supplying the calcium and other elements, [such] as phosphorus and salts for the system, in a diet, [eat] much of *this* nature [of foods]—these may be found to be most helpful:

At least once or twice a week the sea foods may be taken, especially clams, oysters, shrimp or lobster; or these may be alternated or changed [about] to suit the taste of the body. The oyster or clam should be taken raw as much as possible, while [having] the others prepared through roasting or boiling with the [use of] butter would be better than prepared in other manners. Then, a *general* outline:

Mornings: Citrus fruits; [either] cereals or fruits, but do not mix citrus fruits and cereals, though stewed fruits may be taken; or [have] citrus fruits, and a little later [have] rice cakes or buckwheat or graham cakes, with honey *in* the honeycomb, with milk or the like, and *preferably* the raw milk *if* [it is] certified milk!

Noons: Rather vegetable juices than meat juices, with raw vegetables as a salad or the like.

Evenings: Vegetables, with such as carrots, peas, salsify, red cabbage, yams or white potatoes—these the smaller variety, [if eaten] with the jackets [it will be] the better; using as the finishing, or dessert ... blancmange, or Jello, or jellies, with fruits—as peaches,

apricots, fresh pineapple or the like. These [foods], as we find, with
the occasional [eating of] sufficient meats for strength, would bring
a well-balanced diet. Occasionally we would add these [foods] of
the blood building [type], once or twice a week; the pig knuckles,
tripe, and calves' liver, or those [meats] of *brains* and the like. See?

275-45   F.25   2/10/38

*Q-6. Outline diet for three meals a day that would be best for
[this] body.*

A-6. *Mornings:* Citrus fruit juices *or* cereals, but not both at the
same meal. At other meals there may be taken or included with the
others [other cereals] at times, dried fruits or figs, combined with
dates and raisins—these chopped very well together. And, for this
especial body, [a mixture of] dates, figs (that are dried) cooked with
a little corn meal (a very little sprinkled in), then this taken with
milk, should be almost a spiritual food for the body; whether it's
taken one, two, three, or four meals a day. But this is to be left to
the body itself [to decide].

Noons: [Foods] such as vegetable juices, or [these] combined
with a little meat juices and a combination of raw vegetables; but
not *ever* any acetic acid or vinegar or the like with same—but oils,
if [they are] olive oil or vegetable oils, may be used with same.

Evenings: Vegetables that are of the leafy nature; fish, fowl,
or lamb, preferably, as the meats or their combinations. These of
course are not to be all [the foods], but this is the *general* outline
for the three meals for the body.

But for this particular body, equal portions of black figs or Assyrian figs and Assyrian dates—these ground together or cut very fine,
and to a pint of such a combination put half a handful of corn meal,
or crushed wheat. These cooked together—well, it's food for such
a spiritually developed body as this!

935-1   F.Adult   6/14/35

Mornings: Whole wheat toast, browned. Cereals with fresh
fruits. The citrus fruit juices occasionally. But do not mix the citrus
fruit juices *and* cereals at the same meal.

Noons: Principally (very seldom altering from these) raw vegetables or raw fruits made into a salad; not [having] the fruits and
vegetables combined, but these may be altered. Use such vegetables

as cabbage (the white, of course, but very fine), carrots, lettuce, spinach, celery, onions, tomatoes, radish; any or all of these. It is more preferable that they *all* be grated, but when [they are] grated do not allow the juices in the grating to be discarded; these should be used upon the salad itself, [juices] either from the fruits or the vegetables. Preferably use the *oil* dressings, [such] as olive oil with paprika, or such combinations. Even egg may be included in [these] same [dressings], preferably the hard [boiled] egg (that is, the yolk) and it [may be] worked into the oil as a portion of the dressing. Use in the fruit salad such [fruits] as bananas, papaya, guava, grapes; *all* characters of fruits *except* apples. Apples should only be eaten when cooked; preferably roasted and [served] with butter or hard sauce on same, [topped] with cinnamon and spice.

Evenings: A well-balanced cooked-vegetable diet, including principally those things that will make for iron [to be] assimilated in the system.

1568-2   M.51   4/20/38

Q-3. Please give detailed outline of diet for each meal.

A-3. As indicated, the outlines will necessarily change as conditions progress [or improve]. But have rather a percentage of eighty percent alkaline-producing to twenty percent acid-producing foods.

Then, it is well that the body not become as one that couldn't do this, that, or the other; or become as a slave to an idea of a set diet.

Do not take citrus fruit juices *and* cereals at the same meal. Do not take milk or cream in coffee or in tea. Do not eat fried foods of any kind. Do not combine white bread, potatoes, spaghetti—or any two foods of such natures in the same meal.

142-5   M.20 mos.   12/5/28

Do not give the body apples raw, or *bananas* in any form. Rather let *this* be an outline for a diet, though, necessarily, this may be modified occasionally to meet the needs of a *developing* and growing body.

Of mornings: Cereals—these changed from dry to the cooked. Cream of Wheat® or Wheatena®, or Oatmeal, or Grape Nuts®, or Corn Flakes®, or Rice Flakes®—with the cream *mixed*—not full raw. First giving a small amount of orange juice.

In the middle of the day, or noon lunch: Juices (not the meats, but the juices) of meat. Broths or something of that nature, with a minimum amount of sweet.

In the evenings: This may be changed with those of spinach, of lentils, beans, and broths—with those of prune juice, or such. These, of course, may be alternated. Cooked apples, if they are of the Jenneting variety, may be given. None of those of the more woody variety, as those of Ben Davis or of Wine Sap, or of the fall or woody variety. These should *not* be given this body in *any* manner.

Diet (Food)

Food: Acid

1523-3   F.29   3/22/38
Q-5. What foods are acid-forming for this body?
A-5. All of those that are combining fats with sugars. Starches naturally are inclined for acid reaction. But a normal diet is about 20% acid to 80% alkaline-producing.

340-5   F.38   11/14/26
Do not take in the system, then, especially any of those foods that produce an over acidity in the lower end of the stomach—such as pickles, or any food carrying over amount of acid or vinegar, or acetic acid, and never any canned goods having benzoate of soda. This includes relishes and things of that nature.

294-86   M.49   11/22/26
The acidity [was] produced by taking too much sugar in the system in candies and in those properties as were taken before the stomach was filled with foods [at meals]; and then overloading the system at such times brings this condition . . .
Q-2. What properties were referred to as being taken into the system before food was taken?
A-2. Candies—and smoking.

340-12   F.42   5/26/30
Necessary that occasionally the body be put wholly on that of the citrus fruit diet, that the body abstain from too much of the sweets—especially that of the cane sugar variety, though those

[sugars] that are of the grape, or that are fermentation forming, and sweets as come from chocolates or of fruits that do not carry potash—*these* will be helpful to the general system.

Well that the fruit salts at times be taken for the condition in the system, or in the bowel itself. This will produce better clarification.

Also well that the antiseptic [Glyco-Thymoline®] for the intestinal tract [be used], so that those tendencies of exciting the mucous membranes throughout the system do not become infectious from the acidity as has existed there and has been thrown much through the system; else we may form conditions that either will be resultant in the destructive forces for [the] kidneys' circulation or [the] lungs, or both; for rarely (this would be well for *all* to remember) has there ever been a case of tuberculosis without *first* the kidneys going bad.

Food: Alkaline

480-19   F.23   7/12/35

The diet should be more body-building; that is, less acid foods and more of the alkaline-reacting [foods] . . . Milk and all its products should be a portion of the body's diet now; also those food values carrying an easy assimilation of iron, silicon, and those elements or chemicals—as all forms of berries, most all forms of vegetables that grow under the ground, most of the vegetables of a leafy nature. Fruits and vegetables, nuts and the like, should form a greater part of the regular diet in the present . . .

Keep closer to the alkaline diets; using fruits, berries, vegetables particularly that carry iron, silicon, phosphorus and the like . . .

Q-2. *Can immunization against [contagious diseases] be set up in any other manner than by inoculations?*

A-2. As indicated, if an alkalinity is maintained in the system—especially with lettuce, carrots and celery, these in the blood supply will maintain such a condition as to immunize a person.

270-33   M.49   1/24/35

. . . when there is the tendency towards an alkaline system there is less effect of cold and congestion.

808-3   F.27   5/19/35

As indicated, keep a tendency for alkalinity in the diet. This does not necessitate that there should *never* be any of the acid-forming foods included in the diet; for an over-alkalinity is much more harmful than a little tendency occasionally for acidity.

But remember there are those tendencies in the system for cold and congestion to affect the body, and cold *cannot—does not—exist* in alkalines.

Hence the diet would be as indicated. Citrus fruits; or the smaller fruits occasionally with the cereals that are dry (but do not have citrus fruits and cereals at the same meal). Green raw vegetables should be a portion of the diet occasionally. The meats should be such as lamb, fowl, fish, or the like. Occasionally the *broiled* steak or liver, or tripe, would be well.

A well-balance between the starches and proteins is the more preferable, with sufficient of the carbohydrates.

And especially keep a well-balance (but not an excess) in the calciums necessary with the iodines, that produce the better body, especially through those periods of conception and gestation.

798-1   F.48   1/23/35

As to the diets: We would use not too much sweets, but preferably raw vegetables—at least have one portion of one meal each day consist of a combination of raw vegetables in a salad; such as celery, lettuce, tomatoes, peppers, radishes, carrots, beets, spinach, mustard, onions, lentils and the like.

There is the need of such stamina that may be supplied by the combinations of the *green* vegetable forces with the activities in the system. Watercress, especially, is well for the body, and may be included in the salad. This should be eaten at least during one meal each day.

And the rest of the diet should consist of the more alkaline reacting foods. For, in all bodies, the less activities there are in physical exercise or manual activity, the greater should be the alkaline-reacting foods taken.

Energies or activities may burn acids, but those who lead the sedentary life or the non-active life can't go on sweets or too much starches—but these should be well-balanced . . .

Keep an attitude of helpfulness, cheerfulness, hopefulness.

Be optimistic! At least make three people each day laugh heartily, by something the body says! It'll not only help the body, it'll help others.

902-1   2/17/41

The diet also should be considered—in that there is not an excess of acids or sweets, or even an excess of alkalinity . . . there should be kept a normal, well-balanced diet that has proven to be right for the individual body . . .

741-1   M.Adult   11/21/34

As to the matter of the *diet*, keep rather to the *alkaline reacting* foods; and where acids of any building foods are used let them be specifically in nuts and fruits. Naturally, the normal vegetable reaction would be kept in at least one meal during the day.

Food: Combinations

416-9   M.30   7/30/36

Q-3. What foods should I avoid?

A-3. Rather is it the combination of foods that makes for disturbance with most physical bodies, as it would with this [body].

In the [office] activities of the body in its present surroundings, those [foods] tending toward the greater alkaline reaction are preferable. Hence, avoid combinations where corn, potatoes, rice, spaghetti or the like are taken all at the same meal. Some combinations of these at the meal are very good, but all of these tend to make for too great a quantity of starch—especially if any meat is taken at such a meal. If no meat is taken, these [starches] make quite a difference. For the activities of the gastric flow of the digestive system are [of a type that indicate] the requirements of one reaction in the gastric flow for starch and another for proteins, or for the[di-gestive] activities of the carbohydrates as [they may be] combined with starches of this nature—especially [when eaten] in the manner in which they are [often] prepared.

Then, in the combinations, do not eat great quantities of starch with the proteins or meats.

If sweets and meats are taken at the same meal, these are preferable to starches [and meats]. Of course, small quantities of breads with sweets are all right, but do not have large quantities of same.

These are merely warnings. Then, do not combine also the [al-kaline] reacting acid fruits with starches, other than *whole wheat bread!* that is, citrus fruits, oranges, apples, grapefruit, limes or lemons or even tomato juices. And do not have cereals (which contain the greater quantity of starch than most) at the same meal with the citrus fruits.

340-32   F.48   1/7/36

As we find, there is rather an acute condition of cold or congestion from an unbalancing in the alkalinity of the system. Not [an unbalancing produced] by the foods themselves; rather [by] the manner of their combination. For, as indicated, there should not be taken starches and sweets at the same meal, or so much together (that's why that ice cream is so much better than pie, for a body!).

Meats or the like should not be taken with starches that grow above the ground. There's quite a variation in the reaction in the physical body [to such combinations], especially where intestinal disturbance has caused the greater part of the inflammation through a body—as indicated in this case, from those conditions that have been formerly described, through the intestinal tract itself. Hence potatoes or the peelings of same with meats are much preferable to eating bread with meats, see?

2732-1   M.43   4/16/42

Q-3. Please suggest things to be stressed and things to be avoided in the diet.

A-3. *Avoid* too much combinations of starches. Do not take a combination of potatoes, meat, white bread, macaroni or cheese, at the same meal; no two of these at any one meal, though they each may be taken separately at other times, or as a lunch or a part of a [separate] meal. Avoid raw meats, or rare meats—that are not well cooked. Not too much *ever* of any hog meat. Have plenty of vegetables, and especially one meal each day should include some raw or uncooked vegetables. But here, too, combinations must be kept in line. Do not take onions and radishes at the same meal with celery and lettuce, though either of these may be taken at different times, see?

623-1   F.Adult   1/6/33

Mornings [eat] citrus fruit or stewed fruits (as figs, apples, peaches, or the like), but do not serve the stewed fruits with the citrus fruit juices; neither serve the citrus fruits with a dry cereal.

2072-14   F.34   4/17/44

Q-3. What foods can be used with fresh citrus fruits to make a complete meal?

A-3. Any foods that may be eaten at any time save whole grain cereals.

2853-1   F.31   11/19/42

Q-1. What effect has alcohol when you eat raw oysters?

A-1. It produces a chemical reaction that is bad for *most* stomachs. Oysters should never be taken with whiskey.

Food: Cooking

1196-7   M.58   3/30/37

Q-5. Is food cooked in aluminum utensils bad for this system?

A-5. Certain characters of food cooked in aluminum are bad for *any* system, and where a systemic condition exists . . . a disturbed hepatic eliminating force—they are naturally so. Cook rather in granite, or better still, in Patapar Paper®!

843-7   M.54   8/15/38

Q-6. Do I have aluminum or arsenate of lead poisoning?

A-6. Neither of these; though the effect of aluminum—or effect [made] upon the body by foods being cooked in same—adds to, rather than detracts from, the [poisoning] activities in the system.

Hence, as we have indicated for many who are affected by nervous digestion or any overactivity of the nerve forces during the state of [eating or when] digestion [is] taking place, the body should be warned about using or having foods cooked in aluminum. For this naturally produces a hardship upon the activities of the kidneys as related to the lower hepatic circulation, or [affects] the uric acid that is a part of the activity of the kidneys in eliminating same from the system.

303-11   F.49   3/17/36

And in the matter of the diet, keep away from too much greases or too much of any foods cooked in quantities of grease—whether it be the fat of hog, sheep, beef, or fowl! But rather use the *lean* portions and those [meats] that will make for body-building forces throughout. Fish and fowl are the preferable meats. No raw meat, and very little ever of hog meat. Only bacon. Do not use bacon or fats in cooking the vegetables.

462-14   M.57   1/6/42

Q-14. Consider also the steam pressure for cooking foods quickly. Would it be recommended and does it destroy any of the precious vitamins of the vegetables and fruits?

A-14. Rather preserves than destroys.

1223-1   F.29   7/18/36

... [cook] not in aluminum but rather in enamel or glassware. *Not* in aluminum. For with this condition [incoordination], aluminum becomes poisonous to the system. Do not use aluminum ware in *any* form where this body takes food from!

2188-1   F.34   5/7/40

Q-1. Was this poisoning caused from foods cooked in aluminum or copper utensils?

A-1. It was caused from pieces of copper being accidentally cooked in aluminum vessels with food.

Food: Digestion

1710-2   M.23   1/12/39

Q-4. Should I continue taking Alcaroid? If so, when and how often?

A-4. So long as there's a tendency to belch or feel a fullness after the meal, take same ... when this does not occur, leave off.

1710-7   M.27   3/12/42

Q-1. Should Alcaroid be continued?

A-1. If necessary. But if there are the applications made as suggested, these should take the place of much of that which has tended to cause the lack of proper assimilation. If it is necessary, take the Alcaroid, when there is the feeling of indigestion or of too much greases in the digestive area. But adhere to the suggestions made as to the character of diet, and don't eat things you know you shouldn't eat and then expect to be relieved!

558-4   F.32   5/25/34

We would begin taking internally the anti-acid digestant powder known as Alcaroid, at least two doses four hours apart; half a teaspoonful in two glasses of water at each dose.

341-46   M.31   1/26/39

Take an alkalizer, then; and here we will find that Alka-Seltzer® will be very well. For the analgesic here will tend to ease the inclination for the spasmodic reaction in the stomach itself. One tablet; this not taken, though, until after at least two or three of the small doses of Castoria® have been taken.

5545-1   M.41   2/10/30

The water that is taken [by this individual in his condition]—*most* of same should carry those of elm, and this should be prepared just before taking, but should *always* be cool, or cold. Just before the *meals* are taken, [drinking] that of a *mild* tea of saffron should be able to coat the whole of the stomach proper. This will aid digestion . . .

Q-1. What quantity of elm and saffron should be used?

A-1. For each glass of water a pinch between the finger and thumb of the ground [or powdered] elm, stirred well, with a small lump of ice in same; prepared about two to three minutes before it is drunk. Of the saffron—this should be made as a tea, *steeped—as* a tea— and *not* too strong . . . when this is taken, it should be preferably warm, and just before the meal, see? So that, that as first taken, in the system—or into the stomach—forms a coating over the whole of same. If these [drinks] are found to produce *distresses* at any time, *not* the *quality* of the stuff but the *quantity* should be decreased; for these will be effective . . . in *changing* the conditions in the system . . . Charcoal [tablets] should be effective also, to reduce the amount of gas.

2876-1   F.18 mos.   1/7/43

Do give the body Yellow Saffron Tea. This is the regular American Saffron. Put a pinch between three fingers into a crock and pour a pint of boiling water over same. Let this steep as tea. Give [the baby] at least a teaspoonful of this two to three times each day. Make fresh every day.

633-1   M.23   8/16/34

As for the properties to be taken, not a great deal of what would
be called by others medicinal properties; but [have such] as these:
To 3 drams of Yellow Saffron add about 16 ounces of water. Let this
steep as tea for half to three-quarters of an hour; not boiling but just
steeping, see? Use this as a drink three times each day. Take a *glassful* of it in the mornings before any meal is eaten, and before the
evening meal (for we would have the raw vegetables in the middle
of the day), and at night before retiring.

Food: Easily Assimilated

533-6   M.24   9/28/35

*Q-2. Please suggest such predigested foods as would be well for
the body, when these may be taken [as he recovers].*

A-2. First we would take principally fruit juices; such as orange
juice with a little lemon—four parts orange juice to one part lemon;
grapefruit juice, grape juice, pineapple juice. The pineapple may be
combined with the grape juice, if it is preferable.

Then we would begin a little later, in a day or two days, with very
browned whole wheat bread, with a little Ovaltine®, a little malted
milk—the egg may be beat in same, only the yolk of the egg. Junket,
Arrowroot, and things of such natures. These should be [eaten] for
three to four days and then begin with soups—as [soups] of wild
game, potato soup, or cracker soup, and things like that.

Through all the period, then, be mindful that the whole of the
intestinal system is kept open.

2041-1   F.61   11/10/39

In the diets, have preferably more of the liquid and semi-liquid
foods, and those that are almost of a predigested nature; these are
the better for the system . . .

These natures would be preferable: [such foods] as Junket,
Arrowroot, and such natures forming the principal portion of the
diet. Of course, there may be taken the yolk of an egg well beaten,
with a little milk, or with milk and a little sherry or wine or spiritus
frumenti as a stimulant. Not so much of the white of the egg should
be beaten in same, but rather the milk and the yolk and the like.
These will be stimulating. Just a little of this would be taken at the

time, you see, in [doses] rather [as] sips than large quantities. Two or three or four sips—and not spoonsful—taken often.

1208-6   M.3 mos.   10/3/36

In the diet, as the [baby's] body develops, necessary that there be the gradual changing to the greater amount of active [food] forces for the body in its developments.

But *do not* give these other than in a form that may be easily assimilated; as [can be] the calcium and silicon from the orange juice and Gerber's® vegetable juice, or oatmeal that is strained.

Now for the [baby's] body, this doesn't mean spoonsful! but if there is a quarter or half a teaspoonful during the whole day, for the next month, [this] would be sufficient . . .

Do not give sugar in any form other than from fruit or vegetables, until *after* he is at least eighteen months old! . . .

Q-2. *Should Karo® as being prepared in the milk be used?*

A-2. Only as [part of] the formula that has been used.

Sugars will make for the easy assimilation or activity of [a] cold, for it produces acid—which makes the body susceptible to changes . . .

Q-6. *What causes stomach to sour?*

A-6. Sugar.

Food: Fruits

481-1   M.25   7/26/32

If cereals are taken, do not mix these with the citrus fruits—for this *changes* the acidity in the stomach to a detrimental condition; for citrus fruits will act *as* an eliminant when taken alone, but when taken with cereals [they become] as *weight*—rather than as an active force in the gastric forces of the stomach itself.

2072-14   F.34   4/17/44

Q-3. *What foods can be used with fresh citrus fruits to make a complete meal?*

A-3. Any foods that may be eaten at any time save whole grain cereals.

274-9   M.37   1/24/36

Q-2. Is the quart of milk a day, and orange juice, helpful?

A-2. Orange juice and milk are helpful, but these would be taken at opposite ends of the day; not together [for this particular body].

2072-3   F.31   3/18/41

Take plenty of citrus fruit juices; even if this is a part of the meal each day, it is well. With the orange juice put a little lemon—that is, for a glass of orange juice put about two squeezes from a good lemon, not a dry one, so that there will be at least a quarter to half a teaspoonful [of lemon juice added]. With the grapefruit juice put a little lime; about eight to ten drops. Stir these well, of course, before taking.

3525-1   F.44   1/6/44

It will be much better if you will add a little lime with the orange juice and a little lemon with the grapefruit—not too much, but a little. It will be much better and act much better with the body. For, many of these are hybrids, you see.

1208-14   M.2½   2/19/39

Combine a little lemon with the orange juice, or grapefruit juice.

1709-10   F.24   6/21/43

Q-5. Is lemon juice, as being taken now, helpful?

A-5. It is a good alkalizer. Squeeze a little lime in with it also, just two or three drops in a full glass of the lemon juice taken. Best to mix the lemon juice with water, of course. Use half a lemon, or a full lemon to a glass of water, depending upon how soon the lemon is used after it is fully ripened . . .

5097-1   F.28   5/10/44

Have raw vegetables also, but not a great deal of melons of any kind, though cantaloupes may be taken, if grown in the neighborhood where the body resides; if [a cantaloupe is] shipped, don't eat it. The fruits that may be taken: plums, pears and apples. Do not take raw apples, but roast apples aplenty.

1187-9   F.57   6/25/36

. . . we would have citrus fruit juices, fresh; not those that are canned, see? For this body those of the preservatives that are in most are *not* so good.

275-21   F.18   8/18/31
Q-5. *What is raw cereal?*
A-5. Rolled wheat, rye, or oats are usually termed the *raw* cereal.

Food: Vegetables

2602-1   F.38   10/13/41

Have at least one meal each day that includes a quantity of raw vegetables; such as cabbage, lettuce, celery, carrots, onions, and the like. Tomatoes may be used in their season.

Do have plenty of vegetables grown above the ground; at least three of these to one below the ground. Have at least one leafy vegetable to every one of the pod vegetables taken.

3373-1   F.74   11/26/43

Normal diet . . . Use at least three vegetables that grow above the ground to one that grows under the ground . . .

457-14   F.36   5/15/44
Q-14. Does it make any difference whether the Mullein [in Mullein tea] is dried or fresh?
A-14. Does it make any difference whether cabbage is wilted before it is boiled? It should indeed be fresh, not as in people, but as in the vegetable kingdom; not applying to people being fresh, but plants used for medicinal purposes, the fresher, the more active the better.

900-386   M.33   5/26/28

. . . vegetables will build gray matter faster than will meat or sweets!

Q-10. Would it be well for me to eat vegetables such as corn, tomatoes, and the like?
A-10. Corn and tomatoes are excellent. More of the vitamins are obtained in tomatoes [vine ripened] than in any other *one* growing vegetable!

584-5   M.57   10/4/35

Q-2. What has been the effect on my system of eating so many tomatoes?

A-2. Quite a dissertation might be given as to the effect of tomatoes upon the human system. Of all the vegetables, tomatoes carry most of the vitamins in a well-balanced assimilative manner for the activities in the system. Yet if these [tomatoes] are not cared for properly, they may become very destructive to a physical organism; that is, if they ripen after being pulled, or if there is the contamination with other influences [or substances].

In *this* particular body, as we find, the reactions from these have been not *always* the *best*. Neither has there been the normal reaction from the eating of same. For it tends to make for an irritation or humor. Nominally, though, these [tomatoes] should form at least a portion of a meal three or four days out of every week; and they will be found to be *most* helpful.

The tomato is one vegetable that in most instances (because of the greater uniform activity) is preferable to be eaten after being canned, for it is then much more uniform.

The reaction [from non-canned tomatoes] in this body, then, has been to form an acid of its own; though the tomato is among those foods that may [usually] be taken as the non-acid forming. But these [tomatoes] should be of the best in *every* instance where they are used.

Q-3. What brand of canned tomatoes is best?

A-3. Libby's® are more *uniform* than most.

404-6   F.46   1/15/36

Q-7. Should plenty of lettuce be eaten?

A-7. Plenty of lettuce should always be eaten by most *every* body; for this supplies an effluvium in the blood stream that is a destructive force to *most* of those influences that attack the blood stream.

3172-2   F.21 mos.   5/15/44

Q-10. Will the vaccination against smallpox be detrimental?

A-10. Depends upon when it is administered. When [the child] is a little older, give plenty of celery and lettuce, and you won't ever have to vaccinate; or if you will keep the vaccine from milk or cow about the body, vaccine will not take.

457-9   F.34   5/21/42

Q-14. Since onions are supposed to be good for your blood and otherwise, why do they cause such ill-smelling gases?

A-14. From the most foul at times comes the most beautiful lilies.

404-6   F.46   1/15/36

Q-6. What is the food value of raw green peppers?

A-6. They are better in combinations than by themselves. Their tendency is for an activity to the pylorus; not [affecting] the activity in the pylorus itself, but more in the activity from the flow of the pylorus to the churning effect upon the duodenum in its digestion.

Hence it is an activity for *digestive* forces [which results].

Peppers, then, taken with green cabbage, lettuce, are very good for this body; taken in moderation.

2803-6   F.24   12/15/43

Q-5. What foods should be stressed or avoided during pregnancy?

A-5. Those carrying silicon, calcium, those good for the eyes—all of these should be stressed; that is, the salads with carrots, watercress, celery, lettuce, and occasionally tomatoes—though not too many of these, for they will be ripened indoors and *not* as good, but use these occasionally.

All of these [vegetables] may be served with oils or mayonnaise.

These should be stressed and occasionally [have also] artichokes, [and] the oyster plant—these are good in their activities.

840-1   M.Adult   2/23/35

[The raw fresh vegetables] would consist of tomatoes, lettuce, celery, spinach, carrots, beet tops, mustard, onions or the like (not cucumbers) that make for purifying of the *humor* in the lymph blood as this is absorbed by the lacteal ducts as it is digested.

340-31   F.47   6/21/35

Q-5. Does steam pressure cooking at 15 lbs. temperature destroy food value in foods?

A-5. No. Depends upon the preparation of same, the age, and how long gathered. All of these have their factors in the food values. As it is so well advertised that coffee loses its value in fifteen to twenty to twenty-five days after being roasted, so do foods or vegetables lose their food value after being gathered—in the same proportion in hours as coffee would in days.

1586-1   F.77   4/29/38

Do not cook the vegetables with meats to season them; only use a little butter, with pepper or salt or such. And preferably use the sea salt entirely, or iodized salt—this is preferable.

3047-1   M.36   6/11/43

The foods that are of the nature of leafy vegetables, both raw and cooked, are preferable to those of the tuberous nature; though carrots—both raw and cooked—are well.

Food: Gelatin

[Gelatin salads were suggested by the readings for everyone's daily diet, since the gelatin acts as a kind of catalyst to increase the natural body absorption of vitamins. Unfortunately, this information is as little-known as it is significant.]

849-75   M.36   1/25/44

Q-4. Please explain the vitamin content of gelatin. There is no reference to vitamin content on the package.

A-4. It isn't the vitamin content but it is [its] ability to work with the activities of the glands, causing the glands to take from that [which is] absorbed or digested the vitamins that would not be active [in the body] if there is [or were] not sufficient gelatin in the body. See, there may be mixed with any chemical that which makes the rest of the system susceptible or able to call from the system that [which is] needed. It becomes then, as it were, "sensitive" to conditions. Without it there is not that sensitivity [to vitamins].

3429-1   F.52   1/2/44

In the diet [of this body] keep plenty of raw vegetables, such as watercress, celery, lettuce, tomatoes, carrots. Change these in their manner of preparation, but do have some of these each day. They may be prepared rather often with gelatin, as with lime or lemon gelatin—or Jello. These will not only taste good but be good for you.

2520-2   F.38   10/4/41

Have a great deal of such [foods] as liver, tripe, pig's knuckle, pig's feet and the like; a great deal of okra and its products, a great deal of any form of desserts carrying quantities of gelatin. Any of the gelatin products, though they may carry sugars at times, these are to be had oft in the diet.

3051-6   F.46   6/19/44

Q-1. What is the best diet for this body?

A-1. Now that which is a well-balanced diet. But often use the raw vegetables which are prepared with gelatin. Use these at least three times each week. Those which grow more above the ground than those which grow below the ground. Do include, when they are prepared, carrots with that portion especially close to the top. It may appear the harder and the less desirable, but it carries the vital energies, stimulating the optic reactions between kidneys and the optics.

3445-1   F.55   12/4/43

Do be mindful of the diet. Include in the diet often raw vegetables prepared in various ways, not merely as a salad but scraped or grated and combined with gelatin . . .

5394-1   F.58   8/24/44

In building up the body with foods, preferably have a great deal of raw vegetables for this body—as lettuce, celery, carrots, watercress. All we would take raw, with dressing, and oft with gelatin. These should be grated, or cut very fine, or even ground, but do preserve all of the juices with them when these are prepared in this manner in the gelatin.

3266-1   F.48   10/6/43

We would supply to the system those vital forces that may aid in producing in the body-energies that necessary influence for the reviving and regenerating of the body forces. Hence we would take Knox gelatin. One day in the morning take about a teaspoonful thoroughly dissolved in warm water—cooled just a bit but not so that it jells before drinking. The next day in the afternoon take about half a teaspoonful prepared in the same way.

Food: Meat

["Fish, fowl, and lamb, never fried" is a phrase which appears in hundreds of the readings given by Edgar Cayce.]

1710-4   M.24   11/24/39

   Q-3. Please outline the proper diet, suggesting things to avoid.
   A-3. Avoid too much of the heavy meats not well cooked. Eat plenty of vegetables of all characters. The meats taken would be preferably fish, fowl, and lamb; others *not* so often. Breakfast bacon, crisp, may be taken occasionally.

5269-1   F.38   6/17/44

   In the diets: Keep away from heavy foods. Use those which are body-building, [such] as beef juice, beef broth, liver, fish, lamb; all [these] may be taken, but never fried foods.

Food: Meat: Abstinence

5401-1   F.43   8/24/44

   This, to be sure, is not an attempt to tell the body to go back to eating meat; but do supply, then, through the body forces, supplements, either in vitamins or in [meat] substitutes, for those who hold to these [vegetarian] influences—but purifying of mind is of the mind, not of the body. For, as the Master gave, it is not that which entereth in the body, but that which cometh out that causes sin. It is what one does with the purpose; for all things are pure in themselves and are for the sustenance of man, body, mind, and soul; and remember—these must work together, as should be indicated for the body in its interpretation of [its] music. For music is of the soul, and one may become mind and soul-sick for music, or soul and mind-sick from certain kinds of music.

295-10   F.31   1/18/35

   Q-15. Should the body abstain from meats for its best spiritual development?
   A-15. Meats of certain characters are necessary in the body-*building* forces in this system, and should not be wholly abstained from in the present. Spiritualize those influences, those activities, rather

than abstaining. For, as He gave, that which cometh out—rather than that which goeth in—defileth the spiritual body.

Food: Meat: Fowl

1523-8   F.31   1/9/40

Plenty of fowl, but prepared in such a way that more of the bone structure itself is [used] as a part of the diet in its reaction through the system; [so] that better reaction for the [assimilation of] calcium through the system is obtained for same.

Chew chicken necks, then. Chew the bones of the thigh. Have the marrow of beef, or such, as a part of the diet; [eat such foods] as the vegetable soups that are rich in the beef carrying the marrow of the bone, and the like . . . and *eat the marrow!*

1973-1   F.71   7/31/39

In the diet beware of those foods that carry large quantities of fats—as the fat of fowl, though the lean or bony portions would be very well to supply more calcium; as well as fish and those bony portions of same that are cooked to such an extent that these may be masticated also . . . Hence these boiled or broiled or roasted would be preferable for the body . . .

5069-1   M.41   5/8/44

Q-2. Although my teeth seem to be in good condition,could they be partly the source of trouble?

A-2. The teeth are in good condition. It would be very well to take foods to supplement [the present diet], especially foods from which the body may assimilate larger quantities of calcium, such as fish, chicken especially prepared in a way where the bones may be eaten. The feet and neck of the chicken are worth a lot more than the breast, although the breast is more palatable.

Chewing the bones will be worth more to the body in strengthening and in the eliminations. These should be broiled or stewed, but do keep the lid on so that the boiling will not carry off that which is best to be taken.

Food: Meat: Pork

3599-1   F.51   1/21/44
Here [in the condition of this body] we have a result of the absorption of certain food values that arise from eating a certain character of foods.

The character of dross it makes in the body-functioning causes a fungi that produces in the system a crystallization of the muscles and nerves in portions of the body.

These [results] have been [apparent] in the pelvic organs, the whole lumbar-sacral area, portions of the sciatic nerves, the knees and feet—all of these are giving distress.

These [distresses] began as acute pain, rheumatic or neuritic. They are closer to neuritic-arthritic reactions. This is pork—the effect of same.

294-95   M.50   3/16/27
Q-3. What has the body been eating that it should not?
A-3. Meats—in the form of hog meat, see?

3596-1   M.39   1/25/44
. . . keep away from red meats, ham, or rare steak or roasts. Rather use fish, fowl and lamb . . .

Food: Meat: Wild game

2514-4   F.23   12/8/41
Q-1. Is it all right for me to eat rabbit and squirrel, baked or stewed?
A-1. Any wild game is preferable even to other meats, if these are prepared properly.

Rabbit—be sure the tendon in both left legs is removed, or that [part] as might cause a fever. It is what is called at times the wolve [or wolf] in the rabbit. While prepared in some ways this would be excellent for some [specific] disturbances in a body, it is never well for this to be eaten in a hare.

Squirrel—of course, it is not in same. This stewed, or well cooked, is really more preferable for the body, of course—but rabbit is well if that part indicated is removed.

137-30   M.27   11/12/25
. . . never, under strain, when very tired, very excited, very mad, should the body take foods in the system . . . and never take any food that the body finds is not agreeing with same . . .

Food: Minerals

1131-2   M.Adult   10/29/32
Q-13. Please give the foods that would supply these [minerals].
A-13. We have given them; cereals that carry the heart of the grain; vegetables of the leafy kind; fruits and nuts as indicated. The almond carries more phosphorus *and* iron in a combination easily assimilated than any other nut.

840-1   M.Adult   2/23/35
. . . rolled or crushed or cracked whole wheat, that is not cooked too long so as to destroy the whole vitamin force . . . this will add to the body the proper proportions of iron, silicon and the vitamins necessary to build up the blood supply that makes for resistance in the system.

Food: Minerals: Calcium

1968-6   F.30   7/26/41
Keep plenty of those foods that supply calcium to the body. These we would find especially in raw carrots, cooked turnips and turnip greens, all characters of salads—especially as of watercress, mustard and the like; these [are] especially [helpful] taken raw, though turnips [should be] cooked—but cooked in their own juices and *not* with fat meats.

951-7   F.30   10/30/43
Calcios™ is the better manner [in which] to take calcium. It is more easily assimilated, and will act better with pregnancy than any type of calcium products as yet presented. About three times each week, at the noon meal, eat a whole-wheat cracker spread thinly with the Calcios™.

2752-3   F.2   1/17/44
Q-3. Any special care to keep teeth strong and healthy?

A-3. Give her a little Calcios™ or lime water. But Calcios™ would be better, if it is given correctly. About once or twice a week, give the body what would go on about half of a whole-wheat cracker, as though it were buttered. She will like it after the third time, but you'll have a time with her at first.

808-15   F.34   10/5/41

When there is a great deal of fowl taken—that is, of chicken, goose, duck, turkey or the like, and the bony pieces or broths of same are taken—it is not so necessary for great quantities of the Calcios™.

Food: Minerals: Phosphorus

560-2   F.48   5/26/34

The phosphorus-forming foods are principally carrots, lettuce (rather the leaf lettuce, which has more soporific activity than the head lettuce), shell fish, salsify, the *peelings* of Irish potatoes (if they are not too large), and things of such natures . . . Citrus fruit juices, plenty of milk—the Bulgarian [buttermilk] the better, or the fresh milk that is warm with animal heat which carries more of the phosphorus and more of those activities that are less constipating, or [that are capable of] acting more with the lacteals and the ducts of the liver, the kidneys, and the bowels themselves.

Food: Minerals: Iron

1187-9   F.57   6/25/36

Let the iron be rather taken in the foods [instead of from medicinal sources], as it is more easily assimilated from the vegetable forces . . . [*Foods with iron: spinach, lentils, red cabbage, berries, raisins, liver, grapes, pears, onions, asparagus*]

Food: Starches

798-1   F.48   1/23/35

For in all bodies, the less activities there are in physical exercise or manual activity, the greater should be the alkaline-reacting foods taken.

Energies or activities may burn acids, but those who lead the sedentary life or the non-active life can't go on sweets or too much starches—but these should be well-balanced.

416-18   M.38   6/2/44
Q-5. What is particularly wrong with my diet?
A-5. The tendencies for too much starches, pastries, white bread, should be almost entirely eliminated. Not that you shouldn't eat ice cream, but don't eat cake, too. White potatoes, such [foods] as macaroni or the like and cheeses, these eliminate. They are not very good for the body [of this individual] in any form.

Food: Sweets

5218-1   M.35   6/9/44
Do be careful that there are no quantities of pastries, pies or candies, especially chocolate or carbonated waters. These [sweets], as we find, will be hard on the body . . .

4047-1   M.36   4/1/44
Q-4. Are daily heavy chocolate malted milks detrimental?
A-4. Chocolate that is prepared in the present [period of wartime substitutes] is not best for *any* diet.

3180-3   F.20   12/21/43
Keep away from sweets, especially chocolate at this period.

1131-2   M.Adult   10/29/32
Q-15. Suggest best sugars for body.
A-15. Beet sugars are the better for *all*, or the cane sugars that are not clarified.

487-11   M.9   9/8/27
Keep the body from too much sweets—though [have] *sufficient* of sweets to form sufficient alcohol for the system; that is, the kind of sweets, rather than [just] sweets. Grape sugars—hence [grape] jellies, or [sweets] of that nature are well. Chocolates that are *plain*—not those of any [brand] that carry corn starches should be taken, or [not] those that carry too much of the cane sugar. Grape

sugar, or beet sugars, or [sweets] of that nature, may be taken.

307-6   F.55   5/13/33
   Saccharin may be used. Brown sugar is not harmful. The *better*
would be to use beet sugar for sweetening.

808-3   F.27   5/19/35
   Q-13. What type of sweets may be eaten by the body?
   A-13. Honey, especially in the honeycomb; or preserves made
with *beet* rather than cane sugar. Not too great a quantity of any of
these, of course, but the forces in sweets to make for the proper
activity through the action of the gastric flows *are* as necessary
as body-building [elements]; for these become body-building in
making for the proper fermentation (if it may be called so) in the
digestive activities. Hence two or three times a week the honey
upon the bread or the food values would furnish that necessary in
the whole system.

Food: Vitamins

   *[It is typical of the psychic readings of Edgar Cayce that they
should urge the taking of vitamins in food rather than in capsules,
especially when the body may need cleansing. It is also typical of
these readings that they should point out a spiritual lesson to be
found—even in vitamins. (See also "Vegetables" and "Gelatin.")]*

2778-6   F.31   12/9/43
   Q-4. Would it be advisable to take vitamins—in what form?
   A-4. For what? There is being supplied to the body those energies
in their proper proportions. Resistances are being supplied vibratorially [through electro-therapy]. There may be an overabundance of
vitamins. Most of this [vitamin-taking] is fad, save as to what may be
necessary to create a balance [in the diet]. If there is a proper balance in the diet, you do not need extra vitamins. And you are eating
very well! You have a very good diet, a very well-balanced diet in
most meals. We wouldn't upset it. We would keep to the right way.

2533-6   M.37   10/31/42
   Knowing the tendencies [towards weakness in your body], supply

in the vital energies that [which] ye call the vitamins, or elements. For remember, while we give many combinations [for treatments], there are only four elements in your body—water, salt, soda, and iodine. These are the basic elements; they make all the rest! Each vitamin as a component part of an element is simply a combination of these other influences, given a name mostly for confusion to individuals by those who would tell you what to do for a price!

2072-9   F.32   7/22/42

Q-12. What relation do the vitamins bear to the glands? Give specific vitamins affecting specific glands.

A-12. You want a book written on these! They [the vitamins] are food for same. Vitamins are that from which the glands take those necessary influences to supply the energies to enable the varied organs of the body to reproduce themselves. Would it ever be considered that your toenails would be reproduced by the same [gland] as would supply the breast, the head, or the face? or that the cuticle would be supplied from the same [source] as would supply the organ of the heart itself? These [building substances] are taken from *glands* that control the assimilated foods, and hence [require] the necessary elements or vitamins in same to supply the various forces for enabling each organ, each functioning of the body, to carry on in its creative or generative forces, see?

These will begin with A—that supplies portions to the nerves, to bone, to the brain force itself; not [being] all of [the supply to] this [area], but this is a part of [the function of] A.

B and B-1 supply the ability of the energies, or the moving forces of the nerve and of the white blood supply, as well as the white nerve energy in the nerve force itself, the brain for itself, and [supply] the ability of the sympathetic or involuntary reflexes through the body. Now this includes all [such energy], whether you are wiggling your toes or your ears or batting your eye or what! In these [B vitamins] we [also] have that [which is] supplying to the chyle that ability for it to control the influence of fats, which is necessary (and this body has never had enough of it!) to carry on the reproducing of the oils that prevent the tenseness in the joints, or that prevent the joints from becoming atrophied or dry, or [from seeming] to creak. At times the body has had some creaks!

In C we find that which supplies the necessary influences to the flexes of every nature throughout the body, whether of a muscular or tendon nature, or a heart reaction, or a kidney contraction, or the liver contraction, or the opening or shutting of your mouth, the batting of the eye, or the supplying of the saliva and the muscular forces in [the] face. These are all supplied by C—not that it is the only supply, but a part of same. It is that from which the [necessary supplies for] structural portions of the body are [taken and] stored, and drawn upon when it becomes necessary. And when [lack of C] becomes detrimental or [when] there is a deficiency of same—which has been [the case] for this body—it is necessary to supply same in such proportions as to aid; else the conditions become such that there are the [resultant] bad eliminations from the incoordination of the excretory functioning of the alimentary canal, as well as the [functioning of the] heart, liver and lungs, through the expelling of those forces that are a part of the structural portion of the body.

G supplies the general energies, or the sympathetic forces of the body itself. These are the principles.

457.S   F.34   4/23/42

Q-13. What foods carry most of the vitamin B?

A-13. All those that are of the yellow variety, especially, and whole grain cereals or bread.

462-14   M.57   1/6/42

Q-13. Considering the frozen foods, especially vegetables and fruits that are on the market today, has the freezing in any way killed certain vitamins and how do they compare with the fresh?

A-13. This would necessitate making a special list. For some are affected more than others. So far as fruits are concerned, these do not lose much of the vitamin content. Yet some of these are affected by the freezing. Vegetables—much of the vitamin content of these is taken [by freezing], unless there is the re-enforcement in same when these are either prepared for food or when frozen.

Q-14. Consider also the steam pressure method for cooking foods quickly. Would it be recommended and does it destroy any of the precious vitamins of the vegetables and fruits?

A-14. Rather preserves than destroys.

2529-1   F.46   7/6/41

In the matter of the diet throughout the periods [of convalescence]—we would constantly add more and more of vitamin B-1, in every form in which it may be taken; in the bread, the cereals, the types of vegetables that may be prepared for the body, the fruits, etc. Be sure that there is sufficient each day [of B-1] for the adding of the vital energies. These vitamins are not stored in the body as are A, D, and G, but it is necessary to add these daily. All of those fruits and vegetables, then, that are yellow in color should be taken; oranges, lemons, grapefruit, yellow squash, yellow corn, yellow peaches—all of these and such as these; beets—but all of the vegetables [should be] cooked in their *own* juices, and the body [should be] eating the juices with same.

1968-7   F.31   7/28/42   ·

So, keep an excess of foods that carry especially vitamin B, iron, and such. Not the concentrated form [of vitamins], you see, but obtain these from the foods. These [foods] would include all fruits, all vegetables that are yellow in their nature. Thus, lemon and orange juice combined, all citrus fruit juices, pineapple as well as grapefruit. Some of these should be a part of the diet each day. Squash—especially the yellow; carrots, cooked and raw; yellow peaches; yellow apples (preferably the apples cooked, however). All of these carry an excess or the greater quantity of necessary elements for supplying energies for the body, and that are much more easily assimilated by the body. Yellow corn, yellow cornmeal, buckwheat—all of these are especially good. Red cabbage. Such vegetables, such fruits, are especially needed by the body [of this individual].

257-254   M.50   12/18/43

Q-4. Are "B-Plus" vitamins now being taken good, or are there better ones?

A-4. As we find, this depends upon whether the system is in shape, or whether there are such conditions that these [vitamins] may add a [negative] stimulation or become a dross to the body. In the present B-Plus are not very good for the body, unless more cold is eliminated. These [vitamins] taken under such conditions merely add a greater amount of drosses to be eliminated. Thus, when the

[body] cleansings are accomplished and the drosses are eliminated from [the] body, these will be very well [for this body].

341-31   M.23   3/10/31

. . . in the matter of diets—one activity is necessary, if there is to be a mental diet—or is there to be a diet for a well-rounded physically useful, mentally useful, spiritually useful body? But there is the lack of vitamins as B and C, in this body. One, the C,[gives] stamina for mental energies that are carried in the white tissue in nerve energy and plexus. B, as is of calcium, of silicon, of iron. These would be well-balanced, will those of the food values that carry same be taken, but unless the activities physical for the body are such as to put same into activity they become drosses and set themselves to become operative, irrespective of other conditions. (This as aside, but as very well in keeping with the circumstances or conditions.) Vitamins in a body are elements that are combative with, or in opposition to, the various activities of a living organism, and may be termed—and well termed—as those of bacilli of any nature within a human or physical organism. That's what we are talking of or dealing with in this body. Now, when these are taken into the system, if they are not put to work by the activities of the system—either physical or mental—they become destructive tissue, for they affect the plasm of the blood supply or the emunctory and lymph which is another name for a portion of a blood supply in a system. Then, in the meeting of the diet—be sure the activities, physically and mentally, are in keeping with; and do not do these spasmodically, but be consistent—for the physical body, the mental body, the spiritual body, is as "Grow in grace, in knowledge, in understanding."

3511-1   M.35   12/17/43

Have ye not read that in Him ye live and move and have thy being? What are those elements in food or in drink that give growth or strength to the body? Vitamins? What are vitamins? The Creative Forces working with body-energies for the renewing of the body! What speaketh of the spirit? My Spirit beareth witness with thy spirit whether ye be the children of God or not. When there are those physical deficiencies, the body is minus something, but who is to add that which will constitute a complete coordination? Man may only sow, man may only apply, but God giveth the increase, God giveth the healing.

Discipline

3003-1   F.61   5/16/43
Q4. How can I discipline myself at my age to do what is mine to do?

A-4. Repeat three times every day, and then listen: *"Lord, what would Thou have me do today?"* Have this not as rote. Mean it! For as He has spoken, as He has promised, "If ye call I will hear, and answer speedily." He meant it! Believe it!

1537-1   M.38   2/18/38
For this entity should comprehend and *know*, and *never* forget, that life and its experiences are only what one puts into same! And unless the activities, the thoughts are *continuously* constructive, and the experience well-balanced, the entity *cannot, will* not fulfill the purpose for which it came into the present experience . . .

. . . the greater import [from astrological influences for the entity] has at most periods caused or been a confusion rather than causing helpful experiences; owing to [the entity's] not comprehending, not understanding that life *is* a *continuous* thing; and that an individual is *each day* meeting his own self—either in the mental, the material or the spiritual phase of his existence!

Know first and foremost . . . that the Lord thy God is *one!* Then know, too, that thyself is one—thy ego, thy I Am. Thy purposes then, thy heart and thy life must be a *consistent* thing! For if thine eye be single (the I Am; that is, the purposes, the desires—and ye work *at it!*), then thy *whole body* is full of light.

But if ye are attempting to have thy physical body doing just as it pleases, thy mental body controlled by "What will other people say?" and thy spiritual body and mind shelved only for good occasions and for the good impressions that you may make occasionally, there *cannot* be other than confusion!

These as given are not merely sayings; they answer to that which has been and is thy turmoil in the present. Look *within!* For if there is trouble in thy mind, in thy body, in thy spirit—or purpose, or mind; sin lieth at that door . . .

... we find the entity often determined to be very good. And for a few hours or a few minutes it is very well! Then such determination is forgotten, and it's to the other extreme! and he begins to constantly berate self for not doing this, that or the other! He declares that he *will* be frugal; he declares that he *will* be saving; he declares that he *will* do this, that or the other! And before the day or the week or the *hour* (and often before the thirty minutes) is passed, it's the same old story again! And yet each determination is just as strong.

... thy *will*, thy purpose is the deciding factor. Mere [astrological] influences cannot or *do not* cause thee to do this, save that they *are* a part of thee.

But to the manifestation of stability, of good, of truth, of consistency, of patience, of long-suffering, of justice, of brotherly love, of brotherly kindness—that is thy purpose! That is oft thy desire!

Then not of thyself alone may ye do it, but in love, in truth, in honor ye may. For these are thy helpmeets, if ye hold fast to them. They arise from the influence or associations in Venus. Hence ye are oft a hail fellow well met, and sometimes *too* well met by some! Ye are made too oft the *expense* of others, yet this is part of thy experience—if used but properly.

Never then be hardboiled, dictatorial—these get no one anywhere; but in being patient, just. *Demand* of others justice in the same measure as ye *mete* it to others—no more, no less; but all of that! ...

Ye are sensitive to things about you; because ye have lived not only in this experience but in many others a very *extravagant* life in *every* phase of your associations with your fellow man! Hence ye find yourself very sensitive to vibrations, very sensitive to a beautiful figure or a beautiful face; very sensitive to those conditions in which there may be something of the risqué nature, or story; and yet very sensitive towards those things that proclaim the spiritual intents of truth and purposes.

All of these become confusions unless ye regulate thine own experiences in such a way that all of these, while they should have their place in thy experience, may be for construction and not for merely the passing moment or the gratifying [of self].

Have ye not found within—as in thine own body in the present—that the extravagance of thy living has produced those very inclinations that arise in thy digestive forces? Thus thy high blood pressure that is produced within thy body arises from this overindulgence, this overactivity.

And unless ye make reparation, these conditions will overcome thee. How may ye make reparation—by being what? *Consistent!* Oh, what a jewel consistency must be in thine experience, if ye will but take it and *use* it and apply it day by day!

As to the material activities—keep away from those things that *hinder*—such as the effects of alcohol, the effects of riotous living, the effects of indulgence in those things that are of the nature of great quantities of stimulations; whether they be in condiments, excess of sugars, excess of this, that or the other. Or, as just given, be *consistent!* . . .

That to which [the entity]may attain rests within self. *Who* and what is thy belief? In *whom* do ye believe? In self, in the God of nature, in the God of heaven and earth, in the God of Isaac or Jacob, in the God of those that are of the earth-earthy? Whom do ye take in partnership with thee? Upon this answer rests what ye may attain.

Know and behold the Lord is One. Thou art His son, a manifestation of His love, of His patience—in the earth. How art thou using same? As if ye were, or as if ye were only adopted or only a bastard? These be the questions ye must ask and answer within thyself. For ye are loved of the Father, even as ye love thy fellow man. For as ye mete to others day by day, so yet mete to that God ye worship within.

What is thy hope for the future? What is thy hope for the present? These arise from the applications of thy experience and opportunities in the past; not only in the present experience but throughout the eons of years that ye have been conscious of that abiding love that ye have at times so misused, have at others hoped for. *Claim* it then as thine own! . . .

Call on Him while He may be found. For His promises are sure, and though ye may be afar "If ye call, I will *hear!*" This does not portend to become as one long-faced, not enjoying the fruits of thy labors nor the associations of friends; but keeping all in the channel and way of truth and justice and mercy; showing thyself *worthy* of the trust He has put in thy hands . . .

Study to show thyself approved unto Him, a workman not ashamed; rightly divining the words of truth and keeping self *unspotted* from thine own conscience that so oft berates thee! Or keeping thyself unspotted from the world. Do not engage in those things in which question marks are set, not only for thyself but for thy children, for thy Lord.

Drugless Therapy

257-254   M.50   12/18/43

For the hydrotherapy and massage are preventive as well as curative measures. For the cleansing of the system allows the body forces themselves to function normally, and thus eliminate poisons, congestions and conditions that would become acute through the body.

3570-1   M.61   1/17/44

Q-5. [Is there trouble with the] prostate gland?

A-5. These are rather pressures from the lack of peristaltic movement in the lower portion of the colon. Take a colonic irrigation occasionally, or have one administered, scientifically. One colonic irrigation will be worth about four to six enemas.

440-2   M.23   12/13/33

Q-8. Do you advise the use of colonics or Epsom salts baths for the body?

A-8. When these are necessary, yes. For, everyone—everybody—should take an internal bath occasionally, as well as an external one. They would all be better off if they would.

457-14   F.36   5/15/44

Q-7. Are colonics also of value to [this] body when not pregnant, and if so, how often?

A-7. Value to the body when not pregnant, or when pregnant, if necessary.

533-6   M.24   9/28/35

Use a soft tube for the colon tube, [one] that opens on the side rather than on [the] end.

1312-5   F.50   8/11/41

Give a colonic irrigation, using the high tube; not just an ordinary tube, but a colon tube, see? for this must empty the colon, so that there will be a reaction of the peristaltic movement. In the first water use a heaping teaspoonful of salt and a level teaspoonful of soda. In the last quart and a half of water put a tablespoonful of Glyco-Thymoline®.

3420-1   F.57   12/17/43

. . . at least one week out of each month should be spent in beautifying, preserving, rectifying the body—if the body would keep young, in mind, in body, in purpose.

This doesn't mean that the entity should spend a whole week at nothing else.

Choose three days out of some week in each month—not just three days in a month, but three days in some definite week each month—either the first, the second, the third, or the fourth week of each month—and have the general hydrotherapy treatments, including massage, lights, and all the treatments that are in that nature of beautifying, and [for] keeping the whole of the body-forces young.

One week each month is required for sterilizing the body functions. Then, is it a wonder that a week after such [menstruation] would be well for the beautifying, for the replenishing, for the supplying of the building forces for the body's activities?

304-2   M.68   6/26/22

Osteopathic treatment is needed, not chiropractic. If we had wanted this we would have given it. The body does not need adjustment, what it needs is relaxation of the muscular forces . . . Chiropractic treatment is adjustment, not relaxation of the muscular forces.

2524-5   M.43   1/13/44

Clear the body as you do the mind of those things that have hindered.

The things that hinder physically are the poor eliminations.

Set up better eliminations in the body. This is why osteopathy and hydrotherapy come nearer to being the basis of all needed treatments for physical disabilities.

3384-2   M.33   1/22/44

The closer the body will keep to those truths and the dependence on the abilities latent within self through trust in spiritual things, the quicker will be the response in the physical body. For all healing, mental or material, is attuning each atom of the body, each reflex of the brain forces, to the awareness of the divine that lies within each atom, each cell of the body . . .

These adjustments are merely to attune the centers of the body with the coordinating forces of cerebrospinal and sympathetic system.

Thus the body is purified or attuned so that it in itself and nature [do] the healing.

As to how soon you may leave off the treatments depends upon how soon you can trust in your spiritual self, your mental self, to direct your physical being.

5211-1   F.51   6/13/44

. . . for this particular body we would continue with the present chiropractor. We would ordinarily give that osteopathy is more vital, but there are chiropractors and there are chiropractors. This is a very good one; don't lose him! He understands this body.

1684-1   M.65   9/10/38

Not taking drugs, but rather activities; and there must be more *consistent* activity of the body *in the open*—if it will attain to its better physical and mental abilities in the present, and under the disturbing conditions mentally and physically that have gradually grown to be a part of the activities.

Hence walking, golfing, riding—all such should be at some time a part of the activity; or as combined with the hydrotherapy—through the seasons that approach—we would have, with the hydrotherapy and massage, also the handball, the electric horse, the bicycle, as a part of the exercise. For without these, we will find there will be less and less elasticity in the muscular or tendon forces as govern the flow of the impulse as well as the stream of blood supply itself.

3374-1   F.35   11/23/43

The entity should keep close to all of those things that have to do with outdoor activities, for it is the best way to keep yourself young—to stay close to nature, close to those activities in every fom1 of exercise that . . . breathe it into thine own soul, as you would a sunset or a morning sun rising. And see that sometimes—it's as pretty as the sunset!

Drugs

[The following extracts are not intended to represent the findings of the complex field of drugs, hundreds of which, of course, were recommended. These excerpts are, however, typical warnings made to individuals.]

3287-2   F.35   1/11/44
Q-3. Would sulfa drugs help the strep condition?
A-3. And make you worse in other conditions? Yes.

294-209   M.67   6/27/44
There is no infection, as indicated, of tubercular inflammation, but [there are] the adhesions, and these were produced by the after-effects of the sulfa drug. While this [drug], to be sure, destroyed those inflammations of the nature [described] in the lobe of the lung itself, yet it is like saying the operation is successful but the patient died; so it [the sulfa] is successful in eliminating the character of inflammation or the bug which was infectious; but the adhesion in [the lung area] is causing the greater trouble.

1264-1   M.Adult   11/15/32
A bromide of any nature *must* eventually become destructive to the physical forces of the body. A hypnotic of any nature continued to be taken must become destructive to the better functioning of the body.

263-1   F.21   2/6/33
Q-5. Is [the taking of] B.C. Powders injurious to the body? Has the body been injured by taking them?
A-5. As any such powders that act upon the hypogastrics of the system itself as to *deaden* them, they naturally become detrimental to the body—but we will relieve these conditions by stimulating to activity nerve plexuses along the system, both by the [osteopathic]

manipulation and the violet ray® [hand machine, bulb applicator].

3629-1   M.34   2/1/44

Q-3. Were hay fever shots in any way responsible for this trouble?

A-3. Any shots are responsible for most anything! Yes—they are a part of the disorders.

130-1   F.40   10/31/30

Q-1. A mad cat bit the left ankle about four years ago. Treatment was given to prevent hydrophobia. The ankle is swollen and is colored. Has this any influence on the health and bodily organs now?

A-1. This is indicated most in the effect that the serums used in this period have upon the sympathetic nerve system, and affects in the present the *lymph* circulation, *with* the pressures as exhibited in the lumbar and sacral.

With the removal of the pressure, the circulation brought to a nearer normalcy, and clarification of the blood stream, an equalization in the hydrochloric content in digestion, an equalization between the iodine and potash content, *without* too much potash and *less* acid—these conditions will disappear.

Well were there taken, at least once each week, an eighth grain of medicated ash to *produce* oxygen, *as* it is carried in the system. When this is taken, over the sacral and lower limbs apply the ultraviolet ray. Apply same to the sacral region and the back portion of limbs, so that along the nerve impulses *to* the limbs the whole of the ray is carried. Let this be at least thirty-eight inches from the body in the beginning, and not given over two and one-half minutes in the beginning, see?

Q-2. How long will it take to bring the body to normal?

A-2. In three to five weeks, as given, there will be the *definite* change . . . As to the responses from then on, will depend upon the conditions in [the] body itself—the mental attitude, the rate of vibration as is kept . . . Don't eat too much—don't get scared—don't work too fast—don't think too hard! . . .

Q-5. What effect has this condition on the mind?

A-5. This should be indicated from that as has been outlined, as to how the greater effect of those injections of those conditions has been *through* the sympathetic system, which is as the basis of the *imaginative* forces; *not* that the body *imagines* its illness, but that it may be accentuated by suggestion or *relieved* much by suggestion; for only in the lumbar and sacral, as given, do the nerve forces or cerebrospinal centers show their repression, except through *sympathetic* centers along the spine.

The mind is good! It's active!

3580-2   M.41   7/5/44

Q-5. Are the spinal and liver injections he is getting at times good or harmful?

A-5. They are not good.

3539-1   M.59   1/6/44

Q-1. Should I discontinue the shots?

A-1. You'd better, if you don't want to get too much of these and cause a heart stroke here!

631-5   F.37   3/8/35

Q-6. What is the proper method or medicines to apply to correct or eliminate all of these conditions?

A-6. Let's, then, for the moment discard or disregard all that has been given. If there is the desire on the part of the body *first* in itself to have applied and to be consistent and persistent in the applications of those elements and influences necessary, first there must be a change in the mental attitude of the body. There must be eradicated that of any judgment or of condemnation on the part of self as respecting self or *any* associated with the body in *any* manner, either previously or in the present. This must be eradicated from the mind. How? By filling same with constructive loving influence towards self, towards others, and as these are raised within the consciousness of self by the proper thinking, with the less and less of condemnation to anyone, these create the proper surroundings, the proper attitude.

1259-2   F.50   12/18/36

Q-3. What should I do about taking the hydrochloric acid internally? I seem to be much better when taking it.

A-3. If that is the desire of the body . . . For the mental outlook has as much to do with the results as the material applications!

Duty

290-1   F.51   3/3/33

... each individual is an entity, a world in itself, yet each entity is dependent one upon another. Yet each in their own way and manner expressing in their lives that which has become the all-possessing idea or ideal to that individual.

... it would be well then that the body first—in the present—make an analysis of the conditions as related to others, of self as in relations to others, and the ideals that must be the basis for the activities of every individual.

And then, in making such [an analysis], realize that to make another error where error has been or is being made will not make for correction to that which would become helpful to any concerned.

Rather had self be put in the position of being mistreated or maltreated, considering the relationships, obligations and duties that should bind all together toward one common purpose; and continue to be under the expressions that become even at times almost unbearable in the experience, yet knowing that to be the one to make moves for material changes would only bring greater consternation, greater trouble, greater worries on the part not only of self but of others to whom duties and obligations are due.

Consider this truth. He or she that follows in the way of condemning another, makes for condemnation also in their own experience, magnifying conditions; rather than taking that which is as a thorn in the body, as a scar upon the better mental and moral aptitudes of the body-consciousness.

Know that only in Him, who may bring peace and harmony by or through the contacts—the thoughts of self as in relationship to the whole—may there be brought about those better relationships.

To continue to condemn only brings condemnation, then, for self. This does not mean that self's activity should be passive, but rather being constant in prayer—knowing and taking, knowing and understanding that he that is faithful is not given a burden beyond that he is able to bear, if he will put the burden upon Him that has given the promise, "I will be *with* thee; there shall not come that which shall harm thee, if thou will but put thy trust, thy faith, in me" . . .

First make an analysis of self, of self's relationships, of the impelling influences that cause others to act in their manners in the present.

Do not condemn self; do not condemn another; but leave the activities that would bring about condemnation rather in His hands, who requireth at the hands of all that there be meted, "As ye would that should be done to thee, do ye even so to thy fellow man!"

311-4 F.44 9/20/43

Q-4. *When a question comes up as to one's health and other persons' desires, how does one best decide to what extent to protect one's own health or interests, or to give in to another's wishes?*

A-4. As ye would that men should do to you, do ye even so to them. This would pertain to health, to mind, to body, to purpose . . . there are duties that ye owe. Ye desire in some respects, but make the desire only as mutual activities . . .

Be sure you are right, then go ahead . . . Study to show thyself approved unto God. That is why the injunction, know thy ideals. Know the Author of thy hopes, and thy purposes.

Eliminations

311-4 M.28 4/11/31

These [disturbances], as we find, have to do with the assimilations and eliminations of the body. There should be a warning to *all* bodies as to such conditions; for would the assimilations and the eliminations be kept nearer *normal* in the human family, the days [of life] might be extended to whatever period as was so desired; for the system is *builded* by the assimilations of that it takes within, and is able to bring resuscitation so long as the eliminations do not hinder.

3381-1 M.32 12/1/43

Q-4. *Should anything be taken for eliminations?*

A-4. Correct [your eliminations] better by the diet than by taking eliminants, when possible. If not possible to correct otherwise, take an eliminant but [alternate] between one time a vegetable laxative and the next time a mineral eliminant. But these [elimination problems] will be bettered if a great deal of the raw vegetables are used and not so much of meats, but do eat fish, fowl and lamb occasionally—but don't fry it!

849-76   M.37   5/29/44

A vegetable as well as a mineral laxative should be [alternated] in the use of alkalizers of four increasing eliminations through the alimentary canal. It is well for those requiring any laxative to change about. Have a mineral and again the vegetable compound, so there is the better balance kept, and neither will become so necessary or it will not destroy entirely the sphincter activities of the muscular forces of the alimentary canal.

264-56   F.50   8/15/41

Q-2. What is the condition of my intestines and what should be done, or should I continue taking Castoria®?

A-2. Rather than so much of the Castoria® [vegetable base] in the present—for this *can* become irritating, of course—we would occasionally change to other eliminants. As we have indicated for other bodies, it is well to alternate these rather than continuing to take just one type of eliminant. Occasionally, then, we would take the Milk of Bismuth®—a teaspoonful, with a few drops of Elixir of Lactated Pepsin® in same—stirred in half a glass of water. This is to cleanse the system, or to absorb the poisons. Then afterward it would be necessary to take small doses of Eno Salts® or Sal Hepatica. The Sal Hepatica, of course, is partially mineral, while the Eno Salts® is practically all vegetable or fruit salts, see?

3336-1   F.77   11/3/43

Set up better eliminations by the use of those foods that tend to produce better drainages . . . laxative foods such as: figs, a great deal of pieplant [rhubarb] whenever obtainable, raisins (stewed and prepared in other foods), a great deal of the black figs and the white or the purple also, and the prunes and prune preparations.

719-1   M.Adult   4/28/31

. . . there would be first a cleansing of the colon with a colonic irrigation, followed with sufficient antiseptic solutions as to prevent further toxins in the system. Then a thorough cleansing of the alimentary canal, rather by those [substances] of an alkaline nature—[such] as may be found in Milk of Magnesia®, Petrolagar®, Milk of Bismuth®, a combination—as it were—of these[each at different periods]; taking at times small quantities of properties of an alkaline reaction, as an intestinal antiseptic . . . [3 to 5 drops twice daily of] Glyco-Thymoline® or such basic forces which are—as we find—an alkaline antiseptic, rather than acid [in] basis.

Eliminants

Castoria®

[The extracts which follow are all recommendations of Fletcher's Castoria®, the laxative most often suggested by the Cayce readings. In the extracts, chosen at random, it is not only possible to compare the dosages given to individuals whose ages vary from 6 days to 61 years, but to discover yet another way in which the psychic readings of Edgar Cayce show their capacity for detail. During the years from 1934 to 1944, which these references cover in chronological order, it is a matter of record that the formula of Castoria® was changed, and then changed back again. Note how the readings adjusted for the changes, even prescribing combinations of laxatives when necessary.]

773-4 M.31½ 11/23/34

Take a laxative such as found in Fletcher's Castoria®, combined with [California Brand] Syrup of Figs. Take from a small bottle (of 900 drops) a teaspoonful, and add in its place a teaspoonful of the Syrup of Figs.

Give half a teaspoonful every half-hour (shaking well each time before pouring out the dosage), until there is the full [desired] reaction from the alimentary canal.

379-4 F.55 1/15/36

Do not take too much food in the system until there is a thorough cleansing of the alimentary canal.

This would be well to be done with an alternation between the Fletcher's Castoria® and the Syrup of Figs. These should be taken about every half an hour, or an hour apart, until there is the *thorough* evacuation. The dose would be half a teaspoonful, at one time of the Castoria® and the next [time] of the Syrup of Figs.

2015-1   F.6 days   10/3/39

Q-1. What dosage and how often should the Castoria® be given?

A-1. This [should be taken] only if it becomes necessary, you see; and then, of course, only one to two drops at each dose, three to six hours apart, until it has made the correction through the alimentary canal—which will be detected, of course, in the stool.

This [dosage] would have nothing to do, of course, with the frequency of the Glyco-Thymoline® [one or two drops], as these will work together; and the Glyco-Thymoline® is for one thing—the correcting in the colon—while the Castoria® is for the digestive system.

1541-9   F.61   9/4/40

Keep up, or increase, the eliminations. Use Castoria® with Syrup of Figs as an eliminant . . .

Better conditions are brought about by taking this in small quantities and often, you see; about half a teaspoonful every half-hour. These—the Castoria and Figs—may be mixed or alternated.

1523-10   F.31   2/9/40

As we find, there are the after effects of the acute conditions in the body—arising from the lack of proper eliminations of the poisons which were caused from the poisoning [pyrene] as was indicated from an acid.

These, as combined then with the after effects of "flu," with so much of a vegetable laxative [Castoria®], have caused a contraction of the mucous membranes in portions of the colon, as well as jejunum.

2516-1   M.56   6/17/41

Take internally a combination of Syrup of Figs *and* Fletcher's Castoria®, in small or broken doses; half a teaspoonful every half-hour, even if it requires more than 900 drops [or a small bottle of the Castoria®].

Take until there is *complete* evacuation, with an activity of the liver and of the kidneys *from* the taking of these broken doses.

The next morning after these properties have reacted, take two heaping teaspoonsful of Sal Hepatica in a glass of water to flush the system.

573-6   F.Adult   7/3/41

Begin with small doses every half hour of Castoria® and Syrup of Figs. On one half-hour take half a teaspoonful of Castoria®, then the next half-hour take half a teaspoonful of Syrup of Figs.

Continue these, first one and then the other, you see, either one or the other every half-hour, until there are *full* eliminations from the alimentary canal.

The basis of both of these compounds is senna, you see, yet there are active principles in each that will affect the hepatic circulation in quite a different manner—and their combinations are needed.

264-56   F.50   8/15/41

Q-2. . . . should I continue taking Castoria®?

A-2. Rather than so much of the [vegetable base] Castoria® in the present—for this *can* become irritating, of course—we would occasionally change to other eliminants.[Mineral; Sal Hepatica, Eno Salts®; see "Eliminations"]

As we have indicated for other bodies, it is well to alternate these rather than continuing to take just one type of eliminant.

2824-5   M.1 12/15/43

Begin with broken doses of Castoria® or with Caldwell's Syrup of Pepsin (Senna or Fig base); half a teaspoonful every hour until good eliminations are set up.

The Castoria® formula has been changed and is not as complete as the Syrup of Pepsin; hence the suggestion for the Pepsin as a substitute.

2752-3   F.2 1/17/44

Now to cleanse the system, we would set up the eliminations with Castoria®. Taken as it is in the present [1/17/44], it is very good.

2824-6   M.1   2/15/44

We would give the Castoria® in broken doses—ten to twelve drops every half-hour until there are thorough, thorough eliminations.

5734-1   F.45   5/4/44

Begin the laxatives with the use of a vegetable compound taken in broken doses, any that is of the senna base; such as the properties in Syrup of Figs, or Castoria® or Caldwell's Syrup of Pepsin.

Vegetable

457-14   F.36   5/15/44

For a laxative take Senna Leaf [or Senna Pod] tea, using four or five of the leaves placed in an empty cup, and then pour hot water on it and let stand for thirty minutes to forty-five minutes; strain and drink it. Do this about once a week and it will be good for the body, as it does not become habit-forming and is a correct laxative for most individuals—though not everyone.

1523-1   F.29   1/28/38

For the eliminations generally, we would use Zilatone as an activity upon the eliminating system; that the organs of the system may be cleansed throughout. Half an hour after the morning meal take one Zilatone tablet; half an hour to an hour after the noon meal take another; then in the evening about two hours after the meal take *two* tablets. And then leave off for at least two or three days, before this may be repeated again.

357-7   F.33   2/21/36

It would be well, as we find, to use the Zilatone as an activative force for stirring the liver and its activities for the general eliminations. For this will also purify and clarify the gall duct area, stimulating the activities for the general system. We would take two tablets of morning and two of evening, the first day. The next day take only two in the evening. The next day take only one. Then skip two days. Then repeat these . . . We would preferably use the Zilatone tablets as indicated with the effective activities from same upon the liver and kidneys, the gall duct, the spleen and pancreas . . .

462-13   M.56   7/2/40

Q-6. What is a good laxative for this body?

A-6. Eno Salts® is the best laxative for this body, for this is of the fruit nature and not mineral—[not] that [which] would cause disturbance or hardening activities through the conditions in the stomach, as well as through those activities in the liver and kidneys. This also should be taken in just small doses, almost every day, for periods of a week at a time—and will be most beneficial.

Mineral

2526-2 F.41 11/5/41
First, we would use a saline laxative to make for better alkalization of the whole system, and to increase circulation in such a manner as to eliminate much of the poisons from the system, especially in the alimentary canal. Take a heaping teaspoonful of Sal Hepatica in half a glass of water, [first having it] dissolved and then filling the glass [with water]—using a large glass, tea glass or the like. Do this each morning for three to five days—each morning before breakfast, see? Using a large glass and putting the dose in the glass half-full of water at first will keep the properties from overflowing when the solution effervesces. Leave off this [Sal Hepatica] after the third or fifth day, provided there have been good eliminations and the cold has been allayed, also the stiffness overcome. But continue to keep an alkalized condition for the body, and to keep up good eliminations.

2051-7 M.70 3/27/43
Then we would increase the eliminations so as to carry away more of the poisons and toxins from the system. For this body in the present, and with the [work] activities, we would use the mineral rather than [the] vegetable eliminants; especially such as may be found in Upjohn's Citrocarbonates®. This we would take a heaping teaspoonful each morning before any meal is taken. Let it effervesce and drink a full glass of water with the spoonful dissolved in same, and then another glass of water afterwards. Do drink more water.

618-2 F.60 10/2/34
And keep [in your routine] occasionally a dose of Upjohn's Citrocarbonate® and Milk of Magnesia®; not both on the same day, no, but once or twice a week take each of these, or one or the other of these.

678-2 F.49 10/16/34
We would take at times the alkaline properties that may be had from the Upjohn's Citrocarbonates®, taken in periods of one to two

days. These will change the effects of the circulatory system as to
allow better eliminations.

Oil

*[Castor Oil Packs have been recommended hundreds of times
for cases of intestinal adhesions, impactions, appendicitis, etc.,
where some type of congestion needs to be broken up.]*

2434-1   F.65   1/23/41
   . . . begin with the use of Castor Oil Packs, an hour each day for
three days. Use at least three thicknesses of flannel, lightly wrung
out of the Castor Oil, as hot as the body can stand it, and applied
over the liver and the whole of the abdomen, especially upon the
right side of same. Keep the pack warm by using an electric pad.
After the third day of using the packs, take a high enema to relieve
the tensions throughout the colon and lower portion of jejunum,
using a colon tube for same. Have the water body-temperature, and
to each quart of water used (and use as much as three quarts) we
would put a level teaspoonful of table salt and half a teaspoonful of
baking soda, thoroughly dissolved.

1523-9   F.31   1/21/40
   As we find, the acute conditions [in this body] arise from the effects of a poison—pyrene. From this activity the acute indigestion
as produced through the alimentary canal has caused an expansion
of, and a blocking in, the colon areas.
   . . . we would apply hot Castor Oil Packs continuously for two and
a half to three hours. Then have an enema, gently given. It would be
well that some oil be in the first enema; that is, the oil alone given
first, see? Olive Oil would be the better for this; about half a pint; so
that there may be the [necessary] relaxing. And then give the enema
with body-temperature water, using a heaping teaspoonful of salt and
a level teaspoonful of baking soda to the quart and a half of water.
Give this gently at first, but eventually—that is, after the period when
there has been the ability for a movement—use the colon tube. Then
we would take internally—after the Oil Packs and the enema—a tablespoonful of Olive Oil. This, as we find, should relieve the tensions
and relax the body sufficiently to remove the disturbing conditions.

1622-1   F.68   6/24/38

Q-5. Would yeast be good for me to take?

A-5. Yeast is very well, but if the apple diet is used for the cleansing forces as indicated—about once a month [for this particular body]—this would be preferable to the creating of greater disturbances in an already fagged condition in the system. If there is the insistent non-activity of eliminations as well as should be, then, as we find, the [taking of] small quantities of Olive Oil—with the activities of the system would be preferable to [taking] the yeast or cathartics or the like. We would take about half a teaspoonful of the Olive Oil about three to four times each day, when it is taken. This will not only supply nutriment to the digestive tract but will aid in the eliminations, and is an intestinal food.

Environment and Heredity

852-12   F.18   11/15/35

Environs and hereditary influences are much deeper than that which is ordinarily conceded in the psychology of the present day.

For the environs and the hereditary influences are spiritual as well as physical, and are physical because of the spiritual application of the abilities of the entity in relationship to spiritual development.

For the purpose of each soul's experience in the earth is to become one with the Creative Forces that manifest in human experience, if [the soul] will but *apply* [this] in its relationships to its fellow man.

Hence what one is today is because of what one (the individual soul) *has done about* that the soul knows *of* the Creative Force or God *in* its experience, in *whatever* environ or consciousness it—the soul—may manifest.

The environs then in the earth, in any given experience, are those things that make for the emotional body in that experience.

That which is innate, or that [which] finds expression when the individual soul turns to the Creative Force or God within, arises from the *soul's* experience in those environs *about* the earth.

Study these, and it—the study—will make for a great interest, or greater interest, in the *causes* of relationships in the earth; or in that which is termed the genealogy of ideas, of individuals, of nations,

of those things that go to make up *why* individuals are born in this
or that environment. For *that* is true genealogy!

816-3   M.51   2/17/35

For while there may be and is in the experience of every soul
the urge that is termed hereditary and environmental influence,
individuals under the same influence of blood and of rearing (or
environment) will respond or react in quite a different manner.
This is caused by that deeper urge that is seen from astrological
sojourns, as well as the indwelling in the earth under certain or
specific experiences.

541-1   F.47   4/28/34

As each soul enters in the earth, there are purposes other than
that which may be arising from[the] desire of those that physically
are responsible for such an advent.

For, the soul seeks from the realm of spirituality to give expression of that [which] it as an entity or soul may do with its experiences in the mental realm, as well as about that it *has* done in a
physical realm.

Hence the law that is ever present; like attracts like; like begets
like. Hence there is the attraction as from the desires of those in
the physical calling to the sources of generation in the flesh, to the
sources of creation or of spirit in the spiritual realm.

Hence there is often a real purpose in the soul, as in this soul,
seeking a period of expression of self; and finding it . . . when there
is the period of presentation. For, while the physical begins at conception, the spiritual and mental is as the first breath taken into the
physical—that becomes then a living soul, with a physical organism
for manifestation during the sojourn in that particular experience.

Then, what influences such a journey, such an advent of the soul
from the unseen into materiality? Development of the soul that it may
take its place, through the lessons gained in physical experience, in
those classes or realms of soul activity in an infinite world—among
those that have passed in their activity through the various realms;
seeking then (as that which first called every soul and body into experience) that of companionship. Hence we have as much hereditary
and environmental forces in soul's experience (or the developed soul
to such an experience) as we have in the law of the earth, as to that

which is hereditary from the parentage of a body—and the environs of the body, as to what is the trend of thought.

Then, what is the environmental and hereditary influence from the soul-body angle for this particular entity . . . [541]?

The sojourns in the environs about the present sojourn, or in this particular solar system. Not that Venus, Jupiter, Mars, Uranus or any of the planets about this earth's sun have beings or bodies such as are known in the earth's sojourns; but those that are peculiar to their own realm—their own element or position from the solar light, or the light and heat. And yet with those influences about same by the variation in what is called in the earth the effect of the various influences shed from other solar systems, suns, and so forth.

For, much might be given respecting those environs and as to how or why there has been and is accredited to the various planets certain characterizations that make for the attractions of souls' sojourns in that environ. But these are places of abode. As in the earth we find the elements are peopled, as the earth has its own moon or satellites enjoined in its environ, so is it with the other planets. The earth with its three-fourths water, with its elements, is peopled; yes. So are the various activities in other solar systems.

Hence the sojourn of a soul in its environ about the earth, or in this solar system, gives the factors that are often found in individuals in the earth that are of the same parentage, in the same environ; yet one might be a genius and the other a fool; one might be a moral degenerate and the other a high, upright, upstanding individual with an aptitude for influences that may not even be questioned.

Then, such environs *physically* are needed for the development of the soul.

So, the entity here finds these as attributes in the mental forces that lie—as it were—*dormant* or innate in each soul or body manifested in the earth, that may be *drawn upon* when apparently everything else has failed. That stamina of character, that indwelling which is a portion of the soul. That which makes for the abilities of each soul to draw nigh unto Him that *is* light, life, and from or through that source build—in and under all circumstances—that which makes for beauty to any who may behold such a soul's activity; and most of all bring to the soul harmony even under oppression or subjugation by circumstances of a material nature, and beauty and joy to those who may contact such an individual or soul. Becoming a light to many, a pathway that may guide many—even as this entity, this soul, through its indwelling in Jupiter . . . the ability to hold to that hope—and this increased in the knowledge of Him that is light—may bring yet joy and peace and harmony that makes for being content in that place one finds self, and knowing that He may have His way with thee . . . the entity is often burdened by the fact that so many apparently are always depending upon what little resources the entity has from the material standpoint. The entity should declare in self those forces that are ever present, that the supply is of such a nature that it may never diminish as long as there is the holding to the power in His name . . .

So has the entity found in its experience . . . that it must not look back, but ever forward; for that which has been must be again, if there will be the preparations in the *now* for its next cycle of activity. And as to whether same comes in a moment or in an age or in a century, or in forty, what is time or space when thou art in those influences that make for contentment in thine inner soul? save those that wander from the knowledge of embracing the moment. For, only one at a time may be experienced—if they are divided as such. But see and know all rather as One.

Exercise

[Two types of exercises are indicated in the physical readings: general exercises, good for all of us, and specific exercises to correct specific conditions.]

1968-9   F.32   7/25/43
Q-11. Is there any special exercise I should take other than the head and neck exercises?
A-11. Walking is the best exercise, but don't take this spasmodically. Have a regular time and do it, rain or shine

416-3   M.28   5/27/34
It's well that each body, every body, take exercise to counteract the daily routine activity, so as to produce rest. Walking is the best exercise for this body; preferably in the evening.

457-12   F.35   5/25/43

Q-16. Has lack of setting-up exercises in last months been det-rimental to the body?

A-16. Whenever something is begun and then left off, it becomes detrimental—[anything] that should have been kept up!

2823-2   F.33   6/5/43

Q-5. What physical and mental exercises will be beneficial?

A-5. Of course, a [period of] meditation is well always; for the mental attitude has much to do with the general physical forces.

As for the physical exercises, walking is the best of any exercise—and swimming . . .

4003-1   M.45   3/24/44

The exercise that we would follow for this body would be the stretching much in the manner as the exercise of the cat or the panther, or that type of activity; stretching the muscular forces, not as [something that] strains but as [something] to cause the tendons and muscles to be put into position for the formation of strength-building to the body . . .

Q-2. How may "classic" physical development be retained over the longest possible period of years, without sacrifice of health?

A-2. As indicated, through the exercise and diet, and [especially] the character of exercise that follows closely the movements of the cat and its kind.

1523-2   F.29   2/10/38

Of morning, and upon arising especially (and don't sleep too late!)—and before dressing, so that the clothing is loose or the fewer [worn] the better—standing erect before an open window, breathe deeply; gradually raising hands *above* the head, and then with the circular motion of the body from the hips bend forward; breathing *in* (and through the nostrils) as the body rises on the toes—breathing very deep; *exhaling suddenly* through the *mouth; not* through the nasal passages. Take these for five to six minutes.

Then as these progress, gradually *close* one of the nostrils (even if it's necessary to use the hand—but if it is closed with the left hand, raise the right hand; and when closing the right nostril with the right hand, then raise the left hand) *as* the breathing *in* is accomplished.

Rise, and [then have] the circular motion of the body from the hips, and [the] bending forward; *expelling* as the body reaches the lowest level in the bending towards the floor (expelling through the mouth, suddenly). See?

Then of an evening, just before retiring—with the [body prone, facing the floor and] feet braced against the wall, circle the torso by resting on the hands. Raise and lower the body not merely by the hands but more from the torso, and with more of a circular motion of the pelvic organs strengthen the muscular forces of the abdomen. Not such an activity as to cause strain, but a gentle, circular motion to the right two to three times, and then to the left.

470-37   M.54   6/20/44

For those [troublesome] conditions with the sympathetic system, if the body would take the head and neck exercise, we will find it will relieve those little tensions which have been indicated as part of [the] conditions in [the] head, eyes, mouth and teeth . . . don't hurry through with it. But do [them] regularly of morning . . . before dressing.

Rise on the toes slowly and raise the arms easily at the same time directly above the head, pointing straight up. At the same time bend [the] head back just as far as you can. When [you] let down gentle from this, you see, we make for giving a better circulation through the whole area from the abdomen, through the diaphragm, through the lungs, head and neck.

Then let down, put the head forward just as far as it will come on the chest, then raise again at the top, bend the head to the right as far as it will go down. When rising again, bend the head to the left. Then, standing erect, hands on hips, circle the head, roll around to the right two or three times, then straighten self. Again, hands off the hip, down gently, rise again, down again, then circle to the opposite side. We will find we will change all of these disturbances through the mouth, head, eyes, and the activities of the whole body will be improved. Open your mouth as you go up and down, also.

3381-1   M.32   12/1/43

Q-1. What can be done to strengthen arches?

A-1. The massage with [specific] oils will be helpful. Also an exercise each day of a certain character would be well; of morning, before the shoes are put on—before the oil massage is given, of course, but do this daily: stand flat on the floor and spring on the toes, rising gently and springing.

3549-1   F.34   1/14/44

Q-1. How can I improve my vision?

A-1. When we remove the pressures of the toxic forces we will improve the vision. Also the head and neck exercise will be most helpful. Take this regularly, not taking it sometimes and leaving off sometimes, but each morning and each evening take this exercise regularly for six months and we will see a great deal of difference:

Sitting erect, bend the head forward three times, to the back three times, to the right side three times, to the left side three times, and then circle the head each way three times. Don't hurry through with it but take the time to do it. We will get results.

2533-6   M.37   10/31/42

Q-2. How may my eyes be strengthened so as to eliminate the necessity of reading glasses?

A-2. By the head and neck exercise in the open, as ye walk for twenty to thirty minutes each morning. Now, do not undertake it one morning and then say "It rained and I couldn't get out," or "I've got to go somewhere else," and think there aren't those despot conditions that rebel at not having their morning walk!

Eyes

1158-31   F.51   8/31/41

Q-11. Are my bi-focal glasses correct and constructive for me to wear?

A-11. Here quite a dissertation might be indicated, as to give the full or complete answer. Bi-focals are correct, when worn constantly. Bi-focals not worn constantly, the more often become harmful.

3050-2   F.55   12/2/43

Q-1. What should be done to relieve my eyes?

A-1. Bathe these with a weak Glyco-Thymoline® solution. Use an eyecup, and two parts of distilled water (preferably) to one part of the Glyco-Thymoline®. This irritation is a part of the kidney disturbance that has come from the upsetting in the digestive forces.

1968-3   F.29   3/14/40

We would use Murine® as an eyewash about once each week [for this condition]; preferably Saturday evenings or Sunday mornings, so that there is rest from the use of the eyes following same. This is only as a stimulation to the flow of [or from] the mucous membranes about the eyeball itself.

409-22   F.21   10/13/31

Q-4. What should be done for granulated eyelids?

A-4. Use a weak solution of boracic acid. About twice each week use [also] those [poultices] of scraped Irish potato, bound of [an] evening over the eye.

5401-1   F.43   8/24/44

Do add to the diet about twice as many oranges, lemons and limes as is a part of the diet in the present. These also supplement with a great deal of carrots, especially as combined with gelatin, if we would aid and strengthen the optic nerves and the tensions between sympathetic and cerebrospinal systems.

3552-1   F.58   1/12/44

. . . and then in the general diet add a great deal of vegetables that have a direct bearing upon the optic forces through the general system; such as carrots, green peas and green beans, onions, beets. All of these have a direct bearing upon the application of that assimilated for the optic forces.

5148-1   F.55   5/25/44

Q-3. What will help the eyesight?

A-3. These we have been administering, but if gelatin will be taken with raw foods rather often (that is, prepare raw vegetables such as carrots often with same, but do not lose the juice from the carrots; grate them, eat them raw), we will help the vision.

2178-1   F.3   4/25/40

We would have plenty of carrot juice; at least an ounce or ounce and a half every other day—or this much taken in two days, see? Use a juice extractor for securing the juice from fresh, raw carrots.

2004-4   F.7   4/28/42

Q-3. What further treatment should be applied for her eye condition?

A-3. A gentle massage given of evenings would be very well for this body; not necessarily by a doctor but the mother may apply same—if it is done *consistently.* But don't begin it unless it is to be done consistently for at least five days out of a week, and then it may be left off five days, and then repeated. This would be a general massage of Cocoa Butter in the area from between the shoulders to the base of the brain.

And give the body *plenty* of celery, lettuce and carrots. Have some of these in the meal each day—both raw and cooked carrots; as well as lettuce and celery being a part of one meal each day.

5059-1   F.80   4/21/44

Activities through the body [of this individual] have been the result of natural deterioration from age. These [deteriorations] are more in the subconscious self than necessarily through the body itself, but in the present there are specific conditions that are disturbing . . .

For the irritation of the eye itself, until there are better coordinations set up [osteopathically], apply occasionally—once a week, or whenever there is irritation—the Irish potato poultice. Scrape the potato and apply [it] directly over the eye socket, letting it remain on for at least half an hour to an hour. Then remove and wash or cleanse with half water and half Glyco-Thymoline® as an antiseptic to cleanse the secretions as will be drawn from the eye with the application.

341-2   M.16   1/26/24

To reach the seat of the trouble [in the focal plane of vision], remove first the cause. This we find that it is the [impingement] of the nerve branch in the second cervical and third dorsal . . . give first the release to these nerve centers through osteopathic or chiropractic adjustments . . .

5571-1   F.Adult   5/16/29

The [osteopathic adjustments] and the treatment with the Violet Ray® [hand applicator] will materially aid [the eyes] . . . but not treating the eyes longer than one minute.

243-11   F.51   9/3/31

Q-5. Why [is there] the blur over my eyes at times?

A-5 . . . Would be well . . . that occasionally—once or twice each week, before retiring (and be sure it is after a thorough treatment with the vibrator so [that] the body won't wake up!), apply a poultice of *old* Irish potato, well scraped, bandage [this] over [the] eyes, and let [it] remain until morning . . . then wash [the eyes] with a weak solution of an antiseptic . . . *This* will clarify [the eyes].

Also we will find that [the following] used as drops occasionally in the eye will *assist* in clarifying [them]: [Use a] little [bicarbonate of] soda and a little salt in about three times the quantity of water, see?

3884-1   F.Child   1/8/24

Bathe both eyes (externally) with twenty percent solution [Boric] acid. Then apply, in rather sufficient quantity to cover the socket or place of eye, the scraped parts of commonly known Irish potato. Let this be of the larger variety as possible, and one that has not frozen or sprouted. When the inflammation has so packed this solution, or application, as to render it of no service . . . remove this, and bathe with equal parts of ten percent solution of [Boric] acid and ten percent solution of myrrh tincture.

Then apply the Yellow Oxide Ointment to the affected parts, and in the edge of the eye proper, near the tear ducts, you see, so this works in under the lids.

After this has remained for some thirty to forty minutes, bathe again in the twenty percent solution of [Boric] acid, and apply again the potato, scraped, you see.

Repeat these [applications], with only a short interval between, until inflammation is subsided and ease obtained for the physical forces.

Then other solutions will be applied. With the solution of acid, add one part of belladonna, which is the strong solution, and this will be used as drops, in the comer of the eye, and when bathed again apply the potato.

Fame and Position

1901-1   M.38   5/30/39

Ye are in the position, ye have been especially endowed with the faculties and the abilities to be of a service to thy fellow man. Will ye do so that thine own ego may be satisfied; that ye may enjoy the pleasures of thine own appetites for a season; using thy obligations, using thy opportunities as an excuse that ye may gratify thine *own* self?

Or would ye not rather that there be the answer within thyself from thy activities that ye are at-one with that Creative Force, God Himself—that ye may have that peace, that harmony, that satisfaction which comes *only* from living, being, exercising thy abilities in the direction that will bring hope and cheer and patience and love and harmony in the lives of all ye touch?

Not by might nor by power alone, but by love and kindness, and freedom *from* worries that so beset so much from self indulgences.

Think—think on these! For with thy abilities ye may apply same in such a manner that, as ye develop thy relationships with thy fellow may ye *know—know* in thy heart, thy mind, that with what measure ye mete to them it will be measured to thee again.

Think not that there is any shortcut to peace or harmony, save in correct living. Ye *cannot* go against thine own conscience and be at peace with thyself, thy home, thy neighbor, thy God! For as ye do it unto the least of thy brethren, ye do it unto thy Maker . . .

And if there will be first, in the present, the purposing and living in such a manner before God as to walk circumspectly in thine own conscience before Him, and in dealing as through that experience [American Revolution, as Samuel Goldman] with thy fellow man, ye may find—as this world's goods increase in thy hands (as they must necessarily do)—they will not and do not become burdens to thy conscience nor separate thee from thy home or thy fellow man. But rather is the opportunity to serve thy Maker.

Ye have earned that right for much of this world's goods. Do not abuse that; else ye become—in thine *own* conscience—an outcast in this experience . . .

The entity then [Roman land], as one Zelost, made for the perfecting of those that not only enabled this to act as a shield from the poles, the spears and even the swords of the antagonist, but it brought to the entity a place of position among those of the early periods.

And thus from same arises in the present that desire for power, that ye may *control* the activities and the lives of others.

Think of that which has been indicated, that as ye measure to others it will be measured to you!

In thy associations and dealings with thy fellow man, manifest that rule (and not by feelings alone, to be sure), that as ye would that men would consider thee if thy positions were reversed, so act toward thy fellow man.

This is not an idle dream, but is a practical experience that ye may apply day by day.

165-2   M.50   10/10/27

[Background: Benjamin Franklin, in last incarnation.]

Beware, though, of expression in the temper, or in the power of the body physical or mental over the weak, for the urge often comes to exercise such. Never turn same for self's own interest, for—as will be seen through experiences in the earth's plane—much may be lost through aggrandizement of selfish motives. Little of self is held in esteem above others, would there be humble and the contrite heart before the Creative Forces . . .

1710-11   M.28   4/8/43

Q-1. As given, [1710]'s activities in the present may become as a service related to state and nation. What type of activity is indicated?

A-1. Depending upon the application of self. In those directions in which the promptings carry the entity in relationship to same.

Q-2. About when should [1710] expect such a change to take place?

A-2. When he prepares for same, and as he prepares for same.

This does not indicate that he is going to be a lord or judge or principal or the like, but the contribution such as was made by Barak [1710, Barak, of Old Testament in previous incarnation]—which was not as an authority over anyone, but as a director, as a leader for a *principle*, a purpose, an ideal—*under* and *through* the direction of a servant of God!

Get the difference in these. This is not applying to materiality, not applying to material things, but to that having to do with the basic principles of why and how men think and act, in their home, in their relationships to their fellow man!

This is spiritual, *not* material.

5148-2   F.55   5/29/44

Consider for the moment many, as we are given the lessons of how that God Himself chose Saul as a goodly king, head and shoulders above his fellow man, his countenance that was indeed kingly and gifted with prophecy; and yet he allowed himself, because of an exalted physical position, to forget his humbleness before God, even as there had been in his experiences in the earth before, in those days as a son [Seth] of Adam, who had been given that privilege of being the channel through which the chosen of the peoples were to be Abraham, Isaac and Jacob.

3633-1   M.12   1/25/44

In giving the interpretations of the records here of this entity, it would be very easy to interpret same either in a very optimistic or a very pessimistic vein. For there are great possibilities and great obstacles. But know, in either case, the real lesson is within self.

For here is the opportunity for an entity (while comparisons are odious, these would be good comparisons) to be either a Beethoven or a Whittier or a Jesse James or some such entity! For the entity is inclined to think more highly of himself than he ought to think, as would be indicated. That's what these three individuals did, in themselves. As to the application made of it, depends upon the individual self.

Fasting

254-46   12/14/28

[Background: On December 14, 1928, the Executive Committee of the A.R.E. asked in a reading:]

Q-9. Should a program be started for developing assistants to Edgar Cayce?

A-9.This should; for, as has oft been given, the force of that [which] is creative in its nature will *not* defeat its purpose, *provided* the application by that which is a portion of Creative Energy itself

does not misapply that in the way of bringing other than the purport
of that in creation.

This, then, should be begun as soon as there is able to be definite
data given from that [which] has already been accomplished by
that one around whom the present work is builded, and it should
take the form of that as of the giving of the future; yet this must be
approached with prayer and fasting, for such can only be accomplished through prayer and fasting. Not as man counts fasting—
doing without *food;* but one that would abase himself that the Creative Force *might* be made manifest.

This will be presented even as such is made known to those
studying such phenomena, as physically called, in the process of
operation.

*Q-10. Should we take this up with the Scientific Society of
America?*

A-10. No! Take it up rather with God!

295-6   F.28   4/16/32

[Background: In 1932 an individual seeking to develop magnetic
healing abilities wanted to know if going without food would be
helpful in preparation for healing work. The answer she received
throws new light on the subject:]

... fasting ... is as the Master gave: Laying aside thine own concept of *how* or *what* should be done at this period and let the *Spirit*
guide. Get the *truth* of fasting!

The body, the man's bodily functioning, to be sure, *overdone*
brings *shame* to self, as overindulgence in anything—but the *true*
fasting is casting out of self that as "*I* would have done," [replacing
with] "but as *Thou,* O Lord, seest fit ... "

5326-1   F.23   7/5/44

Diet, fasting are well in their place; so is the application of that for
supplying a need, for a supply of energies to build body-forces ...

Q-2. Will more than one fast be necessary?

A-2. This depends upon what ye gain by the study and what is
pointed out to thee in thy meditation. Know God will speak with
thee as ye speak with Him in thy conscience, in thy soul-self, if ye
really desire same.

2072-9   F.32   7/22/42

Q-10. Is there any further information to be given at this time regarding the periodical purifying fast?

A-10. These as we find are to be considered as a general condition, rather than a specific. If there will be kept these in a purely coordination or cooperation with the diets, these will be much better. For, much of this must be from the mental, rather than from the real effects of the properties, or the effect created in the body.

When these become, then, lacking in a supply to the body forces of the amount of fats, it becomes more harmful than beneficial to the physical effects in the body, see?

Faults

5321-1   M.29   7/6/44

We would, though, magnify the virtues, minimize the faults; for this the entity must learn within self . . . there are many, many times when this entity is hard to get along with, stubborn and then at times, for mischief, tends to be different. These make, especially in the home, oftentimes questions; yet innately the entity is a whole soul and a good individual.

There needs to be for the entity, if it would accomplish the more, the analyzing of itself as a whole, and the spirituality given an opportunity for expression. When there are . . . conditions which require thought, the entity is as quick as the next to respond, and yet there are those stubborn periods which become very aggravating to others, and it causes in the experience of the entity troublesome periods. These [conditions] need to be recognized . . . [and] some formula set for self, of ideals and purposes, and [a goal to which] the entity would attain . . .

These are necessary, just as the entity is a good business person, weighing, analyzing all phases of cost and plus and situations which would arise in the carrying on or conducting of such undertakings. This needs to be applied in the experience of the home, in the experience of friendships with others. Not that these are to be made as though lacking in sentiment. For there is very little sentiment at times with the entity, and yet [the entity is] tenderhearted, yet keeping the faith, save when the entity wants to be just different.

In these, then, the entity should take itself in hand and know that the greater faults that ye find in others are reflections of that ye have caused, or are a part of thine own reflection. These should be analyzed and studied by the entity . . .

. . . study self in relationship to an ideal, not just an idea. Do give and take, do not become too self-centered. Do not think more highly of thy opinion than ye ought, and ye will find much better relationships may be established in all phases of relationships in the earth.

3063-1   M.56   6/26/43

There is much to commend. There are those things to be condemned . . .

But know that the truth is applicable in every experience of the entity's life, whether as a shoestring vendor . . . or a director of some great financial institution, or even a leader or ruler over many peoples . . .

. . . material success . . . may become the very stumbling block for soul development. And no soul enters a material experience just to have a good time, or to magnify the ego. For he that is the greatest among his fellow man is the servant of all with whom he comes in contact . . .

The entity naturally is something of a politic; and hence very high strung . . . moody at times. In periods it may be very expectant, and apparently determined in self to embrace every opportunity, and looks upon the association of others as opportunities for glorifying that God within self; and at other periods to be used for thine own self-indulgence—whether used as stepping-stones or not, know that ye may stumble over stepping-stones, even into hell itself, unless these are applied in keeping with the divine law.

. . . in the entity's personality [there is]that of perseverance, beauty, love of beauty and of charm; [also] the ability to correct or control others by the very might of the word, as well as the ability to ingratiate itself into the confidences of others.

These abused become stumbling stones. These used to the glory of God, ye climb up to the greater knowledge and awareness of Him . . .

. . . how *demanding* the entity is at times upon those he loves the most, how exacting! Require not of others that you do not require of self. Excuses do not change the law, and because thou art made in the image of man gives thee no right to denounce woman—for she is of thee also! . . .

Don't take advantage of others because you happen to know a little better what is going to take place. But remember, as ye treat thy fellow man, ye treat thy Maker, whose Face ye should seek . . .

You are a very good gambler, but a very bad loser at times!

. . . the entity was among the descendants of Esau . . . the name was Jared. The entity took advantage of a group. Hence expect a group to take advantage of thee! For what ye measure, it must be, it will be measured to thee. For ye must pay every whit that ye measure to others. And this applies in the future as well as in the past. Do you wonder that your life is in such a mess!

. . . in the present, then, ye will find things pertaining to spirituality, a search for truth, coming nigh unto thee . . . Do not disregard [these experiences] . . . Lay hold on same. Seek Him while He may be found . . .

First, study thyself. Know thy own mind, thine own body, thine own spiritual idea. And unless it be founded—thy ideal—in that which is eternal, the end of whatever you undertake must be distressing . . .

Ye are on trial, to be sure; not necessarily more than others, but ye become so sad and ye become so joyous. Find the happy medium. Find joy even in sorrow, and find sorrow in joy. For the Lord is one God, one Lord . . .

Judge not that ye be not judged. Know thy ideal, and check it with that. Not merely in mind, but put it on paper—see what it looks like! In some instances you'll be ashamed, in others it will open much good for thee . . .

The deep urge is too much of self. Get rid of self. Do not be so dictatorial. Do not demand of others that you do not demand of thyself.

3544-1   M.53   1/5/44

. . . this the entity should adopt as its first principle, in the changing of its life as it goes to seek new opportunities. Quit finding fault with others and others will quit finding fault with you. This is the first thing to adopt in thy new life.

815-2   M.31   4/6/35

For that one cannot endure within itself it finds as a fault in others. That thou findest as a fault in others is thine own greatest fault, ever!

987-4   F.49   11/2/37

Q-7. What is my worst fault?

A-7. What is ever the worst fault of each soul? *Self*—SELF!

What is the meaning of self? That the hurts, the hindrances are hurts to the self-consciousness; and these create what? Disturbing forces, and these bring about confusions and faults of every nature. For the only sin of man is *selfishness!*

262-117   2/27/38

What is that spirit that moves thee to find fault with thy brother, thy neighbor? Is that in keeping with what ye believe? Is that how ye will spend eternity? Is that what ye would have thy Savior, thy God be? Then *why* is not thy life more in accord with that ye profess that ye believe? . . . Ye believe that good and right and justice live *on*, and are continuous in thy experience. Yet ye find fault with what this or that person may have said, may have done . . . or may have failed to say or do . . . Do ye day by day, in *every* way, say, *"Thy will, not mine, be done"?* . . . Not gainsaying, not finding fault! . . . for the Spirit of the Christ will and does direct thee! if ye live the Christ life!

Feet

243-17   F.54   5/8/34

Q-3. Is there anything further I can do to strengthen my feet or prevent them from bothering me so much?

A-3. Do not have too high heels on the shoes, and have plenty of room in them. Bathe the feet in the tannic acid, as we have outlined . . . this will be helpful . . . [See below, 243-33]

[Also use the rubs with the compound indicated. Use all the skin will absorb: To 4 ounces of Russian Oil, White Oil or Nujol add: Witchhazel, 2 ounces; Rubbing Alcohol, 2 ounces; Oil of Sassafras, 5 minims; Tincture of Benzoin, 1 ounce. Shake the solution together before it is poured for massaging, for both the Sassafras and the Tincture of Benzoin will tend to separate from the oils. This may be used to massage the entire body.]

243-33   F.60   4/29/40

As for the limbs—each evening, or at least three to four evenings a week, soak the feet and limbs to the knees in a fluid made from boiling old coffee grounds. It is the tannic acid in [the grounds] that is helpful, which can be better obtained from boiling the old grounds (but not soured). Too much of the new coffee grounds is not well, but [use] sufficient that the water is colored well from the hardboiled coffee grounds. Following such a foot bath, massage Peanut Oil thoroughly into the knee and under the knee, through the area from the knee to the foot, and especially the bursa of the feet . . . if this is done consistently, we will relieve these tensions.

265-15   F.72   4/5/34

Q-1. What will relieve the swelling in the feet and ankles?

A-1. Rubbing the lumbar area with the olive oil and myrrh, so that the circulation may be eased through these portions [of the body] . . . where there are the pressures from long sitting or from lack of activity, [these cause] the tendency for blood to flow to feet without the ability to flow away . . . equal parts tincture of myrrh and olive oil, heating the oil and adding the myrrh, massage this in the lumbar and sacral areas.

779-21   M.46   1/5/35

Q-4. What causes the aching and burning of the feet, especially in warm weather?

A-4. Poor circulation, and acid in the system.

3776-9   F.70   10/9/25

Well if the feet and limbs be bathed in very warm water, to increase the circulation in this portion of system, putting mustard in water when same is done . . .

3776-13   F.70   4/10/26

The condition as exists in the lower limbs, especially in the right leg and foot, is, as we see, greatly produced by that of the calculous places as formed on feet from improper shoes, and from irritation, and the system, attempting to meet or overcome this condition, turns too much of the cuticle into irritation resisting forces in the body, or calluses, or burns, or corns, as may be termed, see? . . . For

that condition as is seen in the limbs and in the feet, we would use
as this: Bathe the limb from knee down with warm olive oil. Then
apply the saturated solution of spirits of camphor, with bicarbonate of soda. Even spread it on, as a very thin layer, see? bandaging
this with a *thin* cloth (not so that the air is excluded entirely thin
cloth) about the limb and foot . . . Let this remain over the evening,
or night . . . Then bathe off in tepid water, and rubbing with this
olive oil again the next morning, see? Then, in the evening, bathe in
tepid water, massage the olive oil in and apply again the solution of
camphor and . . . bicarbonate of soda . . . do not confine the feet . . .
in any shoes . . . that hurt or pinch the feet . . .

903-6   F.26   6/9/28

Q-20. Are high heels harmful [during pregnancy]?

A-20. For the body itself, yes. For that coming [body]—not so
much.

325-7   F.53   5/25/25

Q-5. What will relieve the pain in the feet?

A-5. This . . . [is] produced from poor eliminations through the
system, and the impaired circulation . . . [It would be] well if [the
feet] were bathed occasionally in [a] saturated solution of Sal-
Soda® . . . This, as we see, will gradually correct this portion and will
relieve the strain on the body. Have this [solution] as warm as the
body can stand when the . . . feet are soaked in same, and rubbing
same along the limbs to the knees.

487-14   M.12   5/23/30

*Mrs. Cayce: You will tell us the cause of the soreness and pain
in the heels and back of [the] ankles and what will relieve and
cure same.*

Mr. Cayce:[The pains are caused] partially from growing, partially
from strain. To relieve same, we would have the proper manipulations given to relax same and apply the infrared light for twenty
minutes . . . every *other* day—for five to six treatments. This should
relieve the condition.

Have the manipulations [of the heels, ankles and feet] given just
before the treatments [with the light] are applied.

759-9   M.5   11/6/34

Q-8. What causes the unusual perspiration of the feet?

A-8. The circulation being disturbed, of course, especially through the hepatics, produced by poisons or the attempt of the body to throw off same. This being cut off in the lower portions of the system makes for the accumulations there.

903-16   F.30   7/4/32

Q-13. What will stop the condition that occurs between the toes occasionally?

A-13. Use occasionally witchhazel in its full strength to reduce this [itching]. Bathe—when feet are bathed, and bathe them often—in *salt* water.

287-4   M.62   1/22/25

Q-1. What causes the itching of the toes?

A-1. Improper circulation to the lower portion of the body, a great deal of the condition [comes] from nervous reflex rather than from an existent condition . . . we may use very small quantities of sulphur in [the] shoe.

781-2   M.14   6/9/32

Q-2. What causes the breaking out and itching on [the] feet and how can it be cured?

A-2. This is from the poor eliminations. Local application may be made . . . of witchhazel—when ready for retiring.

480-45   F.26   1/30/38

Q-4. There has appeared between the toes a crustiness. How can I help same?

A-4 . . . the use of the exercises [rising on the toes]—and this with only the stockings or very light slippers on, or the like—these will make a great deal of difference in the general circulation.

Local application of any solutions with alcohol, or the pure grain alcohol—weakened—will remove the disturbance.

Flowers

1877-1   F.44   5/9/39

Flowers—no matter whether they be in or out of season—are well to be oft about the body. The beauty, the aroma, the aliveness of same will make for vibrations that are most helpful, most beneficial.

The body becomes quite sensitive to odors, as well as colors; and especially the colors of purple and coral should be about the body—and rose.

5122-1   F.43   5/17/44

Those activities of the entity should be in or around flowers. For this entity has so oft been the music and the flower lady, until it becomes second nature to work in or with those either in arranging bouquets or corsages, or even the very foolish way of sending to those who have passed on. They need the flowers when they are here, not when they are in God's other room!

In this manner, though, and in this work, may the entity not only minister to others, but it may do so in such a way and manner as for the beauty and the color, even the voice and tone of flowers to come to mean so much to people whom the entity would and could interest in such.

Music and flowers, then, should be the entity's work through this experience . . . flowers will love the entity, as the entity loves flowers. Very few [flowers] would ever find it in themselves to wither while about or on this body . . .

May we indeed inculcate in the lives of others that like the rose, that like the baby breath, like every flower that blooms. For it does its best with what has been given it by man, to glorify its Maker with all its beauty, its color, with all of its love for the appreciation of spring, of the rain, the sunshine, the shadows. And so the man in like manner, with the worries, the troubles, heartaches, the disappointments, may draw closer and closer to God, knowing that this may be done as in the Son. He gave Himself that man might know that appreciation, that love, and how that in meting it to others we come to learn, to know the meaning of disappointments, of little hates, little jealousies, and of how they may grow by entertaining them; and how the joys may grow also just by entertaining them, as do the flowers that God hath given, that man might see His face in the beautiful flowers.

Consider the color, the beauty of the lily as it grows from its ugly muck, or the shrinking violet as it sends out its color, its odor to enrich even the very heart of God.

Consider the rose as to how it unfolds with the color of the day, and with the opening itself to the sunshine, into the rain . . .

. . . the entity should in this present experience give some portion of its time to the culture and preparation and the putting together of [flowers]. The flowers will love it, and so will you! And what they may bring to those who are sick or "shut in" or those who are happy! That they are to see their loved ones that day, that evening.

For it is in such occasions that flowers should be the companionship of those who are lonely. For they may speak to the "shut in." They may bring color again to the cheeks of those who are ill. They may bring to the bride the hope of love, of beauty, of a home. For flowers love the places where there is peace and rest. Sunshine and shadows, yes. There are [varieties] from those [of the] open fields to those which grow in the bog, but they grow.

Why won't people learn the lesson from them and grow, in love and in beauty, in whatever may be their environ?

Friendship

2173-1   F.50   4/19/40

Few realize as this entity that no one individual may have too many friends; that neither is there any individual who has so many friends that it can afford to lose one!

This is a condition—yea, a virtue in the entity; and indeed those may count themselves fortunate who are found worthy of being called friend by the entity. For the entity will be a helpful influence, not attempting to impose nor to superimpose self, but giving that needed to create hope and help in their experiences, under *whatever* may be the circumstance.

Too much stress could not be placed on this, for in same may the entity indeed find that harmony which comes from such experience and application, in that it is not those who seek to do some great deed, or to arouse some throng to such an activity as to revolutionize, but lo—as has been ever given—it is not in the tempest, nor in the storm, but rather in the still small voice.

And this may be aroused by a kindly deed, a gentle word spoken when there is turmoil or strife, a brotherly hand held out, patience—which the entity must learn; with that appreciation of the beauty in its life, in its experience—and in patience ye will glimpse indeed thine own soul and its growth in the presence of thy Maker.

For, know—thy angel stands before Him, ever; and He, thy God, is mindful of thee.

5259-1   F.46   6/8/44

Q-3. Is it a waste of time and effort being friendly with people to whom I am not drawn, associating with them, rather than be antisocial, because so few persons do attract me?

A-3. As has been indicated, it may be an opportunity for thee as well as others. Those to whom you're drawn may be your weakness or may be your strength, depends upon that to which they respond.

3226-1   F.44   9/20/43

. . . we find that the entity is ever ready to help a friend, yet often the entity finds self in the opposite extreme when requiring or desiring a friend to help the entity—the entity feels they have forgotten the friendship shown. These are not true laws. For in the manifestation of spirit and mind and matter, like begets like—if the entity shows itself friendly, there will be friends—if the entity manifests itself in those things pertaining to a universal consciousness, that is the good for all rather than the individual or individual group. Courting favor with others, that there may be favor shown self is not so good—unless it is prompted by a universal desire to be of help in many directions.

951-4   F.24   10/3/39

. . . the entity is oft misunderstood; and the associates and friendships are strained or broken, from reasons that are not always reckoned by the entity.

Know, no soul has ever had so many friends that it could afford to lose a single one; nor yet such a covey or number that it could not add another friend, without even lessening the strength, the love, the power of friendship for all.

For love—as friendship—grows by being showered upon others;

as He so thoroughly demonstrated in His experiences in the material plane . . .

For know, in Him and His ways there is ever a constructive purpose; yes, in His commands—and these are "That ye love one another, even as I have loved you."

243-10 F.50 7/23/30

. . . for the entity has gained much that makes for that as was given . . . "He that is just kind to the least of these, my little ones, is greater than he that hath taken a mighty city."

Glyco-Thymoline®

653-1 F.Child 3/26/32

Q-2. What intestinal antiseptic should be used, when taking alkaline laxative?

A-2. That which is alkaline in its reaction, Lavoris® or Glyco-Thymoline®.

340-7 F.42 1/25/30

Q-2. How would you administer Glyco-Thymoline®?

A-2. About five to fifteen drops at a dose, and give it about twice a day—and take it internally, with water.

3050-2 F.55 12/2/43

Q-1. What should be done to relieve my eyes?

A-1. Bathe these with a weak Glyco-Thymoline® solution. Use an eyecup, and two parts of distilled water (preferably) to one part of the Glyco-Thymoline®. This irritation is a part of the kidney disturbance that has come from the upsetting in the digestive forces.

1688-9 F.31 7/15/42

Q-6. What is the cause of my throat filling with a black mucous?

A-6. The inhalation of those properties about where the body works. But with the gargling each evening and morning with Glyco-Thymoline®, this will aid, and if a little of it is swallowed it will not hurt.

2175-4 F.29 6/28/41

. . . at least twice each week—especially following the periods, but twice each week at other times—we would use a vaginal douche with Glyco-Thymoline® as the antiseptic. Use only the fountain syringe in taking these douches. Use at least a quart or two quarts of the water, body-temperature, and put two tablespoonsful of Gly-co-Thymoline® to each quart of water used [with the douches as a purifier for the organs] . . . we should bring about normal conditions.

1745-4 M.48 5/18/41

. . . have a good hydrotherapist give a thorough, but gentle, colon cleansing; this possibly a week or two weeks apart.

In the first waters, use salt and soda, in the proportions of a heaping teaspoonful of table salt and a level teaspoonful of baking soda [both] dissolved thoroughly to each half gallon of water.

In the last water use Glyco-Thymoline® as an intestinal antiseptic to purify the system, in the proportions of a tablespoonful to the quart of water.

4531-1 F.23 6/27/25

Well too if the gentle massage is gone over the body each day, preferably in morning, that the body may gain an equilibrium in the circulation in nerve and muscular system, applying the mental forces in that direction as we have given, and we will find we will bring the nearer normal forces, increasing the strength and vitality, assisting the body in gaining more of the vision in that portion, or that eye wherein the sight has become so defective. All of these conditions should be cleansed, of course, with those properties that are antiseptics in their reaction, using, however, the antiseptic that is of the alkaline nature, such as is found in Glyco® and in combination of the Glyco® with the antiseptic oil.

Hair

2072-14 F.34 4/17/44

Q-4. What foods or treatments are especially good for bringing more of the luster—reds, coppers and golds—back into the hair?

A-4. Nothing better than the peelings of Irish potatoes or the juices from same. Don't just put the peelings in water and cook them, because most of the necessary properties will go out, but put them in Patapar paper® to cook them.

1947-4   F.32   10/11/39

Q-13. What causes gray hair and how can it be prevented?

A-13. This arises from many, many causes—but it is a general condition of the stimulation to the scalp pores or of the hair itself. It may be worry, it may come from anxiety, it may come from fear or fright, or from—as indicated—lack of elements in the superficial circulation.

In the type of circulation as indicated, as we find here, when the body uses the Violet Ray®, use also occasionally—not every time, but occasionally—the scalp [or comb] applicator, or that which works like a rake through same, see?

3051-3   F.45   9/25/43

Q-9. Will canichrome tablets I take restore color to hair?

A-9. *No!* If the juice of potato peelings is taken regularly (two to three times a week) it will keep the hair nearer to its normal color than all other forms of chemical preparations.

3900-1   F.33   3/25/44

Q-3. Is there any real benefit to be gained from the "gray hair" vitamins?

A-3. Upset stomach is usually gained! If you desire to prevent gray hair, drink at least once each week half a pint of juice prepared from Irish potato peelings. Just the peelings, not the bulk of the potato. This will aid in keeping the correct color in hair.

5190-1   M.35   6/5/44

Q-9. How can I improve quantity and quality of my hair?

A-9. Don't worry about your hair. Worry about what you do with your mind and body. Let the hair, by the very activities, take care of itself. Those who do such, and worry about such, don't amount to much.

5261-1   F.31   6/8/44

Q-2. To keep hair from graying or falling out?

A-2. Don't worry about the hair, just keep it nice and smooth. Take care of it more often with either Drene hair tonic or Olive Oil

Hair Tonic, followed with the shampooing with crude oil and tar soap. These, while making irritation at first will maintain the better conditions for the body.

5334-1   M.51   7/17/44

Q-2. Is there anything I can do for falling hair and to keep it from getting white?

A-2. Stimulate the better conditions of the body and that which ye should retain will be the result. Remember, it is better to have activities of the brain center, than hair.

826-1   M.33   2/12/35

Q-4. How can I improve the growth of hair on my head?

A-4. First, do not eat Irish potatoes; that is, the pulp, but *do* eat the skins of same, and that which is very close to the skins. Also the skins of apples (that are cooked, not raw), the skins of apricots and a portion of same. These supply elements for the activity with the thyroids, that produce for the body the activities of the hair, the nails and those portions of the system.

Then, with the stimulating to the glands as indicated, [using] these [massages] will make for stimulations to same.

Use as a massage the crude oil, cleansing same[from scalp] with a twenty percent solution of *grain* alcohol; not denatured or wood alcohol, but *grain* alcohol; and massage into the scalp small quantities of the white vaseline. These will stimulate growth.

2301-5   M.31   8/27/43

Q-1. To prevent falling hair?

A-1. Don't worry too much about this. Brains and hair don't grow very well together at times anyway.

But we would massage the scalp about once a week with crude oil, and then shampoo with vaseline oil hair tonic or shampoo. This will be effective for this body.

The drinking of the soup made from Irish potato peels will also be helpful. Stew the peels from three or four potatoes in a little water and drink about twice a week.

Also the massaging of the scalp with old coffee grounds would be effective. Of course this would keep the hair colored, but it would be effective to make same grow.

1947-4   F.32   10/11/39

Q-12. What causes dandruff? Can you give a formula for curing it?

A-12. It's poor circulation—and, of course, a germicidal condition which arises from the poor circulation.

Use alternately as a shampoo Listerine® once a week, then the next week a pure tar soap as a wash or shampoo. These would keep the scalp clean and keep down the tendency for dandruff. This will also tend to make a better condition of the scalp and thus preserve or retain, and in some respects gradually keep, the right color for the hair.

1523-3   F.29   3/22/38

Q-8. What treatment should be used to rid hair of dandruff?

A-8. Any of those preparations that are a good scalp cleansing tone; as Lavoris® or Glyco-Thymoline®—or combining these occasionally; and Fitch's Hair Restorer—which dissolves same, and is acid of course; while the first two named are alkaline—and these [factors] are well to be considered—the acid *and* alkaline reaction on the scalp. Of course, oil with vaseline; that is, [applied] as an Olive Oil Shampoo®, with vaseline rubbed in afterwards is very well.

261-2   M.42   9/17/30

Q-5. Is any special treatment recommended for dandruff, and can it be entirely cured?

A-5. If this [treatment] will be used, this may entirely cure same: To water—aqua pura, that preferably of *pure* water—to four ounces of same add twenty minims of 85% alcohol, with that [substance by name] of the Oil of Pine, two minims. This [liquid] should be rubbed thoroughly into the scalp, so that there is the proper reaction from same. Then, with this [scalp area] still damp from same, massage thoroughly into the scalp [a] small quantity of white vaseline. Then wash the head thoroughly with that of a tar soap. Do this about once each week. It will disappear.

Halitosis

5198-1   F.38   5/31/44

Q-1. How can I get rid of bad breath?

A-1. By making for better conditions in [the] eliminations. Take Glyco-Thymoline® as an intestinal antiseptic. Two, three times a day. Put six drops of Glyco-Thymoline® in the drinking water.

This is a throwing off into the lung, into the body-forces, poisons from this changing in cellular activity, or through the body, of lymph forces that become fecal.

4073-1　M.41　4/6/44
Q-1. What brought about the skin condition?
A-1. Poor eliminations and the lack of coordination in eliminations. The activities of the kidneys and the incoordination of liver, and thus through the perspiratory and respiratory system there is the bad breath also; there are the poisons eliminated that should be eliminated through the alimentary canal. Thus the rash.

4550-1　F.Adult　3/27/24
The condition . . . of halitosis is produced from the stomach and from the throat and larynx. In the blood supply to the body . . . this in the lungs proper does not receive the sufficient carbon to supply the system. Hence leaves the whole body under strain at times, and this interferes with the blood supply in having sufficient of those properties to supply the organs in their functioning and in keeping coagulation effective in the system, where organs use the force and energy in their functioning. Hence non-elimination often shows, and through this same condition brings much of the condition exhibited in the intestines and stomach of the catarrhal condition as would be called . . .

Then to give the relief to this body we would first take . . . that which will give the incentive for correction in the body through the digestive organs, and as well through the mental reaction in the system.

Unless the body desires to improve itself, it will continue to enjoy poor health.

5009-1　F.63　4/15/44
Q-1. What causes bitter taste in mouth?
A-1. This is the activity of the liver, with the lack of the gastric flow in the duodenum or regurgitation in the stomach.

1710-1   M.23   10/16/38

Here we find ... there is an inefficiency in the purification or oxidization of [the blood supply] through the activity in the pulmonary system ...

We find that the pressures upon the nerve system—from not so much the injury to the vertebra itself as the connecting forces between the vertebra and in the fifth rib area—are producing conditions where the system, attempting to adjust itself, is gradually building conditions that will be harder to be relieved than if they were removed in the present ... [treatment: osteopathy, heat—wet packs, Codiron; specific outline]

Q-3. Give corrective suggestions for bad breath.

A-3. As indicated, when there is the correction of the repressions in the cerebrospinal system, and there are the better eliminations, these [bad breath] effects should disappear of themselves.

Using the Alcaroid after the meals, or once a day, will cleanse the system and purify the breath. A quarter teaspoonful in a full glass of water, but dissolved first in a small quantity [of water]—is the better.

Hay Fever

261-8   M.45   2/4/33

Q-20. Each year beginning in May and lasting through July, I have hay fever. Is there any way of preventing this?

A-20. Hay fever, as we find, comes from three different direct sources, or the classifications of those who suffer from such a condition may be put under three general heads:

Those subject to odors, peculiar fermentations taking place in the atmospheric conditions throughout or wherever the body may be located. In such cases it is the supersensitiveness of the sympathetic system.

Then there is the class wherein there are physical conditions existent in a body that produce, under the impulses of the atmospheric pressures created at such seasons, the tendencies in that direction.

Then there is the general debilitation that exists, which makes the *whole* body susceptible to the general condition.

This particular body, as we find, is subject to the second class.

So, there should be kept the general condition in the body that we have specified, as to bettering the resistance in the general physical forces.

Also, *(at that particular season)* make specific corrections in the cerebrospinal system. [Osteopathy]

Then, as a cleanser—or a *preventative*, in the form of an anti-septic for the general muco-membrane system (which will reduce the condition about 95%—and that would be well for the body!), prepare this as an inhalant:

In a container twice the size of the quantity, or an 8-ounce glass bottle—preferably a large-mouthed bottle requiring a cork that may be pierced with 2 small glass tubes, one a bulb on the end, where it may be inhaled into the nostrils and into the mouth, put 4 ounces of pure grain alcohol (which should be 190 proof). To this we would add, in the *order* given:

Eucalyptol, Oil of	20 minims,
Canadian Balsam	5 minims,
A solution of Benzosol, a saturated solution.	5 minims,
Rectified Creosote	3 minims,
Tincture of Benzoin	10 minims,
Oil of Turp	5 minims,
Tolu in solution	30 minims.

Keep this tightly corked except when being used. When ready to use, shake [the] solution together and inhale deep into the lungs (as in smoking a cigarette) and into each side of the nostril, night and morning.

With these corrections and minding the diet, you can forget you ever had any hay fever . . .

550-5   M.63   5/15/34

Q-1. What causes apparent hay fever, and sneezing?

A-1. With the corrections that we find will be gained by the manip-ulative measures over the body; that is, from the 9th dorsal upward, we will relieve those pressures that tend to make for an irritation in the muco-membrane of the nasal passages, by the removal of those pressures in the upper dorsal and cervical area that tend to make for this irritation to the bronchi and to the nose.

This is an attempt rather of the circulation to adjust itself under the general strain that has existed and does exist in the system.

Head Noises

5132-1 M.70 5/20/44

As we find, in some times back there were congestions through the area of the throat and that portion of the head which developed into a catarrhal condition.

From the general strain on a weakened system, this catarrhal condition now has attacked the Eustachian tube and thus makes a general pressure on the nerves of the sensory system.

These as we find may be materially aided. We do not find cures entirely, but they may be materially aided.[Treatment: Wet Cell Appliance® and massage]

1523-15 F.33 4/28/42

Q-5. What causes my ears to roar like ocean waves beating in them at times?

A-5. This is from the emotional body. Hence the needs for the head and neck exercise. This is a tendency of the slowing of the circulation through the Eustachian tubes to the auditory forces of the ear. Thus the physical reaction from same. This should entirely disappear if the head and neck exercise is taken.

5140-1 M.40 5/19/44

There will be required the analyzing of self first, as to what purpose, as to what use the body will give to those creative forces that may bring relief from the physical disturbance which exists. Unless these are to be used in a greater service for the Master, of what use will the life be? . . .

Have you listened to the voice of conscience as it has brought corrections to the self? These are parts of the cause of the creation of deposits along the Eustachian tube, which causes the great roaring in the head and ears; that is, in the anxiety the body feels at times through the general mental attitude towards conditions as well as towards people.

1688-7 F.31 8/19/41

Q-3. What is [the] cause of continuous ringing in head and ears?

A-3. Same reasons we have indicated. This is an area in which a great deal *of* lymph is required, through the throat, the nasal passages and the soft tissues of face. Hence specifically the massages with the Peanut Oil, as indicated, are to be given around the neck and about the head, see? But it would be well to massage each joint with same . . . About twice each week, almost bathe in Olive Oil or Peanut Oil; especially Peanut Oil—in the joints, the neck, across the clavicle, across all the areas of the spine, the rib and the frontal area to the pit of [the] stomach, across the stomach and especially in the diaphragm area; then across the hips and the lower portion of the back and across the sacral area and then the limbs themselves. Massage these by dipping the fingers in the oil. Do not sponge off immediately. Do this just before retiring, wipe off with tissue, and then bathe off in the morning . . . if these are kept consistently, we will not only build strength but supply the better circulation throughout the whole body . . . Take not just a few minutes, but set a period and make of it an occasion when the massage is given. Take from thirty minutes to an hour or [an] hour and a half to do it!

1688-9   F.31   7/15/42

Q-3. What is [the] trouble with my left ear? It rings constantly and feels as though it has something in it.

A-3. Those pressures in the cervical and upper dorsal, that should be relieved by those relaxing treatments [Osteopathy]. These are nerves, see?

Healing Through Attitude

[The one characteristic which best distinguishes transcripts of the readings of Edgar Cayce from clinical reports is their earnest insistence on spirituality. The great majority of the readings contained passages which pointed out to each individual his need to be spiritual in order to get well or even to stay well. The following extracts are typical, and they indicate an approach to health which is little studied in modern therapy.]

3384-2   M.33   1/22/44

The closer the body will keep to those truths and the dependence on the abilities latent within self through trust in spiritual things, the quicker will be the response in the physical body. For all healing, mental or material, is attuning each atom of the body, each reflex of the brain forces, to the awareness of the divine that lies within each atom, each cell of the body.

3455-1   F.40   12/5/43

It is not necessary that there be other than a competent and a spiritual-minded nurse; preferably such should be minded toward Christian Science, but willing to use these suggestions [for treatment made earlier in the reading].

For the powers within must be spiritualized. Not that the body [this individual] is not spiritual-minded, but there is the necessity to be spiritual-minded and then [to be] able to gain control sufficiently over the power of mind in the body as to cause the vibrations from the atomic structures to produce health-giving forces, rather than taking the continual suggestions "I'm sick and going to stay sick."

These reactions should be brought about by suggestion as well as [by the necessary physical] application. For know, as was given from the beginning, it is necessary to subdue the earth. Man is made, physically, from every element within the earth. So, unless there is a coordination of those elements of the environs in which the animal-man operates, he is out of attune—and some portions [of his body] suffer. He must contain and command those elements. These [suggestions of physical treatments] are subduing, using, controlling; not being controlled by, but controlling those [material] environs [of this body], and influences about same.

3594-2   M.59   4/1/44

While there are many varied conditions [or suggestions for treatment] given [through this channel] as to diet, as to purifying throat and lungs, as to the effect of properties upon the lymph circulation of [the] throat and head, remember that these have a basis of power, of force.

What is the source of all good? Ask self that. Answer it—don't give just a guess at it. If you don't know, you had better be finding out—you will need it much sooner than you would expect, if you don't pay more attention to it!

Do those things, for it is of the mental and spiritual import. Why would the body be physically improved if it is not for betterment, not merely for self-indulgencies to a greater extent? Why do you seek to indulge the body and the appetites of the body? Why not supply spiritual and mental good for others? You'll get well a heap quicker, life will be more worthwhile, and you'll be better for it. *Don't* ask for the gratifying of appetites!

5081-1   F.31   5/6/44

Do [the things] that [we have suggested] so the conditions will enable the body to better be the nurse, as it is. Administering to others is the best way to help self. More individuals become so anxious about their own troubles, and yet helping others is the best way to rid yourself of your own troubles. For what is the pattern? He gave up heaven and entered physical being that you might have access to the Father. Then what are you grumbling about because you dislike your mother? She dislikes you as much, but change this into love. Be kind, be gentle, be patient, be long-suffering, for if thy God was not long-suffering with thee, what chance would you have?

1807-6   F.40   1/16/44

Do use the period [of electro-therapy] as the period for prayer and meditation. Do keep the attitude in body-mind for those of better creative influences.

Not only be good—be good for something! Do think of others, not altogether of self, but [study] as to how the body may contribute most to that [which is] not merely of pleasure, but of creative forces and influences in the lives of others, also!

2828-1   M.40   10/15/42

For, in part the entity is meeting self, from those of its experiences in the earth. Then, know—deep within self, deep within thy consciousness—*who* healeth thy diseases, *who* giveth thee opportunities. And the trust and the hope, the understanding as may be gained by that analyzing of self from the careful study of the 30th of Deuteronomy, the 14th, 15th, 16th and 17th of John, should be the life. As we find, [the study should be] not as rote but as living, hoping, believing, knowing that as ye may ask—in His name—it may be done in the body . . .

Q-1. How long has this condition been coming on?

A-1. For about ten years.

Q-2. Approximately how long will it be before I will improve?

A-2. How long before tomorrow, Mr.[2828]? How long is the power of God in self? How long does it take thee to do His biddings? How long hast thou kept in the way [being] beyond reproach of thine own self, as well as in the way of being a helpful influence in the experience of each one ye meet day by day?

1967-1   M.24   7/25/39

And, above all, *pray!* Those who are about the body, use, rely upon the spiritual forces. For the prayer of the righteous shall save the sick.

Know that all strength, all healing of every nature is the changing of the vibrations from within—the attuning of the divine within the living tissue of a body to Creative Energies. This alone is healing. Whether it is accomplished by the use of drugs, the knife or what-not, it is the attuning of the atomic structure of the living cellular force to its spiritual heritage.

Then, in the prayer of those—live day by day in the same manner as ye pray—if ye would bring assistance and help for this body.

Hemorrhoids

2823-2   F.33   6/5/43

But the best for the specific condition of hemorrhoids is the exercise, and if this is taken regularly these will disappear—of themselves! Twice each day, of morning and evening—and this doesn't mean with many clothes on! rise on the toes, at the same time raising the arms; then bend forward, letting the hands go toward the floor. Do this three times of morning and three times of evening. But don't do it two or three times and then quit! . . . Be regular with it, each day!

5226-1   F.58   5/26/44

Q-2. Piles?

A-2. Use Tim. And this exercise: Each morning upon arising, before dressing, gradually rise on feet at the same time gently raising hands above head. Then try and touch the floor with the hands. This gradually will raise the whole of the sphincter nerves, but cleanse same in the manner indicated and it will have much to do with correcting these conditions also.

1800-20   9/13/34

Preferable that this [Tim formula] never be put in tin, but rather in the porcelain or glass; and should be in an ounce or ounce and a quarter hexagon-shaped jar, preferably. The directions would be to apply as an ointment to affected portions once or twice each day. Rest as much as possible *after* application, with the feet elevated *above* the head. It'll cure it!

563-5   F.26   3/1/40

Also we find there are those conditions through the alimentary canal, where especially the sphincter muscles and nerves are involved from this disturbance.

Hence the conditions that cause a great deal of itching, and at times the blind hemorrhoids—or protruding of the folds of the lower portion of the anus.

This also at times causes a great deal of distress, as well as—through the thinned condition of the folds—a great deal of bleeding . . .

We would begin with the use of an ointment—as Pazo Ointment™—for injection through the areas where there are the disturbances . . .

Stay off the feet as much as practical until the acute conditions are removed . . .

Keep away from highly seasoned foods, and from any form of drinks that carry carbonated waters or that are of any appreciable alcohol content.

Take more of the liver and beef extracts. Or, the Wyeth's Beef, Iron and Wine will be most helpful; a teaspoonful at each meal taken. Don't take this *unless* the meal *is* taken, but with each meal take same.

Fresh vegetables are better than the dried—so take them fresh whenever practical. [Take exercise outlined above in 5226-1.]

Do not use too much of laxatives, but rather use enemas to have the evacuations each day.

357-4   F.Adult   5/5/33

It will be necessary that precautions be taken, and that this be done with the idea in mind that there must not be too great an irritation to those portions in the system that have caused so much

disorder and trouble, from the tendency of the constipation to produce the hemorrhoids and their resultant conditions in the system.

Hobbies

5177-2   F.65   5/26/44

Then . . . make it a habit, make it a hobby, to at least each day,
speak kindly to someone less fortunate than self. Not that there
should be so much the contribution to organized charity, but have
those charities of self [that] you never speak of, by speaking kindly
to someone each day.

This will let the body rest at night when it hasn't been able to,
with its mental and material worries . . .

But don't forget, as the Boy Scout or Girl Scout oath would be:
Do a good deed every day. This is just being kind, just being patient,
showing long-suffering, gentleness; and we will find much help for
this body.

3188-1   M.23   8/31/43

*Q-7. How much attention may I justifiably give to music, which
I love so much?*

A-7. This should be ever rather as the hobby, fulfilling. For, oft ye
will find the music alone may span the distance between the sublime
and the ridiculous. So it is in the search for God, that haply ye may
find Him, for He is within thine own self.

Q-8. Could I become a fine professional musician?

A-8. As for special service, yes—but this is only one way. Go the
whole way.

5226-1   F.58   5/26/44

Q-5. What hobby do you suggest?

A-5. Get rather the hobby of helping somebody else.

As a hobby, any of these things which would have to do with work
out of doors with flowers or such activities would be well, but do
plan each day to do a good deed, for somebody who is not able to
do for themselves. If it's nothing more than conversation of keeping
company for and with someone who is "shut in" or the like, you'll
find great help for self. Do that.

5108-1   F.30   5/15/44

Q-2. Please suggest a hobby that I would use constructively.

A-2. Stamps. These would be well for the body, and you'll have a very good chance soon for collecting of many such. These ye may study as to what their place is in the nations' accepting or rejecting the Lord, and such a hobby may be made to be far-reaching and worthwhile.

2385-1   M.34   10/23/40

Q-9. What are my musical possibilities, and how much should this expression be stressed?

A-9. Rather as the hobby.

263-18   F.31   6/7/42

Q-4. Should we plan some specific hobby or recreation together, periodically? If so, what?

A-4. This would be a very, *very* good start. Where the planning of recreation, of activity, of thought or study, or interest, is separate, ye grow apart. Where the interest may be together—whether in a hobby, in a recreation, in a study, in a visitation, in an association—ye grow in purpose as one.

Home and Marriage

3051-4   F.45   11/29/43

Q-4. What can [I] do to overcome [my] husband's lack of generosity to [me] financially?

A-4 . . . be just as generous to the husband as [you expect] the husband to be to [you], and these will be more in accord and will bring greater harmony in the relationships throughout the experience.

These each have ideals. Make them coordinate with the material, the mental, and the spiritual lives of each. Know that it must begin in the spiritual. Then material results will be brought into the experience as the mind is controlled towards those ideals set by each as to the spirit with which they will control and act in relationships one to another . . .

Q-8. If [I] adopted some children would it be a blessing to both [my husband] and the children, considering [my] physical condition?

A-8. This had best be determined in selves. If that is the desire of each, let them be wholly in agreement. And where there is agreement, there may be harmony. And if harmony, then it would be for the better welfare of all concerned.

Remember, there are those responsibilities as well as possibilities that arise with the desire for adoption. For, in many instances, and it might be found here, unless this is prompted by a spiritual desire on the part of each, it is better not to attempt such. If it is prompted by the spiritual, then the mental and material relationships will take care of themselves. And these are well, if prompted by the spiritual desire of each—and they are in accord. Without such, be mindful . . .

Q-11. Why are we together in this life and how can we accomplish this mission?

A-11. By each being true to themselves. Ye are together because of those attractions one for the other through relationships borne in other activities. And [each] . . . being true to the ideal and keeping self as one, they make for those activities of the earth, and those portions in which they reside, being better for their living therein.

This is the purpose of each group or each person in the earth. We are to subdue the environs. We are to turn same to helpful forces for those to come.

1470-2 M.29 2/12/38

Q-1. Why has my marriage to the entity now known as [M.A.C.] been blocked each time it has been planned?

A-1. There is a resentment within self, and this . . . must be cleared before choices or a decision may be reached. It *must* be upon the basis of whether or not there would come the fruits of love, of patience, of kindness.

The choice must be made upon that basis. And the *choice* must be within the self. Weigh all phases. See, know—*ask* and ye shall receive from *within!* . . .

Q-3. What will be the effect on my life of this marriage to [M.A.C.]?

A-3. What wilt thou *allow* it to become? This depends . . . upon the choices. If such could or would be picturized for the entity, would it have been that the Father would have said, "I repent that I have ever made man"?

Man and woman are free-willed. What will ye *make of* such an association? If ye choose the right—contentment, happiness and joy. If it is for self and the glorification and magnification of self—inharmony, distrust, turmoils and strife. The law is before thee—and it is *sure!*

939-1   M.28   6/23/35

If there will be kept within the intent and purpose of each *as* is the desire toward each in the present, well! For their minds, their bodies, their desires, are in the present in accord.

Even though there would arise in their experience that which would be of the nature as to cause turmoils, dissensions, even strife, if their hearts and minds are kept—*ever*—in that of being a helpmate one for the other, such would become then rather as stepping-stones for greater opportunities, greater privileges.

Should they either become self-centered, or allow selfish motives to make for demands one upon the other; or become at such times so self-centered as to desire the gratifying of self's desires irrespective of what the satisfying of same might bring into the experience of the other, then these would become as those things that would divide the purpose. And a house divided against itself *will not* stand . . .

Q-3. Do they genuinely love each other?

A-3. In the present. Remember each, love is giving; it is a growth. It may be cultivated or it may be seared. That of selflessness on the part of each is necessary. Remember, the union of body, mind and spirit in such as marriage should ever be not for the desire of self but as *one.* Love grows; love endures; love forgiveth; love understands; love keeps those things rather as opportunities that to others would become hardships.

Then, do not sit *still* and expect the other to do all the giving, nor all the forgiving; but make it rather as the unison and the purpose of each to be that which is a *complement* one to the other, ever.

Q-4. If they marry, will they be happy and compatible?

A-4. This, to be sure, is a state that is *made* so; not a thing that exists. For Life is living, and its changes that come must be met by each under such circumstances and conditions as to *make* the union, the associations, the activities, such as to be more and more worthwhile. Let each *ever* be dependent upon the other, yet so conducting self that the other may ever depend upon self. Thus will they find the associations, the mental forces, the spiritual activities that will bring peace and contentment in such a union . . .

Q-6. It married, what activities and pursuits would they enjoy most in common?

A-6. Those that make for the preparing of themselves for being the complement one to the other . . .

These are the manners, the interests, as this:

"What will prepare my mind the most to be on an equal footing with my husband, that the interests may be as one? so that when there are those things necessary for the more perfect understanding, I would be able to meet him on his own ground?"

The same with the husband should be; not different worlds through their associations, socially, morally or materially, but *ever* as a oneness of service, in a *constructive* manner ever.

Q-7. If they marry, will there be issue; and if so, how many boys and girls?

A-7. This would depend, to be sure, upon their activity in these relationships. This should be kept inviolate. But let rather this be answered from the Giver of those opportunities, those privileges that are in the experience of father and mother. For those that may be lent them are of the Lord. Let such associations, let such desires be, "Not my will but Thine, O Lord, be done *in* and through me" . . .

Q-8. What knowledge of [N.A.T.] and her personality does [939] require to aid him in understanding her?

A-8. Study rather not the whims or fancies that may be gratified, but that which would bring out the best in each . . .

Study each other; not to become critical, but as to become more and more the complement one for the other.

Q-9. What knowledge of [939] and his personality does [N.A.T.] require to aid her in understanding him?

A-9. The same. In the associations let them, as it were, each have their own jobs; yet *all* in common. Leave the office in the office, when in the home. Leave the petty things of the home in the home, when abroad. But have all things in common.

1872-1   F.30   5/5/39

Q-1. Is there anything I can do to make my husband fall in love with me again?

A-1. There needs to be rather those separations there—unless

physical conditions with the husband, in his idea *of* material relationships, are changed by surgery.

Q-2. *Why do we seem to have so little in common, so little to
talk about?*

A-2. As indicated, these are the meeting of self from those experiences through the sojourn just previous to this—when the relationships were rather as father and daughter; yet *brought* relationships
where it required the separate activities for the greater benefit of
each.

And so it may become here, *unless* those activities of a material
nature—and physical conditions—are changed . . . it is a physical
defect—a *physical* condition in that body—the husband . . . not a
mental, not a purposeful one. But the entity must choose for itself,
see?

Do, then, that as indicated. Study within self, first: What is thy
ideal, spiritually—thy ideal home? Nat as to what is the ideal thing
that *others* should do, but the ideal manner that *ye* should do! And
do that!

1523-6   F.29   10/7/38

Then when ye are, either of thee in turmoil—*not* one shall do *all*
the praying, nor all the "cussing"; but *together*—ask! and He will
give—as He has promised—that assurance of peace, of harmony,
that can *only* come from a coordinated, cooperative effort on the
part of souls that seek to be the channels through which His love,
His glory may be manifested in the earth!

Do not let aught separate thee! else it will be the destruction of
thine own selves through *this* experience!

Rather make thy bodies *channels* through which a soul may manifest! and in thy purposes, in thy desires, in thy love of *life*, ye may
show—in that union—that as would bind thee closer yet to Him.

For there is naught else that may bring the understanding, the
comprehension of what thy abilities of each may accomplish, as
being the channels through which a soul—as comes from Him—
may accomplish!

Let, then, thy yeas be yea, thy nays be nay. But keep the way open
for thy better selves, for thy love, for thy respect, for thy faith, for
thy confidence to expand.

Then let each—in thy daily activities—think not on that which satisfies thyself alone, nor yet that which would be indulgence of the other; but rather as to how ye may each become the greater, the better channel for the glory of *life*, of God, of His gifts, of His promises, of His peace, of His harmonies—that they may manifest in thy cooperation one with another.

Hypnosis

2851-1   F.48   11/13/42

The entity would make a good hypnotist, but to the entity's own self this ability had better be used for the spiritual attaining of that the entity may accomplish.

3343-1   M.36   11/1/43

Q-3. *Under hypnosis, could I become a reliable vehicle for the transmission of clairvoyant perception?*

A-3. Best let hypnosis alone, for this body, unless you wish to hypnotize someone else! Practice it within yourself. Let it be self that would be subdued and give the authority to God, not man—through man, but to God.

146-3   M.13   2/23/31

Q-13. *Could hypnotism be used in his case [deaf-mutism, epilepsy]?*

A-13. It might be used, but be *mindful* of who would use same! . . .

Q-15. *Would auto-suggestion be helpful?*

A-15. Most beneficial. This can be given best by mother.

Q-16. *Please give form of suggestion.*

A-16. That as is desired to be awakened. Work *with* one applying the manipulative [osteopathy] forces in this, but appeal *always* to the *inner* being—that being awakened in this formative period of the development of the body, mentally and physically.

This may be as a form, but should be put in the words of the individual making such suggestions. As the body sinks into slumber: May the self, the ego, awaken to its possibilities, its *responsibilities*, that, as I speak to you, in the normal waking state you will respond in that same loving, careful manner this is given [to] you. See?

4506-1   F.50   3/22/21

There has been brought into this physical body here some of the error that is inherent from the parent . . .

Q-1. Who shall put this body under hypnotic treatment?

A-1. One of the people that has a clean mind themselves. The body is good to look at, and it would not be well to put under the influence of one with ulterior motives or desires.

4506-2   F.55   5/21/26

This subjugation should be made by one that gives the massage and adjustments of the centers in the cerebrospinal system, or by one who gives the nerve centers the incentive for normal action.

This may be begun by the one so manipulating, insisting that the body (during the time of treatment) keep entirely quiet, and the operator talk continually, with the suggestion necessary for the improvement in the body, physical and mental, see? for, with these conditions, this would gradually bring about this subjugation with the centers where the cerebrospinal and sympathetic are at junctures with each other, as [are] seen in the cervical, the dorsal, and in the whole of the sacral and lumbar region.

1839-1   M.39   3/7/39

Q-1. What should be done to relieve hiccoughs which he has had for six days?

A-1. Let this be done by suggestion, through such as Kuhn.

3450-1   F.55   12/8/43

Q-4. Would hypnosis help the body conditions[Parkinson's disease]? If so, please give name and address of reliable hypnotist in or near Boston.

A-4. Not as we find indicated here. Spirituality is the most help. Deep meditation, prayer, will be the most helpful.

3619-1   F.54   1/28/44

These arise from an injury received by the body at the cardiac portion of the stomach . . .

As we find here, the relaxings of the body by or through suggestions made as to almost hypnotize the body will help. This should be done by the power of suggestion at the same time that applications would be made for magnetic healing. This may be done by the very close associates of the body . . .

1135-6   M.36   11/11/36

Many an individual, many a personage has given his all for the demonstrating of a truth.

As it has been indicated from the first through *this* channel, there should ever be that ideal, "What does such information as may come through such a channel produce in the experience of individuals, as to not their thoughts, not their relations other than does such make them better parents, better children, better husbands, better wives, better neighbors, better friends, better citizens?" And if and when it does *not*, LEAVE IT ALONE!

284-1   F.51   2/24/33

Throughout the experience the entity gained, for he not only accomplished the feat of living without self but being able to extend to others much of that aid that may be had through the field of activity in bringing about the change of thought in individuals, so as to affect them bodily. Not only as for their influencing to the extent as to heal physical conditions, but bringing about activities that were easily turned at times by others into detrimental influences in individuals' lives.

The entity did not take advantage of others, but saw the advantage taken often. Hence in the latter portion of the experience the entity began to doubt self. Hence the entity may be said to have been among the first in that particular experience to use the abilities for raising the vibrations in self for helpfulness, and also to raise them to the extent as to override the will-influence in the activity of other individuals.

In the present, then, the study of hypnosis, mesmeric and rote influence, is held askant [askance]; yet there are the abilities within self, provided these are basically in that principle gained in self even in that experience—that, when such influences are used for good, it is well—but when they are used for personal gain, bad!

Illness, Why?

[The Cayce readings refer to our having lived on earth several

times before, in the same matter-of-fact way that they refer to in-
testinal adhesions. In discussing the causes of a serious illness
which an individual may suffer, the term "karma" is sometimes
borrowed from the Hindu language to express the familiar
Christian concept, "As ye sow, so shall ye reap." Presupposing
reincarnation, such a reference to "karma" or "meeting self" in
an individual's readings means that his particular experience of
suffering—or of joy—is a case of actually experiencing what he
dealt out to others in a previous life, a situation being reversed
upon him with a justice more than poetic.]

3395-2   F.63   1/15/44

Q-1. Is the ill health which I have been experiencing the past
years the result of mistakes of a past life or is it due to something
amiss in this present life?

A-1. Both. For there is the law of the material, there is the law of
the mental, there is the law of the spiritual.

That [which is] brought into materiality is first conceived in spirit.
Hence, as we have indicated, all illness is sin; not necessarily of the
moment, as man counts time, but as a part of the whole experience.

2828-4   M.41   9/20/43

Remember, the sources [of this body's condition], as we have
indicated, are the meeting of one's own self; thus are karmic.

These can be met most in Him who, taking away the law of cause
and effect by fulfilling the law, establishes the law of grace. Thus
the needs for the entity to lean upon the arm of Him who is the law,
and the truth and the light.

For, while these [conditions in the body] may be sought to be
explained through the defects in the body, read carefully—who
healeth all thy diseases, who bringeth this or that [illness or health]
to pass in thy experience? that through thy experience ye may learn
the more of the law of the Lord, that it is perfect . . .

As has been indicated for the entity, [use] the [ultraviolet] lights
that would aid in checking—even in helping the disturbed area in
the spine by the use of this high vibration. Electricity or vibration is
that same energy, same power, ye call God. Not that God is an electric light or an electric machine, but that vibration that is creative
is of that same energy as life itself.

2828-5 M.41 1/10/44

. . . it was given, "Whosoever sheddeth man's blood, by man shall his blood be shed." That is, in this case, the blood of [this individual's] will, of his purpose, of his physical desire to carry on in his own ways of activity, and by those conditions in the body itself being thwarted. The entity thwarted others [in a previous lifetime] and is meeting it [now] in self. That is karma.

3485-1 M.51 12/27/43

For here we have an individual entity meeting its own self—the conditions in regard to the movements of the body, the locomotories, the nerve ends, the muscular forces. What ye demanded of others [in another experience] ye must pay yourself! Every soul should remember not to demand of others more than ye are willing to give, for ye will pay—and, as most, through thy gills!

288-38 F.29 9/19/34

Q-16. Are all physical weaknesses and ailments caused primarily from breaking of spiritual laws, instead of just physical or natural laws as we know them?

A-16. Rather the combination of each . . . These [weaknesses] come from [as far back as] the first urge which is the meeting of the union of forces that create, as the beginning of inception, and those elements then, that enter in by the feeding—when it begins [to enter the baby's experience] with the changes of same—make for certain indications; and [there is] the functioning of glands, as[their activities] are indicated, that make for the height [of a body] or that make for color, or [act so] as to make for the functioning of various [organic] conditions. Then, it's a combination of [all] these. Yet, as has been indicated, *always* will it be found [also] that the *attitude* of the mental forces of a body finds its inception [or reflection] in those things that come into growth; for what we think and what we eat—combined together—make what we *are*, physically and mentally.

Q-17. For instance, do my weaknesses in the physical body have anything to do with the manner in which I first erred in spirit, hence making it necessary for me to correct inharmony within before attaining [to] a perfect body?

A-17. They are the result of same, of course, throughout the activities in the ages, and [the result especially of] what we do *about* them in any *one* experience or combination of all of the experiences.

3051-7   F.46   6/20/44
Q-2. Since all disease is caused by sin, exactly what sin causes the colon and elimination condition?
A-2. The sin of neglect. Neglect is just as much sin as grudge, as jealousy—neglect.

3395-2   F.63   1/15/44
For God has not purposed or willed that any soul should perish, but purgeth everyone by illness, by prosperity, by hardships, by those things needed, in order [for the individual] to meet self—but in Him, by faith and works, are ye made every whit whole.

3049-1   F.11   6/14/43
But this [treatment] should be done systematically, *expectantly;* not doubting. For what ye ask in His name, believing, and thyself living, ye have already.

2948-1   F.11   4/1/43
Do keep sweet. Keep that attitude of expectancy. Do keep the attitude of hope. And *know* that there is healing in the power and might of the love of God.

Individuality and Personality

4038-1   F.53   4/7/44
With this entity, as with most individuals, the personality and the individuality are not always the same.

5246-1   F.26   5/27/44
Personality is that ye wish others to think and see.
Individuality is that your soul prays, your soul hopes for, desires.

2175-1   F.28   4/23/40
These interpretations are chosen . . . with the desire and purpose that this may . . . enable the entity to analyze and see within self that [which] may be helpful in meeting this, that is called by

some at times, dual personality.

It is rather, though, the personality at times giving expression—influenced from sojourns in the material plane—and at other periods the individuality of the entity giving expression—as urged or ruled from the experiences during the interims between the earthly sojourns.

3590-2   F.57   1/26/44

. . . personality and individuality should have some analysis, so as to give the entity a concept of what we mean by personality and individuality:

Personality is that which the entity, consciously or unconsciously, spreads out before others to be seen of others. As to whether you will say "Good Morning" to Jim or John and ignore Susan or not—these are parts of the personality, because of some difference or because of some desire to be used or needed by *that* others would have to give.

While individuality in that same circumstance would be: I wish to do this or that for Susan or Jim or John, because I would like for Jim or John or Susan to do this if conditions were reversed.

One is for the universal consciousness that is part of the soul-entity's activity.

The other is the personal, or the desire for recognition, or the desire for the other individual to recognize your personal superiority.

These are variations to this individual entity.

. . . the entity finds itself—if it will stop to analyze—a body, a mind, with the hope for a soul eternal, that will constantly, eternally have recognition of those relationships to the universal consciousness or God.

Then, as the entity in this material plane has found, it is necessary physically to conform to certain moral and penal laws of society, of the state, of the nation, even to be termed a good citizen.

Thus, if there is to be preparation for the entity as the soul entity, as a citizen of the heavenly kingdom, isn't it just as necessary that there be the conforming to the laws pertaining to that spiritual kingdom of which the entity is a part? And there has been an ensample, a citizen of that kingdom, the Son Himself, has given the example to the entity as well as to others.

Isn't it well, then, that the entity study to show self approved unto that kingdom, rightly putting the proper emphasis upon all phases of His admonitions, His judgments, His commandments, and thus become . . . a good citizen of that individual kingdom?

These are just reasons within self, if there is the time taken to interpret what ye believe and what ye hope for.

Do not do it just mentally. Do it mentally and materially. Set it down in three distinct columns: The physical—what are the attributes of the physical body? Eyes, ears, nose, mouth—these are means or manners through which the awarenesses of the physical body may become known to others, by sight, by hearing, by speaking, by feeling, by smelling. These are consciousnesses. Then there are the emotions of the body. These come under the mental heading, yes—but there are also those phases where the mental and emotional body is born [of], or under the control of, the physical and sometimes under the control wholly of the mental.

What are the mental attributes, then? The ability to think, the ability to act upon thought. From whence do these arise? Do you use the faculties of the physical being for such? You do in many instances, yet you can think by sitting still—you can think yourself wherever your consciousness has made an impression upon the physical being of what exists. For you can sit in your office and see yourself at home, and know exactly what your bed looks like and what you left sit under it when you left this morning! These are physical, not material at all; yet you judge them by paralleling with that knowledge, that understanding.

The spiritual self is life, the activity of the mental and of the physical is of the soul—and thus a soul-body.

Set down the attributes of each, and as to when and how you use them, and how you change them. What is the ideal of each? Of your mental, your physical and your spiritual or soul body? And as you grow in grace, we will find that the individuality will change—until you become one, as the Father and the Son and the Holy Spirit are one. This is the manner in which you grow.

Then study to show thyself approved unto God, a workman not ashamed, rightly dividing the words of truth, keeping self unspotted from the world; not condemning, even as ye would not be condemned. For as ye pray, as He taught "Forgive me as I forgive others." So in thy condemning, so in thy passing judgment, let it be only as ye would be judged by thy Maker.

4082-1   F.52   4/12/44

The individuality is the sum total of what the entity has done about those things that are creative or ideal in its varied experiences in the earth.

5246-1   F.26   5/27/44

Urges termed astrological would be very far from correct in this particular entity. For, as has been indicated, the personality and the individuality of the entity are quite at variance . . .

[Personality and individuality] need not necessarily be one, but their purpose must be one, even as the Father, the Son and the Holy Spirit are one. So must body, mind and soul be one in purpose and in aim; and as ye ask, believing, so is it done unto thee.

3343-1   M.36   11/1/43

. . . first find self in its relationship to spiritual things. Not of self but of that influence, that power through which man may attain to the greater consciousness of his oneness with the universe, yes— but as of a personal Savior, a personal God—not as an individual. For the individuality of a soul must be lost in the personality of the Christ—in God. These become unified, then, in their activities in relationships with others.

5125-1   F.30   5/19/44

The entity is an individual, individual in itself; that is, its personality and its individuality are nearer one and the same than you will find in one out of a million; and this is well.

As to activities and experience in the earth, we find that these, combined with the astrological urges, give the personality and individuality of the entity; and you won't find another in a million just like it!

Introverts (Suppression)

3564-1   F.44   1/17/44

All of [the physical conditions] are general results of what might be called inhibitions. Or the body being inclined to close in on itself; timid, lack of self-expression . . . the body has been too sedentary in its activities. It should be out-of-doors more; holler, yell more, for the fun of it! The body has wanted to many times and never has to the full extent in its whole experience, since it was sat upon by somebody—it hasn't ever liked very well since.

But the body needs to change its environment, to be where it will meet lots of people and have to do a lot of talking and a lot of explaining to people that you realize don't know near as much as you do, and give to those who think they know a lot. If you will only realize it, you know a lot more than they do—on any subject.

These changes will make a great deal of difference with this body . . .

Do change the environment . . . Don't be afraid of having troubles . . . Know that whatever you want you can have, for the Lord loveth those who love Him and He will not withhold any good thing from such.

3564-2   F.44   1/17/44

Too long has the entity been, as it were, under a cloud; rather timid, rather lacking in self-expression. It needs to get out in the wilds and yell, and hear its own echo back again. Not to be subdued by others who try, or have tried to impress the entity with their importance. For God is not a respecter of persons. And anyone can act the fool by appearing to be important. For the greatest among those of the earth are those who serve the most. But [this] doesn't mean keeping so quiet, being so uncommunicative. For others may give the entity the impression that they want to tell you and show you how, yet the entity all the time really knows much more than most of those who would tell the entity what to do . . .

[There is] the lack of flash and show. If the entity would dress up in a red dress, it could cut a nice caper, and this is not meant as a pun, either!

For the vibrations of such have even been so subdued about the entity that little of the real beauty has escaped, because the love and deep emotion has been kept hid so long . . .

[The entity] has belittled itself, cramped its abilities . . . Turn self loose! It may go anywhere so long as it keeps its faith in the one God, and applies itself in just being kind, patient, showing brotherly love. For these are the things that make the entity, and will make the entity, the handmaid of the Lord our God.

5242-1   M.20   6/3/44

Overcome timidity by having something particular to say. Many individuals talk without saying anything; that is, [anything] constructive, or that which has even meaning, but to the entity they are giving expression of self.

There is given only two eyes, two ears. We should hear and see twice, yes four times as much as we say . . . never boastful, never attempting to be just as the other boys and do what people say because ye may be thought different of.

Dare to be different and you'll find if ye will begin with Deuteronomy 30, [and] Exodus 19:5, you will know the reasons deep within self.

Kidneys

[The Cayce readings have indicated the following directions for use of the Jerusalem artichoke where insulin is needed: Keep the artichokes in a flower pot or imbedded in the ground, so as to preserve them; they will not keep on ice, but need to be in the ground. Eat one about the size of an egg twice a week, once raw and once cooked. Cook in Patapar Paper® so as to preserve the juice, and mix the juice with the bulk of the artichoke when it is eaten, after seasoning it to taste. Eat it with the regular meal; do not make a meal of just the artichoke or eat it between meals. This kind of artichoke carries sufficient insulin to be easily assimilated and yet it is not habit forming. See also Diet: Artichoke, Jerusalem."]

3274-1   F.50   10/9/43

Do use the Jerusalem artichoke at least once a week in the diet, but only cooked in its own juices—or mix the juices in which it is cooked with the bulk of the artichoke; that is, cook it in Patapar Paper® . . .

Q-2. Do I still have diabetes? What remedy?

A-2. A tendency towards same, as indicated from the amount of insulin to be given in the artichoke diet.

1523-7   F.30   4/5/39

Occasionally—once a week or oftener—the Jersulem artichoke should be a part of the diet. This will tend to correct those inclinations for the incoordination between the activities of the pancreas as related to the kidneys and bladder. These [small amounts of insulin] as we find, even in this form, will make for better corrections.

2472-1   M.67   3/26/41

A very positive reaction may be had that will relieve a great deal of this tension, if there will be eaten each day—with the meal—a Jerusalem artichoke; one day cooked, the next day raw; one not larger than about the size of a hen egg. Preferably keep these fresh, not by [their] being put in the refrigerator, but by keeping them in the ground; by necessity protecting them from animals—dogs, hogs, pigs, or the like; for these will scratch them up—as would cats also!

There is needed that booster, or the effect of insulin as may be derived from the artichoke, for the system.

416-17   M.36   11/5/42

Then *do not* take *any* carbonated drinks—of any nature. Coca-Cola®, or such, are well to clear kidneys, but make same with plain water.

5218-1   M.35   6/9/44

... Coca-Cola®, if it is taken without carbonated water, will be beneficial for the body in clarifying or purifying the kidneys and bladder disorder.

5097-1   F.28   5/10/44

Do take Coca-Cola® occasionally as a drink, for the activity of the kidneys, but do not take it with carbonated water. Buy or have the syrup prepared and add plain water to this. Take about one half ounce or one ounce of the syrup and add plain water. This is to be taken about every other day, with or without ice. This will aid in purifying the kidney activity and bladder and will be better for the body.

1148-1   F.40   4/15/36

Take internally the tea as would be made from watermelon seed, prepared as a tea; to reduce this activity through the kidneys' affectations, and to alleviate the quantities of water that accumulate through the abdominal area. The proportions would be half an ounce of the crushed seed to a quart of water, allowed to steep for twenty to thirty minutes. This may be kept and should be taken about a glassful each day.

647-3   F.Adult   7/18/35

We would also make a tea of watermelon seed. Put a tablespoonful of cracked or crushed seed in a pint of water and let steep as tea. Strain and make palatable. This will act upon the kidneys, with sufficient nitre to cause an activity most effective in this *particular* condition. Take a tablespoonful of the tea twice a day for two or three days; then leave off a day or two days, then take again.

1151-2   M.47   5/30/36

Take internally small quantities of watermelon seed tea. Take this about once or twice a week. Crack the kernel, about half an ounce to a pint of water, allowed to steep as tea. Drain off. Take two to three ounces or twice during a week; dependent upon activities of eliminations through kidneys, especially.

951-7   F.30   10/30/43

Q-1. How may pressure on bladder be alleviated?

A-1. Haven't we just been trying to tell you how that the gentle massage is to relieve these tensions? Because of conditions that will be left by the activities of the kidneys, these should be purified by [the] very small doses of watermelon seed tea after the birth [seven months pregnant]. Grind, crack or crush a teaspoonful of watermelon seed and pour a pint of boiling water over same, only using an enamel or crock container, covered. Let this stand for twenty minutes, strain, and then put in the refrigerator. Take this amount during two days. Then don't take any more for at least three to four days afterwards. Then repeat this.

Kundalini

5162-1   M.45   5/27/44

We would not make or take the exercises as to raise the kundaline forces in the body without leaving that kind of an experience that is of a nature to coordinate the activities of such exercises through the organs and centers of the body.

Not that these are not good, but it is not very good to give a child a razor, not very good to use a razor to sharpen pencils and try to shave with same. So it is in the activities of those who disregard the means to an end of bringing coordination to organs of the body.

4087-1 M.6 4/15/44

For as we find this entity has more than once been among those who were gifted with what is sometimes called second sight, or the superactivity of the third eye. Whenever there is the opening, then, of the lyden [Leydig] center and the kundaline forces from along the pineal, we find that there are visions of things to come, of things that are happening . . .

Do not use such for gratifying, satisfying, or even encouraging the entity to use such. But do train the entity in the use of divine purpose, divine desire.

2072-11 F.32 10/3/42

Q-5. Please give advice that would help in those times when there is the beginning of kundalini to rise or there is the circulation of kundalini through the body. What should be the next step?

A-5. Surround self with that consciousness of the Christ-Spirit; this by the affirmation of "Let self be surrounded with the Christ Consciousness, and the *direction* be through those activities in the body-force itself."

Do not seek the lower influences, but the Christ Consciousness.

5028-1 F.30 4/13/44

For the entity takes most every experience by intuition. Easily may the entity, by entering deep meditation, raise the kundaline forces in body to the third eye as to become a seeress; so that it may see the future and the past. But the law of such is that, unless these are used for constructive and never for selfish motives or purposes, they will bring more harm than good.

For there is the expression of creative energies that must be a part of the experience. Don't let the experiences of many turn thee aside, where and when it becomes necessary to raise such; and you will not be able to unless you live that you ask of and seek in others. Let that ye seek be that the law of the Lord God, which is manifested in the Christ, may be manifested through thee.

If the body will do just that, it may become a credit to its own environ and all of those who have the pleasure and privilege of knowing the entity. Abusing it, ye will become a byword, ye will become one not a credit to any. What will this entity do with these abilities? The choice may only be in self.

1861-4   M.33   1/13/40

Q-1. How may I bring into activity my pineal and pituitary glands, as well as the kundalini and other chakras, that I may attain to higher mental and spiritual powers? . . .

A-1. As indicated, first so *fill* the mind with the ideal that it may vibrate throughout the whole of the *mental* being!

. . . *Meditate* upon *"Thy will with me."* Feel same. Fill *all* the centers of the body . . . with that ideal; opening the centers by surrounding self first with that consciousness, *"Not my will but thine, 0 Lord, be done in and through me."*

Law, Universal

3063-1   M.56   6/26/43

The experiences in the earth plane have been quite varied. And while matters pertaining to soul and mind have always been of special interest to the entity, the application of some of those tenets has not been so well for the entity . . .

Think not that, because they may apparently apply only to the mediocre mind, or to those that are of or in a certain faith, that they do not apply to thee. But know that the truth is applicable in every experience of the entity's life, whether as a shoestring vendor or a seller of such, or a director of some great financial institution, or even a leader or ruler over many peoples.

For, the same tenet that applies in one [case] is true in the other. For he that would declare, "If I were so and so, how charitable I would be," or "If I were in this or that position what an effort I would make to magnify this or that," only attempts—in saying such—to give others a high opinion of self, and yet is not fooling even himself or anyone else! For if you give not when you have not even sufficient, though you were blessed with many millions, very possibly you would be much more stingy than you are now—and much harder to get along with—though you declare you wouldn't be! . . .

This is the first lesson ye should learn: There is so much good in the worst of us, and so much bad in the best of us, it doesn't behoove any of us to speak evil of the rest of us. This is a universal law, and until one begins to make application of same, one may not go very far in spiritual or soul development.

5259-1 F.46 6/8/44

The entity was then in the name of Esten, and of those groups who eventually settled in, or for a time in, portions of what is now Wisconsin. Thus we find from its activities and its study with the medicine men of that particular area and period, places look familiar, faces appear familiar to the entity. Not that those who are not familiar are to be forgotten. For nothing happens by chance. There may be opportunities for thee, not only to help others, but to be helped by others.

"For all that ye may ever keep is just what you give away, and that you give away is advice, counsel, manner of life you live yourself." The manner in which you treat your fellow man, your patience, your brotherly love, your kindness, your gentleness. That you give away, that is all that ye may possess in those other realms of consciousness.

And then when an entity attains to the realm of the physical consciousness, such as these may bear fruit in thy life, in thy associations with others.

2448-2 F.25 5/31/41

For, know that what is *truly* thine *cannot* be taken away from thee; nor is any real character ever lost.

Remember these—not merely as axioms, but in analyzing the happenings through the sojourns in the earth: Be mindful of the manner of seed ye sow. For, what ye sow ye also reap. With what measures ye mete, it is measured to thee again. If ye would have love, be lovely—to all. For, in the manner ye mete and ye act toward others, ye are measuring and meting to thy Maker.

Remember, then, that those activities are thy pass-key to the throne of grace. Always, in thy material activities with others, keep God's rain check . . .

Oft has the entity found that so many disappointments appear in others. Know that first rule, a *law* that is eternal: *The seed sown must one day be reaped. Ye disappointed others. Today from thine own disappointments ye may learn patience, the most beautiful of all virtues and the least understood!*

Remember, it is one of the phases or dimensions through which thy soul may catch the greatest and the more beautiful glimpse of the Creator.

For, as He came unto His own and His own received Him not, in patience He brought that awareness [to them]of what they had lost in their lack of appreciation of the opportunities given.

So in thy dealings with others, with thy problems with others, in thy daily associations, in thy home, in thy activities—remember to evaluate *every* phase of an experience and to stress the beautiful, minimize the faults. For, this is sowing the seed of beauty in the spirit of truth; and that, too, will blossom in thy life and in thy dealings with others.

See the funny side—don't be too serious. Remember, He even made the joke as He walked to the garden to be betrayed. Remember, He looked with love upon His disciple that denied Him, even as He stood alone . . .

Let not thy heart be troubled; ye believe in God, believe also in Him—who is able to quicken the life as it flows through thy body, thy mind, thy soul, to a full regeneration in the material world, then hope in the mental, then truth in the spiritual. For He *is* truth, and the light, the way; that each soul may find the way from the darkness back to God—even as He.

3098-2   F.54   1/21/44

For, according to the true law of spirit, like begets like. Thus as harmony and beauty and grace reign within the consciousness of an entity, it gives that to others—and others wonder what moved them to feel different, when no one spoke, no one even appeared to be anxious. This is the manner in which the spirit of truth operates among the children of men . . .

What would one describe, then, as the essence of a sunset, the essence of the beauty of a rose, the essence of friendship, the essence of love? These are indicated in what was given to be part of the offering upon the altar in the holy of holies when there were certain combinations given that were to be offered as the sacrifice, as a sweet odor unto the Lord.

Then, what is that sweet odor in peoples' lives? It is what may be indicated as the essence of love, hope, beauty. These are those things in which people often excel and others pay little attention, yet are influenced by them and it is not known why.

Individuals who live such lives, then, and with all the emotions of nature and of the material world, are indeed those who may be called the children of the Holy One.

3335-1   M.72   11/3/43

Hence, study in self to show self approved unto thy God. What is thy God? Who is thy God? Who is His messenger to thee? What have His messages meant to thee, as to the manner in which ye are to treat thy fellow man? For, as ye do unto others ye do unto thy Maker.

Thus, this attitude reflects itself in thy physical conditions—and don't think it doesn't! It does in every soul-entity . . .

Meet the problems of the day in the light of thy desires as thy Father-God would meet thee with thy own shortcomings with thyself. Meet these [problems] in thy relationships to others. No, not idealistic. Make thy relationship to God practical in thy relationship to thy fellow man.

961-1   M.55   7/25/35

For that creative force, that spirit that *prompts* the activities in a material world, arises within the heart, the soul of each individual in meting out to its fellow man.

For one may not hate his brother and love his God; one may not worship his God and hold malice or envy against his brother. For these are of *One*, and the Law of One must carry through.

As ye sow in spirit, so may the mind build that ye reap in materiality. As ye sow in materiality, so may that mind build to make for dissension or a paralleling of an activity in the spiritual import. They are interchangeable.

2970-1   F.48   4/22/43

Know that thy body, thy mind, thy soul, is a manifestation of God in the earth—as is every other soul; and that thy body is indeed the temple of the living God.

All the good, then, all the God, then, that ye may know, is manifested in and through thyself—and not what somebody else thinks, not what somebody else does! For, that is a nice way of the devil in his workshop—"Do because somebody else does! Think of that because somebody else does!"

The Lord thy God is *One*—as thou art one . . .

For, we are—physically—that we have digested for the body.

We are mentally that which we have thought, but it hasn't added one whit to the physical, has it?

We are spiritually that we have digested in our mental beings.

And if He walk with thee, ye will never be alone!

3175-1　F.42　8/25/43

Entertain Him then oft in thy mind, in thy activity. For, the applications of His tenets are simple; yet in the world of reality oft become as mountains:

Patience, love, kindness, gentleness, long-suffering, brotherly love. There is no law against any of these. For they are the law of consistency in the search for peace. For they of themselves bring peace, and they are what He gave into the world with the offering of Himself to be the mediator between man and God.

2620-2　F.41　11/24/41

It is true for the entity, and for most individual souls manifesting in the earth, that nothing, no meeting comes by chance. These are a design or pattern. These patterns, however, are laid out by the individual entity. For, there are laws. For law is love, love is law. And He hath not willed that any soul should perish, but hath with each temptation, each trial, prepared a way of escape . . .

It is true, then, that there are latent and manifested urges, manifested abilities, manifested virtues, manifested faults, in the experience of each entity. These faults, these virtues may be pointed out, yet the usage, the application of same is of free will—that which is the universal gift to the souls of the children of men; that each entity may know itself to be itself and yet one with the universal cause.

Thus the pattern, the book of life is written by the entity in its use of truth, knowledge, wisdom, in its dealings with its fellow man through the material sojourns. Also during the interims between such sojourns, there are consciousnesses, or awarenesses. For, the soul is eternal, it lives on, has a consciousness in the awareness of that which has been builded.

987-4   F.49   11/2/37

. . . to bring hope, to bring cheer, to bring joy, yea to bring a smile again to those whose face and heart are bathed in tears and in woe, is but making that divine love *shine—shine—in* thy own soul! Then *smile*, be joyous, be glad! For the day of the Lord is at hand.

Memory

987-2   F.47   8/9/35

Q-4. How can I improve memory and concentration?

A-4. Study well that which has been given through these sources on meditation. Through meditation may the greater help be gained.

4083-1   M.55   4/12/44

Q-2. Why has [my] memory seemed poor—when [I] really [have] a very good memory—and [I seem] unable to develop original ideas?

A-2. Have ye used thy memory as a creative thing? Only that which is creative grows. Thy memory, remember, is as the Way has given: "If ye apply thyself, I will bring to thy remembrance all things since the foundation of the world." What is lacking? It is thine own coordinating of thy mind, thy body, thy soul-purpose to the first cause, the first principle, love. For God so loved the world that He gave His own, His own Son that ye, as an individual, might have access to the Father.

69-2   F.48   10/22/29

Q-5. Why is it difficult for me to remember?

A-5. It isn't difficult! It's rather trained in self *to forget!* See the differentiation between forgetting and remembering is—*memory*—is the exercising of the inner self as related to thought. To acknowledge that the memory is poor, is to say you don't think much! The forgetting is to say that the thought becomes self-centered, for memory is thought—even as thought is memory, brought to the forefront by the association of ideas.

189-3   F.42   4/22/37

Q-1. What can the entity do to sharpen her memory of names, directions, people?

A-1. . . . associate same with places, conditions, circumstances . . .

So in sharpening the memory, the associations of same with places, dates, times, make for the drawing as it were of the whole picture.

3343-1   M.36   11/1/43

Q-8. Why do I find it comparatively easy to hold the details of some subject in mind while I am teaching it, and then after a lapse of but a few months have such a vague recollection of the details which were once so familiar?

A-8. The abilities to live today! And you possess it, but it is the way to live.

1711-2   F.59   3/4/40

Q-1. What should be done for loss of memory?

A-1. The memory is not lost. There isn't such a thing as loss of memory—there is only the need for making the individual aware of that to be brought to material activity.

With the stimulations to the centers between the sensory forces of the body—that is, the sensory nerve system between the shoulders and to the head and neck—by the massages . . . it will aid in making the sympathetic system and the cerebrospinal system better coordinant—or capable of better memory, better ability to recall that desired to remember . . .

1965-2   M.58   5/2/41

Q-5. What will help the memory?

A-5. [The treatment indicated], with the mental attitudes. Remember, it requires the concerted activity of body, mind and purpose—or spirit, to remember that you mustn't get mad, that you mustn't hold grudges, that you mustn't hold animosities, that you mustn't allow self to get riled. Thus with such exercising of the mind, with a bettered body, there is a better memory.

5022-1   M.9   4/10/44

Q-1. Are we too drastic with him or are we not sufficiently drastic in our disciplinary methods?

A-1. . . . There are pressures that cause animosities, hates, rebellion in the body, because of the manner in which there are reflexes to the brain. Not that there isn't the brain, but there are such in-coordinations in regard to suggestions as to cause the body to be rebellious and to forget.

Mostly when individuals forget it is because something within themselves, all their inner consciousness, has rebelled—and they prepare to forget.

2598-1   F.64   10/6/41

. . . the reflexes to the reactions in the sensory forces are gradually being impaired, so that the lapse of memory is gradually coming about, or the inability to retain a visualized reflection . . .

1581-2   M.12   3/26/39

Q-3. Will you give me suggestions as to how to improve my work in school, and my memory?

A-3. Let that be rather as this: That which ye would attain in the studies as to that which is a text, a thesis or a theory—mull same, as it were, in thy mind, in thy consciousness. Then lay it aside and meditate rather upon its application . . . Do this especially just before ye would rest . . . or in sleep. And ye will find thy memory, thy ability to analyze, thy ability to maintain and retain greater principles, will be thy experience.

For remember that the principle is throughout physical, mental and spiritual alike . . . Hence in the physical application ye pass to, through the physical eye, or through the ear, or through the sense of consciousness, that as of a physical law, or as a physical thesis, as a physical theory. This ye pass for judgment to thy mental consciousness, and in the laying aside of thy physical consciousness the spiritual attributes record same as it were upon thy real self . . .

Q-6. I have had flashes of past lives—a Norseman, a Spaniard about the time of Ponce de Leon, one of being on Columbus' ship, a Roman soldier, an American Indian. Are these impressions from past incarnations? Please explain.

A-6. As just indicated, the body is body, mind, soul. *Heed* these impressions. These are flashes at times of material experiences that have been an influence—just as has been indicated as to how ye may develop to apply thy mind in thy studies, or in any endeavor that ye undertake—these become a part of the real self.

These are, in instances, material experiences as sojourns. For as has been indicated, not all of the dwellings [incarnations] in the earth have been given [in the life reading].

For, as the illustrations: Ye experienced much of the Indian experience through the Salem sojourn—that is, by associations.

The Ponce de Leon and the Spanish—these ye will find, as ye interpret deeper, are one.

And the flashes as from the Norseman—a real experience.

Menopause

2792-2   F.43   11/20/42

Q-2. Would one sick and nauseous menstrual period indicate anything?

A-2. This only indicates that there is the readjusting of the activities of the organs and their functionings.

Q-3. Has menopause any direct bearing upon my condition?

A-3. The weakness is a part of the attempt of the system to adjust itself under those changes coming about . . .

Q-7. Approximately how long will it take for the menopause?

A-7. This depends upon the response of the body. It usually requires at least twelve months—or nine months.

313-17   F.52   1/18/39

We would continue occasionally with the douches; especially just before and after the periods; using the Atomidine® in same—about a teaspoonful to the quart of water. Have the douche at least body-temperature . . .

Q-4. Why is [the] pulse so rapid at times?

A-4. As just indicated, this is the effect of the disturbance through the upper hepatic circulation; which causes a quick return or flow as it were of the circulatory forces from the heart to the liver; quickening the pulse as well as the nerve tension in the periods that are preceding the menopause.

Q-5. Is this why the menstrual period is irregular?

A-5. This is a portion of the disturbance.

Q-6. What is [the] trouble in left ovary?

A-6. The inclination for the poisons, or a sympathetic effect from the poisons from the system.

Hence, as indicated, the necessity of cleansing first the alimentary canal and stimulating more normalcy in the hepatic circulation, as well as using the douches to purify the conditions through the pelvic organs and their activities. This should aid a great deal.

Of course, the use of the electrically driven vibrator over the body of evenings would be especially helpful in equalizing and causing a better circulatory force; especially using the sponge applicator across the abdomen and pelvis, and even across the lower portion of the lumbar area.

538-29   F.50   9/24/30

Those conditions, as we find, [that] are producing distresses in the present have to do with the organs of the pelvis, as with those of the eliminating system, and unless there are precautions taken to prevent those accumulations there must be plethora or tumor, or such natures [that] are indicated in such conditions. But if drainages are set up in the system through the stimulation of the centers from which eliminations in the pelvic regions take place, as well as through the alimentary canal—(without causing prolapsus of any nature in the colon, as to produce irritation in the region of the organs of the pelvis, through which such inflammation passes)—we will find the conditions would be improved.

These, we find, would be through the continued stimulation of the muscular forces through manipulation in the lumbar, sacral, and the general system—with the use of those laxatives, not so much of cathartics—and with . . . stimuli through the vagina [with] the violet ray® . . .

The violet ray® . . . with the vagina applicator—we would take at least twice each week—Tuesday and Thursday.

Q-2. How long at a time should this be used?

A-2. Three to five minutes. Set up drainages with the manipulations, see? When pains become severe in the bearing down pains, then we would use the hot packs—a combination of mutton tallow, camphor, turpentine—and this on flannel—with salt, hot salt, as the heat, see?

Q-3. Should this be applied across [the] back?

A-3. Where the pain [is]—across the back.

1100-28   F.44   4/7/40

Then, there needs be only the precautions as to plenty of exercise in the open each day; walking as the preferable character of exercise, as well as the specific exercise morning and evening to aid in keeping the body muscular forces and the body figure in proper order and shape.

The activities as related to diet—keep well rounded as to food values.

Occasionally—once in two weeks or the like—have a general osteopathic adjustment as a *relaxing* treatment; not as a stimulating but as a relaxing of the general nerve and muscular tension that naturally comes with such changes as are active in the system in the present.

As to activities in crowds or the like—do not get in crowds where there is the rush, the push or the like; but being in pleasant company and several in crowds, very good for the body.

These as we find are the general conditions; for it is the period of change in the general activities of eliminations and glandular forces of the body itself.

Do that . . .

Q-1. Is this the cause for the cessation of the menses?

A-1. As has been indicated.

Q-2. What causes discomfort around heart area?

A-1. As just indicated, the general change in the pressures throughout the system. Hence the character or type of manipulations that would be given as a *relaxing*, and not as a stimulating activity to the whole general body, see?

Q-3. Please give some further advice which will be helpful to me.

A-3. Do *these*, as we find. Of course, keep the mental attitudes towards all helpful influences, not only in a general manner but make some rather specific activity daily, as it were, towards some helpfulness to some individual.

Menstruation

[As a means of relief from severe pain in dysmenorrhea, the applications of salt packs and tincture of Laudanum and Aconite have been frequently recommended. Packs of this sort are made by quilting heavy or coarse salt into a pad and then heating the pack in an oven.]

578-4   F.22   9/30/35

The salt packs (heavy salt, you see, heated) on the abdomen,

lower portion of the abdomen and over the edge of the pubic bones
. . . and on the spine across the lower lumbar and the sacral area.

2803-4   F.24   7/26/43

In the periods when there is great pain, paint the pubic center—
using a small brush—with a combination of four parts tincture of
Laudanum to one part Aconite. Then apply a heavy pack of salt, heated, in a sack, you see. This will relieve the contraction that is caused
in the tubes and the pain through the vagina and the ovum's activity.

It will be necessary to obtain [the solution] from a doctor, or by
a doctor's prescription . . .

578-4   F.22   9/30/35

*Q-2. Please explain fully the reason for cramps at menstrua-
tion.*

A-2. Contraction of the uterus. And this is caused by the muscular forces that supply nourishment to the ovarian channels and
the Eustachian valve or the Fallopian tubes. Hence [have] those
[osteopathic] relaxations and the general [body-building] conditions as indicated that would be the necessary applications for
correction.

2602-2   F.39   6/21/42

Q-8. Why are the headaches at the time of my monthly period?

A-8. These are part of the clogging that is a part of the general
eliminating system. As indicated, see, there are channels or outlets
for the eliminating of poisons; that is, used energies, where there is
the effect of the activity of the circulation upon foreign forces taken
in breath, taken in the dust, taken in particles of food or those activities that come from such as these—from odors or the like. These all,
by the segregating of same in the system, produce forces necessary
to be eliminated. We eliminate principally through the activity of the
lungs, of course, and the perspiratory system, the alimentary canal,
and the kidneys. Then, as in the case of women—as here—we find
that such periods of the menstrual flow cause congestion in certain
areas until the flow is begun, or until there is the beginning of the
let-up of same. This, then, of course, clogs some portions of the
system. The headaches are the signs or warnings that eliminations
are not being properly cared for. Most of this, in this body, comes

from the alimentary canal, and from those conditions that exist in portions of the colon itself—as to produce a pressure upon those centers affected from such periods. Hence the suggestion for the osteopathic corrections, which aid but which do not eliminate all of those conditions which are as accumulations through portions of the colon. Consequently, the colonic irrigations are necessary occasionally, as well as the general hydrotherapy and massage.

Do these things, as we have indicated. Keep the mental attitude of a useful, purposeful, directed life; keeping the Creative Forces as the ideals and principles—or in that direction of using the abilities to be helpful to others.

Migraine Headaches

3400-2   M.39   1/23/44

Here we find some complications—the effects of or the beginning of migraine headaches. Most of these, as in this case, begin from congestions in the colon. These [congestions] cause toxic conditions to make pressures on the sympathetic nerve centers and on the cerebrospinal system. And these pressures cause the violent headaches, and almost irrational activities at times.

These, as we find, should respond to colonic irrigations. But first, we would x-ray the colon, and we will find areas in the ascending colon and a portion of the transverse colon where there are fecal forces that are as cakes.

There will be required several full colonic irrigations, using salt and soda as purifiers for the colon; and we will find that these conditions will be released.

The first cleansing solution should have two level teaspoonsful of salt and one level teaspoonful of soda to the gallon of water, body temperature. Also in the rinse water, body temperature, have at least two tablespoonsful of Glyco-Thymoline® to the quart and a half of water.

Also we would use the Radio-active Appliance each day for at least an hour, letting this be the period for meditation and study for the analyzing of self. Keep the attachment plates very clean, polishing them with the emery paper each time before attaching to the ankle and the wrist, and polishing them each time when taking them off.

Do have the osteopathic adjustments to relax the areas in the 1st, 2nd and 3rd cervical, in the 6th dorsal, and in the lumbar axis.

Do these and we should bring help for this body . . .

Q-1. Is any of this trouble due to allergy?

A-1. Some of it is due to allergy, but what is allergy? These are the effects of the imagination upon any influences that may react upon the olfactory or the sympathetic nerves. If we will cleanse the system, as we find, we should bring better conditions.

Do the things indicated here.

Q-2. What mental factor is responsible for the disturbance in the subject's head?

A-2. Those pressures, as indicated, between sympathetic and ce- rebrospinal system, and these arise from the condition in the colon. X-ray it [the colon] and you'll find it.

3400-1   M.39   12/9/43

Then, in the life purpose—be serious with self. Are you living the purposeful life that you would have others to see? This is not a ques- tioning of you. The question is in self! For each soul gives account for the deeds done in the body . . . To whom do they account? The divine within their own selves!

And then do you wonder that you have aches and pains, troubles and worries? You are meeting your own self.

Thy labors are well. Keep them in that way of doing that you would have others do to you. Give your office something to be proud of, by the manner in which ye treat those serviced from there.

Moles, Warts and Cysts

573-1   F.Adult   6/6/34

Q-3. What treatment would remove the mole on my chest, or is this advisable?

A-3 . . . The massage with the Castor Oil twice each day; not rubbing hard, but *gentle* massage around and over the place. And it will be removed.

678-2   F.49   10/16/34

Q-1. Should moles on the back be removed? If so, by whom and what method?

A-1. As we find, these are not to be disturbed to the extent of any material or outside influence. The massaging . . . with just the Castor Oil will prevent growth, and—if persistent with [massaging] (not bruising same)—will remove same entirely.

487-22   M.20   4/15/38

Q-1. What causes the warts on the hand and how may they be removed?

A-1. This . . . happens to most every individual in those periods of the change that comes about for glandular reaction; and it is the effect of the localizing of centers that attempt to *grow*—as they do!

As we find, they may be removed by touching same with a 20% solution of Hydrochloric Acid. But do not pick at them as the discoloration takes place, and as they begin to deteriorate! Rather let them wear off than pick at them, see? for such [picking] would allow too great a chance for infection by the irritating, and cause disturbance; otherwise they will disappear. In touching them with the Acid it is preferable to use either a glass pestle (that is, a small round piece of glass) or a broomstraw.

3121-1   M.39   7/31/43

As we find, these we would do in the present: First, we would give [the suggestion] that there be prepared an ointment from the leaves of young Plantain, at this particular season of the year [July], growing in the vicinity where this body lives [Ky.]. Yes, it is this herb that you desire oft to get rid of, in the yard, garden or walk. But do not use the seed, so much, in the ointment. Gather the tender leaves, about the quantity that may be crammed, not too tightly, into a pint [measuring] cup. Then put this into a quart enamel container (with an enamel or glass top) and add one pint of sweet cream, poured off the top of milk. Cook this until it is rather thick. Do not allow to burn. Then use it as an ointment over the areas where these protuberances gather at times—for they do vary. They become as warts or moles, that become infected and sore and run. This ointment will tend to dry same.

288-51   F.36   10/15/41

Q-1. What caused, and may anything be done to eliminate the red spot on my nose?

A-1. This is from a broken cell. Do not irritate [it] too much, or this may turn to a mole or wart—which would be a disfiguration to the body.

We would keep a little camphor, or camphor ice on same of evenings.

1523-5   F.29   5/23/38

Q-9. What causes the lump on the left eyelid?

A-9. An accumulation from broken cellular tissue. This as we find will disappear as there are the corrections for the flow of circulation through the whole of these areas [osteopathy] . . .

1424-4   M.50   9/18/37

Q-5. What causes the little place on his eyelid, and what will remove it?

A-5. Cyst as from a breaking of cellular forces. Massage with the pure Castor Oil.

Motherhood

5090-1   F.40   5/16/44

When there are those preparations for such, do this to insure conception, if this is desired at a special period (and those periods just before the menstrual period are the preferable for conception [for this body]): Put into a hot basin of water a sweet gum ball about the size of a small agate, or say the end of the thumb, in hot boiling water. Sit over this for some ten minutes, and you needn't fear, there will be conception.

457-8   F.34   4/23/42

Q-19. Is there a definite number of days before the period within which it [conception] must occur?

A-19. If there is the study of how conception takes place, it will be understood that this takes place only when there is the flow from the ovary of the mother and there is the spermatozoa of the male present.

Whether it's [a matter of] days or hours or the minute! It may be a day, it may be an hour, it may be ten minutes, it may be two days. But this depends upon *when* there is the flow—not of the menstrual period but from the ovary.

2977-2   F.37   3/31/44

Q-1. May I still hope to be able to have a child, or should I give up the idea entirely?

A-1. Let this rest rather with the ideals and purposes for same, making of self a better channel; physically, as well as mentally and spiritually. This will renew and keep the hope for the body.

Too oft individuals are too prone to look upon conception or childbirth as purely a physical condition. Rather should it be considered as it has been from the beginning, that life—sources of life—is from the one source . . .

Remember how Hannah prepared herself, and as to how others—as Mary—prepared themselves. There are many [such cases] recorded, and there are many others of which nothing is heard, and yet there was the long preparation. For God is to each entity, individual. He must become [to each] Father-God. For as the Master indicates, "Our Father." He has become this to those who seek to be a channel through which God may bring life for a purpose.

Then make thyself a channel, physically, mentally, spiritually. To be sure, law applied. For in the beginning of man, in his becoming a living soul in the earth, laws were established and these take hold. But lose not sight of the law of grace, the law of mercy, the law of patience as well. For each has its place, especially when individual entities consider and seek, desire, that they be channels through which life, God, may manifest.

2803-6   F.24   12/15/43

Q-7. What mental attitude should I keep always before me during the coming months [of pregnancy]?

A-7. Depends upon what character of individual entity is desired. More beauty, music—if that is desired to be a part of the entity; art, and the like. Or is it to be purely mechanical? If purely mechanical, then think about mechanics—work with those things. And don't think that they won't have their effect, as the impressions give that opportunity.

Here is something that each and every mother should know. The manner in which the attitude is kept has much to do with the character of the soul that would choose to enter through those channels [of birth] at the particular period.

This has been indicated as the attitude, "If ye love me and keep my commandments, I will love you—as ye do unto others, ye do unto me." Does this seem strange, or isn't it consistent with God's plan of creation? That attitude held, then, during these periods, presents the opportunity for the type of character of soul seeking expression.

Q-8. Would my working outside the home now be injurious to the child?

A-8. This is the formative period. Hence it depends upon what character of individual you hope to have! One that will be a work-a-day, material-minded one looking for the making of money, the making of position, the making of this or that? Not that this would necessarily be the outward attitude, but [it would be] the real innate attitude deep within the soul of the entity attracted.

457-9   F.34   5/21/42

Q-40. Does intercourse while carrying child interfere with the physical or spiritual development of the child?

A-40. After three months, yes.

457-14   F.36   5/15/44

Q-2. Will giving birth always be easy for me or can this vary with each child?

A-2. Has been with this body due to the care taken before child-birth. If mothers would only know that a good gynecologist of the osteopathic school would save more mothers from hard labor! as it has with this [mother]; though to be sure, the mental attitude as well as the physical activities cause variations at each birth.

951-7   F.30   10/30/43

Q-4. Where and by whom should the baby be delivered?

A-4. Better that it be by a specialist from the osteopathic profession.

1208-2   M.5   days   6/26/36

Q-3. Any special food to be avoided by the mother?

A-3. As has been indicated, *fats* are the most detrimental to *all* infants in this developing [and nursing]stage. And *anger!* Keep [the mother] from *anger!*

457-14   F.36   5/15/44

Q-1. Is there an average period of time necessary between birth of one and conception of another?

A-1. Two years at least.

457-12   F.35   5/25/43

Q-13. Is there any way to keep down the size of the baby without causing any detrimental effects on either mother or child?

A-13. Who knows how to create the body better, the Creator or the man?

Music

2780-3   M.10   12/11/43

Q-8. Should he study a musical instrument; if so, which instrument would be preferable?

A-8. Music should be a part of each soul's development. There's not a great deal of music in this entity . . . The piano would be well, or the banjo, for this entity.

3053-3   F.11   11/11/43

Q-6. What course of studies should I pursue in secondary and higher education?

A-6. Music! History of, the activity of, all of those various forms. If you learn music, you'll learn history. If you learn music, you'll learn mathematics. If you learn music, you'll learn most all there is to learn—unless it's something bad.

5265-1   F.58   5/29/44

Q-7. Are music, poetry, art, just worldly and illusory?

A-7. Know [that] they are of the realms of creative energies which are of the Maker . . . Embrace Him, while ye may, in music, in art . . . do keep the music of the spheres, the light of the stars, the softness of the moonlight upon the water as upon the trees. For nature in its song, as the birds, as the bees make music to their Creator, contributed to man.

3386-1   F.38   12/3/43

Then, sing a lot about the work—in everything the body does.

Hum, sing—to self; not to be heard by others, but to be heard by self.

5401-1   F.43   8/24/44
For music is of the soul, and one may become mind and soul-sick for music, or soul and mind-sick from certain kinds of music.

1406-1   F.14   7/13/37
Hence as the attuning of music . . . arouses emotions in the body to an unusual degree, well that there be choices made as to what the emotions are that are aroused by the character of music . . . For there is a way that seemeth right to a man, but the end thereof taketh hold upon hell. As to the experiences then that arise from [music], choose that which is constructive in the experience, and know it must partake of that which brings peace to the soul and not gratifying of body or of an emotion of the body alone.

5253-1   M.24   6/2/44
Remember . . . music is the one element which may span the distance between the sublime and the ridiculous. That which may arouse violent passion, which may soothe the beast of passion, as that which may make for thoughts of home, of heaven, of loved ones, the laugh of a baby, the tears of a beautiful woman, of depicting these in manners in which they would become unusual and give the opportunity for the entity not only to give out, but to find in helping others, in bringing more and more of the thoughts of good, thoughts of home, thoughts of heaven, thoughts of mother, thoughts of those things which bring at times sadness, at times joy, but always helpful influences into the experiences of individuals. For as ye pour out self, in a way to be of help to others, ye are the greater help to thyself.

3659-1   F.10   2/15/44
Do learn music. It is part of the beauty of the spirit. For remember, music alone may span that space between the finite and the infinite. In the harmony of sound, the harmony of color, even the harmony of motion itself, its beauty is all akin to that expression of the soul-self in the harmony of the mind, if used properly in relationship to body. Not that music is to be made the greater portion of thy life, but let much of thy life be controlled by the same harmony

that is in the best music . . .

Nails

5104-1   M.38   5/12/44

. . . for the condition of toes and nails, use baking soda moistened with Castor Oil. Put this under the points or edges where ingrown toenails give disturbance. This may make it sore for one time, but rub off with Spirits of Camphor. These may make for roughening, but it will rid the body of those tendencies of ingrown toenails.

5068-1   M.21   4/24/44

Q-2. [What can be done about] the infected toenails?

A-2. These applications suggested will be the more helpful, but as an ointment here we would use Carbolated Vaseline and then the Cuticura Ointment® over same.

5192-1   M.12   6/9/44

Q-3. What causes the deep ridges in thumbnail and what treatments . . . ?

A-3. These are [results of] the activities of the glandular force, and the addition of those foods which carry large quantities of calcium will make for bettered conditions . . . Take often chicken neck, chew it. Cook this well, the feet and those portions of the fowl, and we will find it will add calcium to the body. Also eat bones of fish, as in canned fish. Also parsnips and oyster plant; all of these, of course, in their regular season. Wild game of any kind, but chew the bones of same.

2518-1   M.29   6/26/41

Also a lack of calcium is indicated in the body, by the very color or nature of the toenails and fingernails, and even [by] the condition which exists at times in the hair on various portions of the body . . .

Take small quantities internally each day of calcium, in the form of *Calcios*™; at least for periods of five days at a time, leaving off a few days and then taking again, and so on. Take just the quantity as would be spread on a cracker, whole wheat cracker preferably.

2448-1   F.24   2/8/41

Q-9. What can I do to keep my fingernails from splitting?

A-9. Add the vitamins necessary so that the glandular forces, and especially the thyroid, are improved. Take [also] a few doses or drops of Atomidine® occasionally; say once a month, just before the [menstrual] period, take one drop of Atomidine® in half a glass of water before the morning meal, for three to five days. Also massage the fingernails with Atomidine®. It may stain for a bit at first; but get the system going better and we will find this will be different.

475-1   F.16   1/2/34

Q-2. What should be done to correct the nail-biting habit?

A-2 . . . this is the effect of nervousness—from the gnawing that has been indicated that has been existent for some time in the system . . . And with these corrections, and with the tendency for the body to watch or be careful with self, this [habit] may be eliminated . . . For, if we take away the cause the habit is more easily changed. For, we correct habits by forming others! That's everybody!

2988-1   F.37   5/6/43

Once each week . . . us the Atomidine® as a massage for the soles of feet and as a dressing for the [ingrown] toenails . . . Lift up the nail and put small parts of cotton saturated with Atomidine® under the edge of the toenail . . . Use this at least once each week.

Names

457-10   F.34   5/21/42

Q-12. What is the meaning of names? I have been told that Martha should be my real name. Is there a reason why?

A-12. This comes rather as to the minds and purposes of those who give names to their offspring.

Names, to be sure, have their meaning, but as given by the poet, a rose by any other name would be just as beautiful or just as sweet. So may such be said of [names].

Yet, as given by Him, names have their meaning, and these depend upon the purposes when such are bestowed upon an individual entity entering the earth's plane.

Have ye not understood how that in various experiences individuals, as their purposes or attitudes or desires were indicated, had their names henceforth called a complete or full name, meaning or indicating the purpose to which the individual entity or soul had been called? So, all of these have their part. They are not *all*, as indicated. For, *all* is one. One is all, but each individual is impressed by the various phases of man's consciousness in materiality. [Names], as we find, have varying degrees of effect upon the consciousness or the awareness of individuals. For, "My Spirit beareth witness with thy spirit" is complete in itself . . .

Q-15. When would it be best to choose a name for the child?

A-15. When ye have determined as to the purpose to which ye hope, and which ye will, which ye are willing to dedicate [the child].

1877-2   F.45   4/18/40

Q-5. What is the symbolic meaning of the name Elcor?

A-5. As may be found in scripture itself—one who *joined* doubt and faith!

137-13   M.26   1/30/25

[The name] Edwin, meaning that of a peacefulness, defender of peacefulness, carrying both the condition and implied forces from same. David, rather that of the gift from the higher forces, or a Son of the Father. One, especially, endowed with gifts from the higher forces.

1523-6   F.29   10/7/38

Q-9. Should [1650] and [1523] change their names? If so, what names would be suggested?

A-9. They each are significant of that they have to meet in each other. *Hold* that thou hast!

5023-2   M.45   7/18/44

The body would do well to change its name [with those suggestions given in this reading] from Carl to Michael . . . and then start over again and do more lecturing and living up to that.

808-19   F.35   6/15/43

Thus as indicated in the name It-El-Sut: El indicates "the child of the divine," or El meaning God, as would be the interpretation today. "It" indicates the woman, and "Sut" the name. A woman God-child, then.

2015-3   F.15   days   10/12/39

Before that we find the entity was in the Egyptian land, among the daughters of the Priest [Ra Ta] . . . the entity became as one set apart, as one worshipped—because of being the offspring of the Priest's companion in exile . . . in the name Os-Is-El, or "God manifest in person."

Nature

3374-1   F.35   11/23/43

Thou has read oft that as the tree falls, so will it lie. Hast thou interpreted what this means, not alone in material conception but in spirit? Study same—it will mean something different, even in the light of this . . .

One may never tell a rose to be beautiful nor a violet to give off its fragrance, nor yet a sunset or the storm or the wind to add their voice to the songs of nature. Yet music and nature, and beauty of all kinds, appeal much to this entity. Have you wondered why? Have you used or abused such? These you must answer within self, as you may in viewing the words of truth, the whiteness of the lily and the voice of Him—who was attempting to give the lesson that our whole trust is in God and not in the material things of the earth.

Ever be a worker, as the bee, yes—but in that way in which it is ever a contribution to making thy portion of the earth a more beautiful place for men to live in.

For the smile of a baby, the fragrance of the rose, is but a reflection of God's care for man. Would he but learn the lesson of these little things! For it is the foolishness of man that is the wisdom of God, and the wisdom of man that is the foolishness of his Maker . . .

. . . beauty, love, music, nature, are those things that answer the most to the entity. The beauty of friendship, the beauty of associations, the beauty of the landscape, the beauty of the storm, and yet a fear creeps in when there is a closing in about the entity . . . from the lack of the full trust in Him.

The experiences in the earth are indicated not merely as periods of sojourn but as periods in which the soul has grown or been warped by what men would call circumstance or environ. Yet the will of a soul attuned to God may change the circumstance or the environment, as indicated in the lily; in fact, all the forces even in nature itself. For all the beauty is of God, all the love is of God. All of those that abide in same, then, are manifestations of His love. These nourish, these cherish in all of thy dealings with thy fellow men . . .

The entity should keep close to all of those things that have to do with outdoor activities, for it is the best way to keep yourself young—to stay close to nature, close to those activities in every form of exercise that breathes in the deep ozone and the beauty of nature. For you may breathe it into thine own soul, as you would a sunset or a morning sun rising. And see that sometimes—it's as pretty as the sunset!

Keep these in thy activities, and it will make for the greater experiences in thy life . . .

The entity was among those children who gathered first that day when He stood beside the sea and later spoke from Peter's boat. The entity was then a girl in the early teens who heard those words of the Master. When it allows itself in the present, these words can bring into the experience the greater realization of the beauties of water, the loveliness of clouds in the sky, of the storm, the snow, the sleet, the hail. All of these speak to the entity of the closeness, the loveliness of the Master's promises to the children of men.

Keep ever faithful to that, of the beauty that is wrought even from the contemplation . . .

Look to Him, and let thy prayer oft be—live it—be it:

Lord, here am I! Use Thou me in the way Thou seest I may best fulfill the purpose Thou hast for me in the earth now.

. . . attuning to the vibration of flowers, the song of birds, the wind, the hail, the sleet, the snow. These in their roughness, yea in their quietness. All of these are appealing.

Open thy heart to God, surrounding self with the consciousness of the promises of the Christ—"If ye love me, ye will keep my commandments, and I and the Father will come and abide with thee." And as this is felt and spoken in body, in mind, visualize the coming of the Christ . . .

Obesity

903-16   F.30   7/4/32

Beware of sweets and of condiments. These are those [foods] that are the flesh producing, or the weight producing for the body.

288-38   F.29   9/19/34

Q-11. Why is it hard to increase weight in portions [of the body] and decrease it in others?

A-11. The natural tend or trend in the development of the foetus . . . in its inception, and then the general activities have been in these directions. This would go more into the psychological than the pathological conditions, to be sure, as we have indicated through these sources respecting the associations throughout the sojourn of the entity and its bodily forces in the earth.

3240-1   M.33   9/26/43

. . . there are tendencies that unless these are taken into consideration may cause a great deal of trouble. These arise primarily from a condition which involves the glandular forces of the system, tending towards the creating of sugar in too great a quantity for the activity of the circulation between kidneys and liver and their effect upon the activities of the locomotion of the body.

And this will increase the weight to such an extent that hindrances would arise in a form either of deterioration in the muscle and tendon forces of the body or in the activities that would affect the heart, the liver and the kidneys.

There is a subluxation . . . that exists in the 9th dorsal, the 6th and 7th dorsal. One is in one direction; the other in the other [direction]. This we would correct osteopathically.

Also we would keep better activities by the use of the Jerusalem artichoke as a part of the diet three times each week. Prepare this in a special way . . . Use one about the size of a hen egg, cooked in its own juices and served in its own juice—being prepared in Patapar Paper®. Boil in the Patapar Paper® then mix the bulk of the artichoke with the juices (after taking off the peeling) and season with a little butter and salt, and a little pepper if so desired, and eat all of it.

Do not take this without having the osteopathic corrections, for these are to work in unison.

If these are done, we should have better activities for this body.

3413-2   F.33   4/22/44

Q-2. Are there any exercises that I can take to keep my weight down that will not be detrimental to my back?

A-2. Take grape juice regularly four times each day, about half an hour before each meal and before retiring. Use three ounces of pure grape juice (such as Welch's®) with one ounce of plain water, not carbonated water. This with the [recommended] sweats or the baths will keep down the weight as well as remove poisons.

457-8   F.34   4/23/42

Q-15. Why should [the] body take the grape juice?

A-15. To supply the sugars without gaining or making for greater weight.

2096-1   F.22   2/17/31

While the effects that are created in [the] system from the disturbances at present do not cause such a great inconvenience, other than . . . too much avoirdupois—or obesity—the conditions in the *eliminations* are those *most* to be warned of; for they must eventually turn to a condition which would be detrimental to the heart's action, either through the conditions in the kidneys and lower limbs or through the kidneys and the sugars created in [the] system; for already we find—while the glands have somewhat to do with the disorders that are produced, these are rather general than so specific in their natures—the eliminations are those that cause the disorders in the lower portions of the system; feet, ankles and limbs, as well as those that produce a tendency for *portions* of the body, especially, to be out of proportion to the body as a whole.

These conditions . . . may be aided the most were the body to be more mindful of the diet; not as an extremist, no—but as one that would have the corrections made in the general eliminating system . . .

. . . this would be . . . an outline for the corrections of the physical conditions, that may later produce hindrances in the general physical health of the body:

We would begin first with those colonic irrigations, one every ten days until four or five are taken, which will overcome this tendency of constipation through the system . . .

We would also, at least twice each week, have those sweat cabinet baths, with a thorough rubdown afterwards, [using] any of the eliminants—or, prepare as this: Take Russian White Oil, 1 pint; alcohol, 1 pint; witchhazel, ½ pint. Mix these together and massage the body with same following the baths, see? Well to occasionally leave off the oil rub and to use the salt glow (that is, rub the body with salt).

For the matter of the diet we would use citrus fruits, or stewed fruits, or the whole dried or dry cereal. Do not combine same! That is, when one is used do not use the other—but these may be changed or altered, as this: The juice of two to three oranges, or one grapefruit, with dried toast following, with either Ovaltine® or a cereal drink. Little coffee, little milk or little tea may be taken.

For the noon meal, preferably green vegetables—with any of the oil dressings. All *green* vegetables, see?

Of evenings, we would take fish, honey (in the honeycomb)—not too much; *cooked* vegetables; no potatoes of *any* character; no tuberous roots of any character, but any of the green vegetables *cooked*, or of the *dried* vegetables that grow above the ground— *cooked*. Little ice cream, or none. Little or no butters. Buttermilk may be taken occasionally, but be mindful that it is not taken with too many of the vegetables.

The [osteopathic] manipulations, or corrections, we would take at least *once* each week for at least sixteen to twenty treatments. These manipulations will be as much of a gymnastic exercise of the extremities, as well as the correction of those subluxations that exist in the lumbar and in [the] upper dorsal and cervical region.

Odors

274-7   M.36   6/2/34

So many things we find surround this body and its associations. Odors! . . . there's a kind of an ivy; it isn't like the strawberry, yet it is; it isn't just a ground ivy that runs, but an ivy that blooms. The leaf of this the body should study in its associations, for it would make an odor that would be so unusual and effective and worthwhile, as well as being that which he should use . . . or have about him often . . .

Does the odor of an orris compound affect every individual alike? Or does the attar of roses or the essence of clover or of honeysuckle or crabapple or the like affect [everyone] the same way and manner? No. To some it would bring repellent influences; to others it would bring experiences that have been builded in the inner self. Hence it is given to some that they *adorn* themselves in body with those things which appeal to them, to make themselves appealing to others, and yet the very things that to *them* are an appealing expression would be abhorrent to others . . .

For, there is no greater influence in a physical body (and this means animal or man; and man, presumptuously at times, is the higher order of same) than the effect of odors upon the olfactory nerves of the body. They have made much of the developments for the body. Look at the difference in your New Englander that smells of earth . . . and those in the other climes where they have smelt hot peppers and swamps. Watch the difference in the characterizations of the individuals, or the temperament of same. Nothing has had much more influence than such in the *material* life . . .

How many of those that usually open an egg that's been buried for five to ten million years can, by its analysis, tell you what its composition is, or what the fowl or animal fed upon that laid it? This body can! . . .

If there were opened a sarcophagus in the form of an activity where the feet of such an animal or man or body were chemically analyzed, as related to the odors and their active influences upon the body itself, would it not be possible to indicate as to what had been the means or activities of such a body during that experience in the earth? and as to what were the principal food values? Such abilities would lend much to many of these. In opening a tomb wherein there had been the form of classifications or activities in a temple service, [the entity] would be able to tell whether there had been such sacrifices required as the destruction of animal life or of man, or whether there was used the odors of flowers, trees, buds, or a combination. How valuable would such an one as this body be to many engaged in such work? Not a great many who go into such things see except as a general thing . . . while the body—if turning its abilities in this direction—would be more of the analytical . . .

Q-10. Would you say that my present occupation as chemical engineer in charge of research and production in a perfume and cosmetic concern is a sound one, viewed from the same angle?

A-10. A sound one, viewed from the same angle; would be particularly interested in those activities and things as indicated . . .

Q-12. Is there any other advice that would be of benefit to me along these lines at present?

A-12.There's *so much* that may be given! And we would try to find this—we will go back to this—that we may.

There is—from certain characterizations of soil and climatic conditions, as well as other influences—not an ivy, and it is an ivy; its bloom is purple, its leaf is shaped round instead of oblong—as the strawberry, but it's not poisonous—and it should be sought by the body.

While the fleur-de-lis may have been as a pathological[?] symbol, the scientific would be more from the blossom and leaf of this particular flower—as an interest for this body.

274-10   M.37   1/25/36

Oft thou hast heard, "Let not thy good be evil-spoken of." How, why, may such occur?

Thou speakest . . . one manner and livest another life. Thou proclaimest in thy experience that thou believest this or that, and then thou dost proceed to act as if it didn't exist!

Q-2. Why have I been unable to find the fragrant ivy . . . ?

A-2. Seek and ye shall find; knock and it shall be opened unto thee. Study *all* of those of the ivy family, including what has been called the geranium. For this is of *that* family, including what has been called the geranium. For this is of *that* family, or the stock from which *man* hath brought the varied forms or representations of that plant . . .

In much of thy seeking (as thy advanced thought is so determined, or accepted by many), the synthetic odors, synthetic reactions from varied forms of vegetation or grasses have been accepted; yet these are much like accepting shadows—for the *real* thing!

Q-3. Regarding the fragrant ivy, could you give more precisions?

A-3. As just indicated. Follow the stock from which there has been the propagation of those various plants, with all their *varied* odors.

From what did the plant *obtain* its ability to produce in the one that of lemon, in another orange, in another lavender, in another violet?

Its parent stock was given, not by man but by the very Creative Forces, the *ability* to take and make that which becomes as an essence that *responds* to or sets in vibration the olfactory influences in the mucous membranes of the body of man; determining it to be *setting* in motion that which has such an influence!

For as has been indicated . . . there is the ability to make odors that will respond, and do respond, to certain individuals or groups; and many hundreds *are* responding to odors that *produce* the *effect* within their systems for activities that the psychoanalyst and the psychologist have long since discarded—much as they have the manner in which the Creative Forces or God *may* manifest in an individual!

What meaneth they of old when saying, "This hath ascended to the throne of grace as a sweet savor, a sweet incense before the Maker, the Creator," but that that within the individual is made aware of that estate which he had before he entered into flesh and became contaminated by the forms of matter in such a manner? For odor is gas, and not of the denser matter that makes for such activity in individuals' lives as to make for the degrading things.

Again, what meaneth He when He gave, "I am loath to thy sacrifices and to thy incense, for thou hast contaminated same with the blood of thy sons and daughters in the manner in which thou hast led them astray"?

The mixing of those things, then, became as stumbling blocks. What did Jeroboam, that he made the children of Israel to sin, but to offer rather the sandalwoods of the nations or the Egyptians that made for the arousing of the passions in man for the gratifications of the seeking for the activities that would satisfy his own indulgence, rather than the offering of those things that would make for the *glory* of the Lord's entrance into the activities of the individual?

What bringeth the varied odors into the experience of man? Did lavender ever make for bodily associations? Rather has it ever been that upon which the angels of light and mercy would bear the souls of men to a place of mercy and peace, in which there might be experienced more the glory of the Father.

Yet what bringeth mace and allspice and the various peppers but that which would arouse within man that of vengeance? Why?

These are of those influences that build such *in* the experience [of an entity].

Then *indeed* through the study of those things that have been indicated for this body, this soul . . . there may come that which may be builded even as the music of the spheres, so that it may act upon the body in the varied forms of its development and experience.

Hast thou ever known the odor from a flesh body of a babe to be the same as the odor from a body that has been steeped in the sins of the world, and has become as dross that is fit only to be cast upon the dunghill to become again that through which there may be gained those activities in a sphere of opportunity for a soul expression?

Then, just as these may answer for the varied stages of an individual development, there should be those things that make for such an activity.

Look about thee; and thou may understand how that one of the canine or cat family may—through the very spoor of its master or one of its kind—determine not only the days of its passage but as to the state of its being, interpreted as to its ability for procreation within its own self. This ye see and have taken little thought of.

How much more, then, may there be brought into the experiences of individuals that which may answer in their preparations (body and mind), through the varied effects that may be obtained in the entity or individual entering into an activity that becometh it as a son of a living God?

Dost thou put upon the body of the harlot the same that thou findest upon the altar of thy Lord? Dost thou find upon those entering at birth the same as upon those passing at death? Far apart be these, yet it is as in every law—*just* the reverse side of the same thing!

Q-4. Could you give some information on the relation of the sense of smell to the other senses?

A-4. These apply as has been indicated in that just given. Study these, not only from the manner in which they affect the body in the various stages of its development but from that they have reflected and do reflect in the activity of that kingdom just below thee—yet so often with the appearance of being far above many of those that have made themselves beneath the animal kingdom!

2823-3   F.34   1/8/44

For this body—not for everybody—odors would have much to do with the ability of the entity to meditate. For the entity in the experiences through the Temple of Sacrifice became greatly attuned through the sense of smell, for the activities were upon the olfactory nerves and muscles of the body itself. For there the protuberances were taken away.

379-3   F.54   9/17/35

. . . the odors which would make for the raising of the vibrations would be lavender and orris root. For these were those of thy choice in the Temple of Sacrifice. They were also thy choice when thou didst walk with those who carried the spices to the tomb.

2175-6   F.32   10/17/42

Choose whatever manner that befits thine own consciousness, whether this is from odors or otherwise. And if odors are chosen, choose sandalwood and cedar to be burned.

In such an atmosphere much of those things that were a part of the experience through those periods of meditation may be brought back.

Osteopathy

902-1   2/17/41

Let this be considered in relationship to osteopathy: As a *system* of treating human ills, osteopathy . . . is more beneficial than most measures that may be given. Why? In any preventive or curative measure, that condition to be produced is to assist the system to gain its normal equilibrium.

It is known that each organ receives impulses from other portions of the system by the suggestive forces (sympathetic nervous system) and by circulatory forces (the cerebrospinal system and the blood supply itself).These course through the system in very close parallel activity in *every* single portion of the body.

Hence, stimulating [the] ganglia from which impulses arise—either sympathetically or functionally—must then be helpful in the body gaining an equilibrium.

2524-5   M.43   1/13/44

Q-1. What is the state of my health and what measures should I take to improve it?

A-1. . . . Clear the body as you do the mind of those things that have hindered. The things that hinder physically are the poor eliminations. Set up better eliminations in the body. This is why osteopathy and hydrotherapy come nearer to being the basis of all needed treatments for physical disabilities.

1968-7   F.31   7/28/42

When there is the tendency for the least acidity in the system (which may be indicated by the metallic taste in the mouth), do have a good osteopathic adjustment, and ask that eliminations be set up better, see? This should take care of the sinus.

3624-1   F.39   1/31/44

One of the best methods, even for the osteopath, whether he's ever tried it or not, he will find what it will do here: When the body is upon the back for the treatment, raise the head and place the [osteopath's] fist on the 3rd cervical, and let the body rest full weight, even pressing gently—not hard, but gently—until the body does relax. Hold the fist there for a minute, two minutes, and after a while it may be two and one half to three minutes. This will drain, as it were, the whole system, setting up better eliminations throughout the whole body.

3384-2   M.33   1/22/44

Q-2. How long should the osteopathic treatments be continued?

A-2 . . . it will be necessary to keep up the osteopathic applications in series, with a few days rest between. These adjustments are merely to attune the centers of the body with the coordinating forces of [the] cerebrospinal and sympathetic system. Thus the body is purified or attuned so that it in itself, and nature, does the healing. As to how soon you may leave off the treatments depends upon how soon you can trust in your spiritual self, your mental self, to direct your physical being.

1710-10   M.28   2/20/43

Osteopathic or Swedish massage, with particular reference to such centers [sympathetic and cerebrospinal systems], is beneficial at times. Since not many of the masseurs know the centers, it is better to use the osteopathic treatment. These are beneficial, whether once a week, once in ten days, twice a month, ten times a year, or forty times a year. When needed, take them!

Palmistry

416-2   M.28   4/29/34

Q-14. What value is there in palmistry? To what extent may it be relied upon?

A-14. As we have given in regard to any and every omen, it is an indication—yes. As to whether or not it will come to pass depends upon what the body, the mind of such an one does *about* that it knows in relationships to itself.

It may be depended upon, then, about twenty percent, as being absolute—and about eighty percent "chance" or what a body does with its opportunities.

The same as may be said about an individual that has prepared himself to be a medium through which there may be expressed an excellent executive. How much does the preparation have to do with the body being an excellent executive? About twenty percent, and the application is the rest!

It is just so with all activities. For the will of a soul, of a body, is supreme—even as to whether it makes of itself a channel for the spiritual influences in its experience or for the selfish desires of its own body . . .

O if souls, bodies, everywhere, would gain that knowledge that the abilities to be sons of God or of the devil lie within self's own individual will!

For, as has been given of old, "I am persuaded that neither principalities nor souls, individuals nor conditions, may separate me from the love of God save myself." To be that He would have thee be, in all that thou doest and hast done from day to day, is being then a channel—and being used by Him, rather than using the blessings He has given thee for thine own undoing.

5259-1   F.46   6/8/44

For, we have unusual abilities in this entity, dependent upon how the entity may use same, as to whether these [abilities] become hindrances in the material and mental life, or whether they grow to be useful for enlightening and helpful in the experience for others . . .

Thus, we find an entity who has been given unusual abilities, especially in the realm of the fields of mysticism, occult or psychic science; science and psychic here indicating or meaning of the soul of the entity . . .

Thus those abilities . . . should be guided by, prompted by spiritual aspirations and not by imagination or of that activity as of wishful thinking on the part of the entity or by the desire of these whom the entity might aid.

The entity, then, should study the lines especially of hands, of the shape of hands, of the shape of fingers, of all forms which pertain to same, as we shall see why through those particular periods of sojourn of the entity.

But if the entity allows its own consciousness to be the prompting and unless that prompting is free, from spiritual understanding from the higher sources, or that source from which all life, help, aid, immortality, forgiveness, blessings come; unless it is guided through those and not of self alone, do not undertake same . . .

Use the hands, the lines, the fingers and formations then, merely as signs or symbols, not as of prompting of self . . .

. . . do not listen to voices, or rappings outside of self; do *not* use incense or music or automatic writing, for too many may desire to use this entity.

Do interpret from that which may be gained from these: Exodus 19:5; Deuteronomy 30; St. John 14, 15. These interpret within self; apply them in self.

Analyze hands, yes. Use this as a means for help to others.

Physiotherapy

257-254   M.50   12/18/43
Q-7. How often should the hydrotherapy be given?
A-7. Dependent upon the general conditions. Whenever there is a sluggishness, the feeling of heaviness, oversleepiness, the tendency for an achy, draggy feeling, then have the treatments. This does not mean that merely because there is the daily activity of the alimenta-

ry canal there is no need for flushing the system. But whenever there is the feeling of sluggishness, have the treatments. It'll pick the body up. For there is a need for such treatments when the condition of the body becomes drugged because of absorption of poisons through alimentary canal or colon, sluggishness of liver or kidneys, and there is the lack of coordination with the cerebrospinal and sympathetic blood supply and nerves. For the hydrotherapy and massage are preventative as well as curative measures. For the cleansing of the system allows the body forces themselves to function normally, and thus eliminate poisons, congestions and conditions that would become acute through the body.

635-9   F.52   12/11/37

As we find for this body, the Hydrotherapy Bath would be well; which would be to lie in great quantity or a tub of water for a long period—this being kept a little above the temperature of the body; then followed by a thorough massage by a masseuse. This would be better than adjustments *or* deep treatments, though it will be found that with the massage along the spine, with the body prone upon the face, these would—with the knuckle on either side of the spinal column—tend to make many a segment come nearer to normalcy, by being so treated after having been thoroughly relaxed for twenty to thirty minutes *in* the warm or hot water, see?

1947-6   F.32   6/10/40

Q-12. Are there any other mechanical devices I should use in connection with my physical development projects for others?

A-12. This will depend upon the individuals. For, each individual is ofttimes found to be a law unto himself—although there are general principles that work throughout. As we find, this will depend upon what type of mechanical applications are needed for the individual conditions. Of course, the general devices as used for weights or exercises, or elasticity, or any of the *general* things are the better. These fit the more, and can be varied to fit the individual the better.

Q-13. Are there any better devices than the McGregor beauty cabinet?

A-13. As we find, this is such that it can be used in a way there are few, if any, that are better.

4003-1   M.45   3/24/44

Some disturbances are indicated in the digestive forces of the body. These are from the lack of proper eliminations even though there are regularities. With the variations that occur from bodily exercise and the general changes indicated in the body, the eliminations need to be increased from these angles. This may be done in no better manner than by having colonic irrigations occasionally and by including in the diet such things as figs, rhubarb and the like.

Hydrotherapy and physical exercise, combined with these, should bring the better conditions for the body. These are the manners in which the body, or any individual body, may keep better activities.

Pinworms

308-1   F.8   4/3/33

. . . the disturbance saps the vitality and the resistance . . . the basis of this—why the system is not able to *meet* the disturbances—is through a specific condition; WORMS! . . . not the ordinary stomach worms, but rather the string worm, or hair worm, through the jejunum; or in portions of the lower stomach and in the digestive system. Hence we find a little temperature occurs at times. There are days when the body will feel well and strong. A little exercise depletes the activities. The appetite will be ravenous at one meal, and then there will be several meals when nothing just suits exactly . . .

. . . for a few days (three to four), keep the body rather quiet. This doesn't necessarily mean it is not to have movement or activity about the house, or even a little bit out of doors, but not too much of *any* nature. And the principal diet during that period would be a little coffee or tea, and principally green cabbage—for the first day, see?

Then begin with small doses of Fletcher's Castoria®, taking half a teaspoonful every half hour until half a bottle has been taken. Then take a pellet of Calomel and Santonin, followed by another in about two and a half hours. That is, take two doses. This is already prepared, you see—Calomel, Santonin and Nux Vomica. These are prepared in lozenges. Take two of these, about two hours apart.

When the bowels have moved properly, then begin with the rest of the Castoria®, taking at this time—besides the half a bottle left— at least *another* half bottle. When the bowels have been flushed, then begin with a well-balanced diet that will make for nerve and blood-building forces for the body. This would be as an outline, though it may be altered somewhat to suit the tastes; but be mindful that—for at least three to four weeks, no candies, cakes or pies are taken:

Mornings—citrus fruit juices; corn cakes or buckwheat cakes that are well buttered, and if a syrup is to be used on same, use honey—but at least half of those eaten at a meal should be without it. Or, this may be altered to stewed fruits, mixed fruits, figs, prunes, or rhubarb may be made as one meal—that is, the morning meal, see?

Noons—a sandwich of chicken or mutton, or lamb, or veal; or there may be included in this the whole wheat toast with milk that has been brought not to a boil but *almost*, or make into milk toast. Or, there may be taken at this meal the juices of meats or the juices of vegetables; but, preferably *without* the meats or the vegetables, see?

Evenings—at least three of the evening meals each week should be of calves' liver with eggs (and only the egg yolks used); with grits and gravy, or rice and gravy—or other cereals of the same nature. And cooked vegetables, as any of the *leafy* vegetables that are palatable for the body, or cooked in such a manner as to *be* palatable; that carry iron, and silicon, and sulphur, and the like, for the developing body. Fish and sea foods, or the shell foods may be used at the same meal . . .

. . . for the day—before this is begun—the principal diet would be a little coffee or a little tea, and *green* cabbage! that one day! Then begin with those other properties.

324-6   F.4   5/29/36

First, then, we would give the course of Fletcher's Castoria®. Then one day, during the whole day (though she may be hard to stay with), give only scraped raw cabbage. Then, preferably under the directions of a physician, give Santonin and Calomel. There should be only one dose, as we find, or it may be divided into two doses; and would not be of too great a quantity. This should rid the body of these tendencies for this upsetting and for the increase in the circulation . . .

Make for a diet that is not irritating and distressing to an already upset stomach.

The massaging of the neck, head, shoulders, with the alcohol—or alcohol and olive oil—will relieve these tensions that produce the irritation through the neck and head.

The causes, though, should be eliminated . . . Until the course is completed, or until there are at least two or three good activities from the alimentary canal [give the Castoria®] . . .

Nothing wrong with the sex development. This is rather the irritation that naturally arises from such parasites as indicated in the intestinal system.

2015-10   F.3   11/30/42

As we find, conditions are very good. There are those tendencies and indications of some pinworms. These, as we find, unless there is a great deal—or considerable amount of green, raw vegetables taken, will tend to increase.

These will be eliminated if there will be taken rather regularly some lettuce and some of such natures of green raw vegetables, raw carrot, raw fruits.

Unless such can be taken, it would be necessary—as we find— to give the body, under the direction of a physician, Santonin and Calomel. This, of course, may upset the body for a day or so, but the little tendencies for nausea, sleeplessness, loss of appetite, are arising from those disturbances through the intestinal tract. They are indicated in the present only in portions of the jejunum . . .

Q-4. How did the trouble of pinworms originate, or what caused it?

A-4. Milk! You see, in every individual there is within the intestinal tract that matter which produces a form of intestinal worm. This is in everyone. But with a particular diet where the milk has any bacillus, it will gradually cause these to increase, and they oftentimes develop or multiply rapidly; and then they may disappear, *if* there is taken raw, green food.

Q-5. Would you change the kind of milk she drinks?

A-5. It isn't so much the change in the kind of milk that is needed. Rather add the raw, green foods as indicated, or give those properties as would eliminate the source of same. But it is better, if it is practical, to induce the body to eat lettuce and celery and carrots—even a small amount. One leaf of lettuce will destroy a thousand worms.

Poison Ivy

2441-3   F.36   8/28/41

We would apply Ray's solution® . . . take internally small doses of Atomidine®, to assist in purifying the system: one drop in half a glass of water each morning before any meal is taken, for a period of eight to ten days.

Also we would take a good eliminant [Eno Salts®, 1 heaping teaspoonful each morning for eight to ten days] for flushing the system from the poisons and accumulations that naturally come with an irritation in the superficial circulation.

1770-4   F.50   8/23/39

Q-5. Is there a remedy for poison ivy which you could suggest?

A-5. The very tender shoots of same made into a mild tea and taken internally as a tonic would prevent poison ivy being effective [for this body].

When it has been attracted, or is effective in the circulation, take small quantities of Atomidine® internally—one to two drops in water for four to five days, and leave off. And bathe in a weakened solution of same, or bathe the portions thus affected.

One is a preventive, the other—of course—is to eliminate same from the system [when the poison has entered].

261-33   M.51   8/29/38

As we find, the specific or acute conditions arising as a rash are the effects of contact with poison ivy.

We would for this particular disturbance in the present: Bathe off the affected parts with a weak solution of Atomidine®, the proportions being about a teaspoonful to half a glass of water. Sponge off same with a tuft of cotton.

Then, after sponging off with the tuft of cotton dipped in the weak Atomidine® solution, we would apply—full strength—the tetrachloride solution, or that [which is] found in the combination of the prescription D.D.D. in the [commercial] solution, see? Apply this two or three times a day—just patted on with a tuft of cotton.

For four or five days it would be well to take internally two drops of the Atomidine® [full or commercial strength] in half a glass of water, before the morning meal . . . Then, be precautions as to the diet, in the general manner as we have indicated for the body.

1635-2   F.3   8/11/41

Hence, first prepare a compound containing a small quantity of Podophyllum, in this manner:

Podophyllum.. ½ grain,
Leptandrin.. 1 grain,
Sanguinaria .... 1 grain.

Mix these ingredients and make into five pellets.

Take two a day, one in the morning, one in the afternoon.

On the third day, after the last pellet has been taken on that morning, you see—begin with Fletcher's Castoria in broken doses—a quarter teaspoonful every thirty minutes throughout the entire day, or until there are thorough eliminations.

Poliomyelitis

[An example of the priceless information secured through the readings of Edgar Cayce is the suggestion of Atomidine®* as a preventive against poliomyelitis. This suggestion was made not only to individuals but in a reading on the disease itself.]

2015-8   F.2   9/16/41

Q-2. What can be done as a precaution to keep her from contracting Infantile Paralysis, which is prevalent in the vicinity?

A-2. Every other day give one drop of Atomidine® in half a glass of water, before the morning meal. Keep this up for five doses, skip five, and repeat—continuing in this manner through the winter.

Q-3. Would this also be a dosage to prevent a grown person from contracting Infantile Paralysis?

A-3. For a grown person take two drops *every* day for five days, skip five days, and so on.

363-1   8/4/36

[Background: Special reading taken on Poliomyelitis]

---

*See footnote on p.43.

In considering this dreaded disease, owing to the fatality, especially among the young, considerations will be given, then, to all
phases of this disturbance.

From the very nature of the condition, the indications are as a
whole that it (the inflammation as produced) is of the emunctory
and lymph circulation.

Hence it is infectious as well as being able to be carried by persons, or [it] is a carrier disease, also.

And it arises (in the individual) from the condition that exists
from what may be termed as *body* or bodily-infectious.

When conditions are at a balance[in a body], where there is that
effluvium that is thrown off through the circulation and the activity
of the superficial circulation, these [skin areas] become irritated
mostly by lack of perfect cleanliness. The infectious forces entering
are also [enabled to do so] by the depleting of these particles or ef-
fluvia of the blood itself; which [means that they] attack, then, the
mucous membranes of throat, eyes, mouth and nasal passages, but
may [also] be absorbed by the emunctory centers—from the groin,
under the arm, the knees, the elbow.

These are the sources, then, thee are the manners, then, of the
infection, of the condition that arises—whether from contact or
whether from the air.

As we find, then, this is of [a] glandular *inception*, or is [of a
type] as indicated where [or by the fact that] there may be many in
a household [exposed to the germ] and only a few in same become
affected. It then needs be [or this indicates] that the *glands* of the
same [are] more active than [the glands of] others.

And there is then, as has been indicated, the greater possibility
for the prevention, the stamping out of same, by the use of those
properties in the system, upon the system, [and] about the household where [or by which) there is a *cleansing* for the glands, stimulation to the activity of the circulatory forces, and [the effect of] an
antiseptic and a [general] cleanser as well.

[The combination of qualities], as we find, is better [found] in that
compound called Atomidine®, as we have indicated. The sponge
bath of same for the elders, for the nurse, or for those about; especially [around] the arms, the groin and [such] portions of the body.
A spray of a fifty percent solution of commercial strength [Atomi-
dine®] for throat, nasal passages and the like. And the taking of same

internally by those that apparently have been exposed to the conditions; one to two minims morning and evening . . . in periods, and then a rest period [from it], and then take again. These will prevent, as we find, the greater inroads. These are the properties, as we find, that will combine with the system as in a *general* way and manner.

Ready for questions.

Q-1. Is the spray of alum, picric acid, etc., which is being used extensively in Montgomery [Alabama] effective in preventing the disease, or is this spray harmful?

A-1. It would be found in some instances to be harmful. For the activity of the picric acid is effective to the mucous membranes, but the activity of the alum combined *with* same may close [areas] for [throwing off] other infectious forces that may later find a sympathetic reaction through the body.

But where [individuals are] exposed, this is very good—for the whole of the emunctory circulation becomes engorged in its first inception.

Q-2. Will you tell us more about the germ itself that causes this disease?

A-2. It has been given; it may be separated if it's looked for in the perspiration of those [areas] through which, where, it begins!

Q-3. In using Atomidine® in sponge bath, what proportions?

A-3. As has been given [for spray 50%].

We are through for the present.

Possession

1183-3   F.56   1/22/38

Q-6. What causes him to lose control of himself?

A-6. Possession! . . .

Q-17 . . . What is meant by possession?

A-17. Means *possession!*

Q-18. Does [possession] mean by other entities, while under the influence of liquor?

A-18. By others while under the influence [of liquor] that causes those reactions and makes for the antagonism, and the very *change* of the activities. For this body (the husband), if there could be a sufficient period of refraining from the use of alcoholic stimulants and the diathermy electrical treatments used, [such treatments] would drive these conditions out!

But do not use [electrical treatments] with the effects of alcohol in the system—it would be detrimental! . . .

Q-19. Is he crazy or mentally deranged?

A-19. If possession isn't crazy, what is it?

1572-1   F.50   4/18/38

While those activities that have been taken by the body produce some conditions that are beneficial . . . they have caused and do assist in producing the exciting of the glandular forces in their activity, as related to the genital system. Thus, as combined with the pressures upon the nerve system, distorted and disturbing conditions are caused for the body . . .

Q-1. What causes the burning sensation which comes over me, as if someone has put "the power" on me?

A-1. . . . this is the incoordination between the cerebrospinal and the sympathetic nervous system. And as the glandular system is affected as related to the genitive system, and especially affecting directly the center above the puba, there is produced—with the toxic forces in the system—this burning, and the *effect* of *possession!* . . .

Q-3. Should anything be taken for the glands?

A-3. There's already been too much [taken], as has been indicated!

5221-1   F.53   6/9/44

. . . the body is a supersensitive individual entity who has allowed itself through study, through opening the [gland] centers of the body, to become possessed with reflexes and activities outside of itself . . .

Q-3. How did I happen to pick this up?

A-3 . . . the body in its study opened the[gland] centers and allowed self to become sensitive to outside influences.

Q-4. What is it exactly that assails me?

A-4. Outside influences. Disincarnate entities.

3421-1   F.40   12/27/43

. . . there has been the opening of the lyden [Leydig] gland, so that the kundaline forces move along the spine to the various centers that open . . . with these activities of the mental and spiritual forces of the body . . . The psychological reaction is much like that as may be illustrated in one gaining much knowledge without making practical application of it . . . Now we combine these two and we have that indicated here as a possession of the body; [a] gnawing, as it were, on all of the seven centers of the body, causing the inability for rest or even a concerted activity—unless the body finds itself needed for someone else. Then the body finds, as this occurs, the disturbance is retarded or fades—in the abilities of the body to exercise itself in [giving] help for others.

3380-1   M.50   11/30/43

Here there is the attempt of possession . . . begin and read the 30th of Deuteronomy . . . Then read the 19th of Exodus and the 5th verse, and know it applies to self.

Psychic Development

1947-3   F.31   9/4/39

. . . the body was first a cell by the union of desire that brought activity in that influence about which the growth began.

Then of itself at birth into materiality the consciousness gradually awoke to the influences about same of body, mind and soul, until it reached the consciousness of the ability for the reproduction within itself of desire, hope, fear.

And the whole of creation, then, is bound in the consciousness of self. That influence, that force is the psychic self.

As to how same, then, may be developed within self:

Each entity enters materiality for a purpose. That all the experiences in the earth are as one is indicated by the desires, the longings as arise within the experience of that which makes for the growing, the knowing within self—*mind!* Thus does the entity, as a whole, become aware that it, itself, in body, mind and soul, is the result—each day—of the application of laws pertaining to creation, this evolution, this soul-awareness within, consciously manifested.

What is the purpose of entering consciousness? That each phase of body, mind and soul may be to the glory of that Creative Force in which it moves and has its being.

And when this influence, this growing self becomes such, or so self-centered, as to lose sight of that desire, purpose, aim to be *to* the glory of its source, and seeks rather *for* self, then it errs in its application of the influences within its abilities for the application of mind within its own experience . . .

Then, as has been said: There is before thee this day life and death, good and evil. These are the ever present warring influences within materiality.

What then, ye ask, is this entity to do about, to do with, this ability of its own spiritual or psychic development; that may be made creative or may bring creative or destructive forces within the experiences of others?

"My Spirit beareth witness with thy spirit as to whether ye be the children of God or not." This becomes, then, that force, that influence for comparisons; as the entity meditates upon its own emotions, its own influences, these become very apparent within itself for comparisons.

Do they bespeak of kindness, gentleness, patience—that threshold upon which godliness appears?

Desire may be godly or ungodly, dependent upon the purpose, the aim, the emotions aroused.

Does it bring, then, self-abstinence? or does it bring self desire?

Does it bring love? Does it bring long-suffering? Is it gentle? Is it kind?

Then, these be the judgments upon which the entity uses those influences upon the lives of others.

Does it relieve suffering, as the abilities of the entity grow? Does it relieve the mental anguish, the mental disturbances which arise? Does it bring also healing—of body, of mind—to the individual? Is it healed for constructive force, or for that as will bring pain, sorrow, hate and fear into the experience of others? . . .

And as these are applied, so may the entity come to apply its psychic abilities, its love, its desire, its hopes, *spiritualized* in self-effacement by placing God's *glory*, God's *love*, in the place of self; bringing hope, *hope* and *faith* in the minds and hearts, the lives of others . . .

These are the purposes, these are the desires, these are the manners in which the mental may be applied for the soul and spiritual development; and in the manner, "As ye do it to the least of these, thy brethren, ye do it unto me," saith the Lord . . .

Q-2. Through what method or manner should my psychic abilities be expressed?

A-2. These . . . will be different with varied or different individuals. Did He teach those at the well the same as those in the mount, or by the sea? Rather as He was given utterance, so gave He to others.

As has been indicated, the entity will find there are intuitive forces aroused by these applications of these purposes and desires. To some it will be healing, cooling the brow of those who are ill. To others it will be counseling as to this or that which disturbs their mental association, their moral lives, their material concepts. To others it will be as directing them to bear *their* cross even as He. For in Him does the burden become light, and the cross easy.

Q-3. Would it be possible for my psychic impressions to come through picture flashes?

A-3. These may come in varied forms. Possible; but know, as has been indicated, the tempter is ever about. That influence stands. Study well that which has been indicated here, and as ye apply it ye will know as to whether these influences of flashes, influences of writing, influences of speaking, arise from creative forces . . .

Q-4. How may I recognize correct urges or hunches for action?

A-4 . . . remember . . . many poisonous vines bear beautiful flowers. But what manner of seed? In what way are they constructive? Do they give a supply? Think on these. There are few even of the foods for the body that are not of the seed of that sown for fruition.

Q-5. May I develop the power to heal others?

A-5. As indicated, this will *oft* be a part of thy experience. For, as indicated, the entity has the ability *innately!* As to how it manifests same, this becomes the job of the entity. To *create* in the minds of those it meets a desire for a worshipfulness toward the entity! What are the fruits, what are to be the fruits of these?

These depend upon what the entity does with that mind seeking—ever seeking light. Give the light—whether it is by song, by vision, by instruction, by healing.

Q-6. How may I develop psychic power for warnings of danger, difficulties to be avoided and opportunities to be taken advantage of, for myself, my children and others?

A-6. Let these be rather the outgrowth of the spiritual desire, rather than beginning with material manifestations, see?

For, these *are—to* be sure—a part of the whole, but if they are sought for only the material sustenance, material warning, material satisfaction, they soon become dead in their ability to be creative . . .

Purpose in the Earth

826-11   M.36   1/11/38

. . . first [consider] the purposes for which an entity enters a material experience—and why: In giving such there must be given then some premise that is acceptable or stated as being a practical thing or condition in the experience of the entity; that it may be a part of the entity in fulfilling that purpose in the present experience.

The entity or man then is physical, mental and spiritual; or the physical body, the mental body, the spiritual body.

The spiritual is that portion of same, or that body, that is everlasting; that is a portion of all it has applied in its mental experiences through the sojourns in the environs of which the entity or soul or spirit body is a part.

From whence comes then this spirit body, that we find in consciousness in the present; aware of the physical attributes, aware of at least a portion of its mental abilities, its mental capacities; only catching a glimpse here and there in the application of spiritual laws or spiritual truths of the spiritual body?

The spirit is of the universal consciousness, or God; that which is the First Cause; that which is manifested in all the varied forms and manners that are experienced in the activities of the individual in this particular sphere of activity or phase of consciousness in the present.

Why the entity—why the spirit of this entity? A gift, a companion—yea, a very portion of that First Cause.

Hence the purposes that it, the entity, the spirit body, may make manifest in materiality or in physical consciousness the more and more awareness of the relationships of the mental body, the physical body to eternity, infinity, or the God-Consciousness.

Why? That is the purpose, that is the gift, that is the activity for maintaining its consciousness throughout matter, mind or spirit.

For as is the consciousness of the entity in materiality, when there is such a diffusion of consciousness as to change, alter or create a direction for an activity of any influence that has taken on consciousness of matter to waver it from its purpose for being in a consciousness, it loses its individual identity.

What, then, is the purpose of the entity's activity in the consciousness of mind, matter, spirit in the present? That it, the entity, may *know* itself to *be* itself and part of the Whole; not the Whole but one *with* the Whole; and thus retaining its individuality, knowing itself to be itself, yet one with the purposes of the First Cause that called it, the entity, into *being*, into the awareness, into the consciousness of itself. That is the purpose, that is the cause of *being*.

Then the natural question to the entity becomes, "What may I do about same? In what manner, in what way may I apply myself as an entity, as an individual, to fill that purpose whereunto the First Cause has its influence, its way, its purpose with me?"

In such an activity then the body-physical, the body-mind, must be taken into consideration; with its faults, its fancies, its faith, its purpose, its abilities in every manner, and in every influence that has been and is a part of that mental or spiritual or material consciousness.

It has been given the entity as to much which or unto which it may attain; as each entity bears an influence into and unto the Whole, and is influenced by same according to the will and purpose of the entity in the individual or the moment's expression. For the choices are continually being made by the body, the mind, *upon* those things that are within *themselves* taken within the consciousness, the awareness of the entity.

Not that there are not *other* influences also that are aware only to the higher portion of the mental and spiritual self. For in the *body* few are aware of even the heartbeat, the fact of assimilation, the fact of distribution, the fact of building or of degeneration.

In the purpose then or premise; it is that:

Mind is the Builder, being both spiritual and material; and the consciousness of same reaches man only in his awareness of his consciousnesses through the senses of his physical being.

Then indeed do the senses take *on* an activity in which they may be directed in that awareness, that consciousness of the spiritual self as well as in the physical indulgences or appetites or activities that become as a portion of the selfish nature of the individual or entity.

It behooves the entity first in its premise then to know, to conceive, to imagine, to become aware of that which is its ideal . . .

These meditated upon then, these kept in the ways that ye know. It is not then that ye *know* as a physical consciousness, but that ye *apply* of good, of that which *is* of God, that makes ye know that consciousness of His walks with thee.

For thy physical self may only see the reflection of good, while thy spiritual self may *be* that good in the activities of thy fellow man in such measures that ye bring—what?

Ever, *ever*, the fruits of the Spirit in their awareness; long suffering, brotherly love, patience, kindness, gentleness, *hope* and faith!

If ye, in thy activities in any manner with thy fellow man destroy these in the minds, in the hearts of thy fellow man, ye are not only slipping but ye have taken hold on the path of destruction.

Then so live, so act, so *think* that others *seeing* thy good works, thy hopes that ye bring, thy faith that ye manifest, thy patience that ye show, may *also* glorify Him.

For that cause, for that purpose ye entered into the materiality in the present.

To what, ye ask, may ye attain—and how may ye attain same? That is only limited by thyself. For He, the Father-God, loveth all alike; but that ye find within thy mind, thy body, that would offend, pluck it away! For thy will as one with His may do *all* these things in *His* name!

Then, to what heights may ye attain?

That height to which thy consciousness is ever clear before the throne of thy awareness with Him; which is to know the glory of the Father through thy dealings with thy fellow man; which is to know—no sin, no sorrow, no disappointments in Him.

Oft is He disappointed in thee, but if thou dost bring such into the minds, the hearts, the lives of others, what is thy reflection but these same experiences?

But to love good, to flee from evil, to bring the awareness of the God-Consciousness into the minds and hearts of others is *thy* purpose in this experience.

1722-1   F.20   11/1/38

Each soul in entering an earth's experience does so through the graciousness, the mercy of the living Father, that the soul may become such that it may be in that association, that relation to the Creative Forces or the Father which was, is, the will of the Father in bringing such into consciousness in the first or beginning.

In entering then, each soul enters with the influences both latent and manifested that have been a part of the experience of the entity. This to be sure includes then relationships with others.

Then what is the purpose of each soul entering a material manifestation? That it may be a witness-bearer for and unto the glory of the Father which has been manifested through the Son, even Jesus; in making then those activities through and in which such may be the purpose, the desire of the individual entity.

It is not then that there may be the satisfying of the mental or material body, or mind. It is not to the indulgence of, nor to the glory of self alone, but that—through the very activities of the body and mind—the fruits of the spirit of truth may be manifested in the material experience.

These truths, these experiences, only find expression in relationships with others. Just as He hath given, "Inasmuch as ye have done it unto the least of these, thy brethren, ye have done it unto me—inasmuch as ye did *not* these things unto thy brethren, ye did them not unto me."

Hence in the relationships, the meetings with others in *whatever* form or manner, such as not coincidental but are rather as purposeful experiences.

Then there must be the filling of the purpose, if there will be the glorifying of His love, His truths, His presence, by that done to and through the activities with the fellow man whoever, wherever such may be; in such a way and manner that His glory is made manifest in thy dealings with thy fellow man.

Look then into thine own heart, thine own mind. See thyself, as it were, pass by. What is thy desire? What is thy purpose? What—and *who*—is thy ideal?

The analysis of such can only be drawn by self. And use as the measuring stick of thyself those truths, those purposes.

What gave He as the whole law? To love thy God with all thy mind, thy body, thy purpose; and thy *neighbor* as thyself! This is the whole law.

And the manner of execution of same is in that as He gave, "As ye would that men should do to you, do ye even so to them."

These are the principles, these are the basic truths upon which joy, peace and understanding may be thine; and thy life, thy activities, thy associations with others will ever be beautiful, peaceful, harmonious.

And as ye do these, ye will find more and more the glory of His presence abiding with thee day by day!

This does not preclude that ye have joy, but that ye have joy and have life and have it more *abundantly*—and not in a manner that ye have or do become or may become subject to those things which would bind or hinder thee in thy thought, thy purpose, thy activity.

Let thy prayer, thy meditation then be—as ye choose this day whom ye will serve whether the fleshpots of thine own carnal self or the duties, the joys, the harmonies of Him who has given, "Come unto me, ye that are disturbed or heavy laden—take my purpose, my yoke—learn of me, and ye shall find rest unto thy mental, thy material, thy spiritual self."

"Let my life be so filled with the desire to be a channel of blessings to others that it may show forth the Lord of Lords, the King of Kings."

Relaxation and Sleep

1711-1 F.57 10/18/38

Q-2. What may be done to enable me to sleep through the night?

A-2. Purifying of the system . . . will relieve the tensions upon the nervous system in such a way that the functions of the body will bring the normal rest for the body.

This is much preferable to attempting to take or to apply influence [of drugs] that become an abhorrence to the bodily functions. For, as is understood—if the body takes the time for thought—physical rest is the natural means of the mental and spiritual finding the means of coordinating with the activities of the mental-physical in the body, see? Hence rest is necessary, but that which would be *induced*—unless it becomes necessary because of pain or the like—is not a *natural* rest, nor does it produce a regeneration for the activities of the physical body.

2067-3 F.52 9/3/40

Q-3. Why am I so dependent upon sleep, and what do I do during my physical sleep?

A-3. Sleep is a *sense*, as we have given heretofore; and is that needed for the physical body to recuperate, or to draw from the mental and spiritual powers or forces that are held as the ideals of the body.

Don't think that the body is a haphazard machine, or that the things which happen to individuals are chance! It is all a law! Then, what happens to a body in sleep? Dependent upon what it has thought, what it has set as its ideal!

For, when one considers, one may find these as facts! There are individuals who in their sleep gain strength, power, might—because of their thoughts, their manner of living. There are others who find that when any harm, any illness, any dejection comes to them, it is following sleep! It is again following a law!

What happens to this body? Dependent upon the manner it has applied itself *during* those periods of its waking state. Take *time* to sleep! It *is* the exercising of a faculty, a condition that is meant to be a part of the experience of each soul. It is as but the shadow of life, or lives, or experiences [in the earth], as each day of an experience is a part of the whole that is being builded by an entity, a soul. And each night is as but a period of putting away, storing up into the superconscious or the unconsciousness of the soul itself.

Q-4. What is the best way for me to get to sleep?

A-4. Labor sufficiently of a physical nature to tire the body; not mentally, but physically.

5177-2   F.65   5/26/44

Q-1. Why can't I get a decent night's sleep, and what should I do about it?

A-1. Take the [treatments of] hydrotherapy and massage at least, as given, once or twice a week, but extend them over a long period, as after those [indicated] periods of recreation or rest or change. Then when the body returns from such periods have a few more, every week or so have at least one or two of these, for varied periods, and we will find much better conditions. But don't forget, as the Boy Scout or Girl Scout oath would be: Do a good deed every day. This is just being kind, just being patient, showing long-suffering, gentleness; and we will find much help for this body . . .

404-6   F.46   1/15/36

Concentration upon relaxation is the greater or better manner for *any* body to relax. That is, SEE the body *relaxing*, CONSCIOUS-LY! Not concentrating so as to draw *in* the [spiritual] influence, but [in such a way] as to let all of the tension, all of the strain, flow OUT of self—and find the body giving—giving—away.

416-9   M.30   7/30/36

Q-6. Am I working too hard for my best physical welfare?

A-6. Few people have ever injured themselves by work. Many have by worry as combined with work. But take the periods of rest and recuperate properly. Do not overtax the body-physical and then make for, by those periods of relaxation, the acting in the manner ... of burning the candle at both ends. Do not do those things physically or mentally that would make for, from the using up of physical energies, greater destructive conditions in the mental and soul forces. And we will find, as has been indicated, a greater physical ability—and work won't hurt anyone.

3120-2   F.33   8/11/44

Q-4. What should I do to ease nervous condition?

A-4. Just relaxing of the body at regular periods is the best. This is much better than depending upon outside influences. Extra amount of B-1 vitamin taken will be the better way and manner, but perfect relaxation [is the best remedy]. Have a period when you forget everything—not necessarily to go to sleep to do so—but if you go to sleep during those periods, very well, but let the recuperation come from deep within self.

440-2   M.23   12/13/33

Q-6. What are best hours for sleep?

A-6. When the body is physically tired, whether at noon or twelve o'clock at night!

816-1   M.51   2/7/35

Q-9. How much sleep does this body need?

A-9. Seven and a half to eight hours should be [taken] for *most* bodies.

1861-18   M.38   4/17/44

Q-3. Is there any way of sleeping on the back without snoring?

A-3. Not that has been invented yet!

288-41   F.31   5/16/36

Q-3. May anything be done to correct or prevent sleeping with mouth open?

A-3. Close it!

Q-4. When asleep, how may this be done?

A-4. Make the suggestions to self as going to sleep. Get the system balanced. And this will be done.

2514-7   F.23   5/25/42

Q-5. Why can't I sleep at night?

A-5. This is from nervousness and overanxiety. Of course, keep away from any drugs if possible, though a sedative at times may be necessary. Drink a glass of warm milk with a teaspoonful of honey stirred in same.

2051-5   M.69   1/31/42

Q-6. Why do I have difficulty in sleeping after four o'clock in the morning, and how may this be controlled?

A-6. This is as a habit and a part of a physical reaction. This should not be attempted to be controlled, but rather *used* advantageously. If ye are aroused, use the period of the first thirty minutes—at least—in direct meditation upon what thy Lord would have thee do that day. You'll soon learn to sleep more than the next hour!

Rheumatism and Sciatica

4517-1   F.Adult   3/25/24

. . . toxins . . . are carried in the system that should be eliminated through their proper channels. Hence there are portions of the tissue we find becomes surcharged with these elements until it brings distress to various portions of the body, in joints, in muscular forces, in tissue; especially that in head and neck, and in the ligaments to locomotion at times . . .

In the nerve tissue and centers we find much of this strain comes, for this is involved in the circulation and the [dissemination] of those forces, as an element in the system brings these strains on the various portions of that governed by the circulation in its course through the system, and attacking those portions that are the weaker or as the cycle of vibrations change in the cellular producing or produced portions of the body for the use in the physical forces. The centers involved direct we find come from the tenth and eleventh dorsal. These we find feed those tissue and nerve supplied to the intestinal tract, so that the system has gradually come to absorb these toxins from the system, and being carried then in circulation distributed to various portions of the body. There are different conditions locally that assist in this, these centers and this intestinal condition, near the Peyers gland region; however, being that from which the condition has arisen. This we see in turn has affected the pneumogastric and hypogastric centers, until the hepatic circulation through kidneys has become involved. Hence to the portions of the system, where the glands, as in tonsils and thyroids, have become involved and produced local conditions . . .

Twice each day take this: Level teaspoonful effervescent phosphate of soda, with three drops of syrup of sarsaparilla, with one drop of oil of white pine.

Take those vibrations each day that will he found in the violet ray®,and massage those portions of the system that will force the elimination in kidneys, liver and in intestinal tract, and correct those centers where ligaments and tissue is impinioned.

Do this, and be persistent with these. We will relieve these conditions.

Q-1. How should the violet ray® be given?

A-1. To those parts especially that are affected at the present time; throat, cervicals and spine, with the extremity centers. That is, the plexus centers of locomotion; brachial center, sciatic center, solar plexus center, forward and back, for at least seven minutes each day; that is for the whole system. Do that.

4517-2   F.Adult   8/18/24

. . . the poisons in system so clog the tissue as to produce the pressure on centers and on the tendons as to make the troubles and distresses through portions of the body. This we see is produced from the system not eliminating properly, and the suggestions as were given have not been carried out and adjustments made for the system as were given, neither has the diet been adhered to as it should have been when conditions were improved in system.

For the present condition we would, where the strain and stress is on the system—that is, the joints, the ligaments, those portions which cause the distress to the body—bathe these well in saturated solution of Bicarbonate of Soda. Then bind about these parts, so as to drive this solution in, very large packs of heavy sea salt, heated, so the body can have the reaction from this heat, making as hot as body can well stand. This will bring relief . . .

We would take into the system those properties as found in Toris Compound. This . . . take in full strength. Also . . . in the food values those of predigested foods, that the toxins in system may be well absorbed, taking at least once every third day at least one tablet of Honey Charcoal, as is prepared by Battle Creek Sanitorium.

Scar Tissue

487-15   M.15   1/6/34

Q-2. Any other condition that needs correcting at this time?

A-2 . . . If he wants to relieve much of the scar tissue on the left limb, we would use sweet oil combined with Camphorated Oil (equal parts). Massage this each day for three to six months and we would reduce the most of this.

Q-3. Would it be to the better physical condition of this body to remove this scar tissue [from the burn]?

A-3. Any scar tissue detracts from the general physical health of a body, for it requires a changing in the circulation continually. Not that the massage would injure the body, but would make for better physical health generally.

1567-4   F.57   11/29/43

Q-5. What will improve scar [from a burn] which causes pain in chin?

A-5. Camphorated Oil, with occasionally carbolated vaseline. This should be put on before the oil is rubbed in.

5092-1   F.30   5/16/44

As for scars, rather let the scars be removed from the mental and spiritual self. To undertake such through those activities of anyone altering these, we will have worse scars. Let the scars be removed from the own mental, the *own mental and spiritual self.* Turn to those things of making application of the fruits of the spirit of truth;

love, patience, gentleness, kindness, long-suffering, brotherly love, putting away those little tendencies for being "catty" at times or being selfish or expressing jealousy and such.

Let that mind be in thee as was in Him, who is the way and the truth and the light, and we will make the light of love so shine through thy countenance that few, if any, will ever see the scars made by self-indulgence in other experiences . . .

Q-1. What can be done to correct excessive oiliness which has resulted in acne and scarring?

A-1. Just read what we have been giving.

2015-10   F.3   11/30/42

Q-2. Will continued use of Camphorice gradually eliminate scar on arm (resulting from severe burn two years ago)?

A-2. Camphorice, or better—as we find—Camphorated Oil. Or make the own Camphorated Oil; that is, by taking the regular Camphorated Oil and adding to it; in these proportions:

Camphorated Oil .... 2 ounces
Lanolin, dissolved .... ½ teaspoonful
Peanut Oil .... 1 ounce

This combination will quickly remove this tendency of the scar—or scar tissue.

440-3   M.23   12/18/33

Q-4. Are the scars on the legs or stomach detrimental in any way to the proper functioning of the body?

A-4. Little or no hindrance. These may be aided in being removed by sufficient time, precaution and persistence in activity; by the massage over those portions of small quantities at a time of Tincture of Myrrh and Olive Oil, and Camphorated Oil. These would be massaged at different times, to be sure; one one day and the other the second day from same—see? In preparing the Olive Oil and Tincture of Myrrh, heat the oil and add the myrrh—equal portions, only preparing such a quantity as would be used at each application. The Camphorated Oil may be obtained in quantity.

Seasickness

887-2   F.25   6/14/35

Q-10. What will prevent . . . seasickness while en route [via boat to Europe]?

A-10. Use a preparation (which is well for all) compounded in this way and manner:

Limewater, 1 ounce; Cinnamon Water, 1 ounce; 10% solution Iodide of Potassium, 20 minims; 10% solution Bromide of Potassium, 20 minims.

This to be sure, does not keep *indefinitely,* but is good for three to four weeks. Have [it] prepared just before leaving, then.

When necessary to take, use a teaspoonful in half a glass of water. This may be taken three to four times a day. Keep quiet.

Well to take a thorough purging during the next week, [so] that the system may be in a normal equilibrium.

288-47   F.35   12/16/40

Q-7. What causes, and how may I prevent, sickness while traveling [by car]?

A-7. By keeping an equilibrium or balance within the system, and changing the mind's attitude.

Talk! Don't just sit—without talking! Find those influences of interest from without, and there will not be the unbalancing from within, see?

106-7   F.48   4/20/25

[Suggestion:] . . . You will also have the specific condition as results from train sickness . . . You will tell us a specific remedy for this trouble, and if same may be used with others . . .

As to the conditions as relating to [train sickness], these we find are much of the psychological conditions of the body, yet for this, and other bodies, there may be prepared that which would eliminate the greater portion of this condition, when the mental forces are kept with the correct equilibrium in body.

They would be found in this: To 2 ounces of a 2% solution of limewater, add 2 ounces of a 10% solution of cinnamon water. To this 10 minims of a 10% solution of Iodide Potassium, with 5 minims of 10% solution Bromide Potassium.

The dose of this would be 3 to 5 drops in water, taken every 1, 2, 3 or 4 hours, according to the needs of the condition of the body. This we would find will offer the correct balance in the system for nausea as is produced by the motion, for the action of same is of a nerve condition, produced by unbalancing of the hypogastric and pneumogastric plexuses, producing nausea, headache, to the body. This we find would work direct with the system as in this: The lime-water offering the reaction in gastric juices to produce elimination, the cinnamon offering the sediment and sedative for the gastric juices, while the Iodide and Bromide act as the sedimentary forces for the nerve system, pneumogastric and hypogastric each being acted upon in a different manner by the two in the combination with each other in this manner.

With these we would find the greater benefits to those of such conditions. Do that.

Q-1. Would this remedy be beneficial in seasickness?

A-1. Any condition wherein the body is set in undue motion or position. Be well for dancers, or seasickness, or train sickness, or auto trips; any wherein the body is unduly positioned.

Service

416-2   M.28   4/29/34

Q-16. Just how can I affiliate myself with those fostering the [A.R.E.] work . . . ?

A-16. Speak kindly, speak in convincing ways and manners of that which is thine own experience. For, each soul must apply—especially spiritual, but also mental truths in its own experience. With all of those that are sincere in their endeavors to make known that which is the birthright of every soul through such information, that not only makes for the less and less of self but the more and more of that Christ Spirit that gives life, light and understanding to those that seek Him; then—in the closer relationships, in an aid here, in an aid there—these will bring about contentment in the experience that makes peace and harmony in the souls of all.

1877-2   F.45   4/18/40

Q-6. Is there any way in which the entity at this time could serve her Father-God, as she has an intense desire to do so?

A-6. As indicated, it is not by might, nor by some great deed . . . nor by something that may be spoken of by others, but as He has given so oft, it is here a little, there a little, line upon line, precept upon precept; *sowing* the fruits of the spirit, *leaving* the fruition of same to God! So oft do individuals stumble over their own abilities, because of not seeing, not experiencing great revolutions because of their attempts. Remember, as it was told to those of old, as it was told to *thee* by those who answered when ye beheld Him enter the glory of the clouds, the sky, "Think not He has left thee, for His promise has been, Lo, I am with thee always, even unto the end of the world" . . . Faint not—but keep the faith.

165-22   M.60   5/29/37

Q-9. What time and activity should be devoted to helping Miss [1376]?

A-9. . . . each entity must stand upon its *own inner* developments to bring peace or harmony. So long as any is leaning upon another, or so long as self is leaning upon another, there *cannot* be the full or complete control of self.

1957-1   F.32   7/17/39

. . . do not be afraid of giving self in a service—if the *ideal* is correct. If it is for selfish motives, for aggrandizement, for obtaining a hold to be used in an underhand manner, *beware*. If it is that the glory of truth may be made manifest, *spend it* all—whether self, mind, body, or the worldly means—whether in labor or in the coin of the realm.

1599-1   F.54   5/29/38

For until ye are willing to *lose* thyself in service, ye may not indeed know that peace which He has promised to give—to all.

243-15   F.53   12/12/32

. . . when there has been and is made the best possible effort that self may give to do that which is in keeping with His will (as is understood by self), leave the results in His hands; for whom the Lord quickeneth may be turned into those channels . . . which will give the channel for the better service to self, to others. *Make known* the desires to . . . [those] connections that may be had. Then wait ye on Him.

887-3   F.25   6/18/35

Keep ever, all, in the attitude that—in thy service to those thou would entertain—something is given out that arouses helpful hopefulness in the experience of the individual or the group or the masses that ye would entertain. For whether ye preach a sermon, or whether ye entertain . . . let it be done with an eye-singleness of *service*, of *joy*, of helpfulness to thy fellow man . . . let each and every program contain something of a *spiritual* awakening; not only for self, but as ye give, as ye do unto thy fellow man, ye are doing unto the God in thyself.

Sin

3395-2   F.63   1/15/44

Q-1. Is the ill health which I have been experiencing the past years the result of mistakes of a past life or is it due to something amiss in this present life?

A-1. Both. For there is the law of the material, there is the law of the mental, there is the law of the spiritual. That brought into materiality is first conceived in spirit. Hence as we have indicated, all illness is sin; not necessarily of the moment, as man counts time, but as a part of the whole experience. For God has not purposed or willed that any soul should perish, but purgeth everyone by illness, by prosperity, by hardships, by those things needed, in order to meet self—but in Him, by faith and works, are ye made every whit whole.

281-2   10/16/31

Q-7. Please explain why the Master in many cases forgave sins in healing individuals.

A-7. Sins are of commission and omission. Sins of commission were forgiven, while sins of omission were called to mind—even by the Master.

815-7   M.39   12/3/42

If the soul were at all periods, all manifestations, to keep in that perfect accord, or law, with the "over-soul," or the First Cause, or the Soul from which it comes, then there would be only a continuous at-onement with the First Cause.

But when an entity, a soul, uses a period of manifestation—in whatever realm of consciousness—to its *own indulgencies*, then there is need for the lesson, or for the soul understanding or interpreting, or to become aware of the error of its way.

What, then, was the first cause of this awareness?

It was the eating, the partaking, of knowledge; knowledge without wisdom—or that as might bring pleasure, satisfaction, gratifying—not of the soul but of the phases of expression in that realm in which the manifestation was given.

Thus in the three-dimensional phases of consciousness such manifestations become as pleasing to the eye, pleasant to the body appetites. Thus the interpretation of the experience, or of that first awareness of deviation from the divine law, is given in the form as of eating of the tree of knowledge.

Who, what influence, caused this—ye ask?

It was that influence which had, or would, set itself in opposition to the souls remaining, or the entity remaining, in that state of at-onement [with the First Cause].

What, then, is the first cause of man's expression? That he may know himself to be himself and yet one with the Father; separate, yet as Father, Son and Holy Spirit are one, so the body, the mind, the soul of an entity may also be at-one with the First Cause.

Q-2. What is the "soul lesson" that I am "asked" to receive from the severance of relations with Miss [2700]?

A-2. All forms of sin or lessons may be implied in the word selfishness. To illustrate in the immediate conditions; and this becomes the application of that implied or intended to be pointed out in the lesson or in the facts above:

In thine own experiences in the earth, in relationships with this entity, ye possessed the body without regard to the unfoldment of the soul of this entity, in its relationships to the First Cause.

Now: The lesson is—though in the *mind*, there are the needs for encouragement, love, the associations for the better activity of the body. Are these to be in mind or in reality—reality meaning soul?

Hence a lesson becomes necessary. As to whether it is to be rectified in this present experience depends upon choices taken in relationships to mental and material activities.

As is oft expressed, the spirit is willing, the motivating force of a soul-entity is willing, but the body, ego, mind, the impelling force to or through which consciousness arises and makes the entity aware through the emotions of mind and body, has its lesson to gain.

Q-3. Wherein was I failing her, or failing my own soul and its progress?

A-3. Doth God point out thy failings? The law is perfect. Study to show thyself approved unto an ideal. Have ye an ideal—spiritual, mental, material? Do ye keep the faith as ye profess in thy knowledge? Knowledge without works is sin. Sin lieth at thy door if ye fail to keep the faith.

These questions may be answered only in self. *No one* made anyone a judge! Thy higher, thy soul self is ever the judge. And thy angel—as everyone's angel, or the shadow of that it is possible for thee to be—stands before the throne, *ever*, to make intercession—through Him who hath shown the way.

What manner of consideration and activity have ye given? Only such a case may be presented for that judgment.

The spirit is willing, the flesh is weak; the *mind* is oft zealous, jealous, faithless.

Q-4. How may I repair the damage I, by whatever acts or thoughts you may find, caused to be created in our association?

A-4. As just given—study to show thyself approved unto *God;* not to man, nor to an individual.

Do *right*, not as in thine own sight but as in the sight of the law of God, the soul—that seeks its union with, that awareness of its oneness with, the Creative Force.

852-12   F.18   11/15/35

. . . selfishness is the besetting sin of man. Tolerance, faith, patience—*these* be expressions that may make for the happiness that all are crying for. Yet so few are willing to pay the price for same—which is tolerance, patience, and *selflessness* in the expressions to its associates, its fellow man, its activities in the earth.

243-10   F.50   7/23/30

. . . being afraid is the first consciousness of sin's entering in, for he that is made afraid has lost consciousness of self's own heritage with the Son; for we are heirs through Him to that Kingdom that is beyond all of that that would make afraid, or that would cause a doubt in the heart of any. Through the recesses of the heart, then, search out that that would make afraid, casting out fear, and *He* alone may guide.

Sinusitis

2794-2   F.34   5/19/43

As we find, there still are irritations existent throughout the
alimentary canal—from the effect of the sinus disorder. We would
use the Glyco-Thymoline® packs over the nasal passages, or sinus
passages. Saturate three to four thicknesses of cotton cloth, or
gauze, in warm Glyco Thymoline®, and apply over the passages,
allowing such a pack to remain on for fifteen to twenty minutes
at the time—and keep up until the passages are clear. Apply such
packs whenever there is any distress—either in the sinus or in the
digestive system. Such packs may also be applied over the abdominal area to advantage, as well as over the face, see?

Also we would take Glyco-Thymoline® internally, two to three
drops in half a glass of water about twice a day (and drink a glass
of water afterwards), until the system has been purified.

5147-1   M.53   5/24/44

In meeting the needs, then . . . First, we would have prepared an
inhalant. Take at least a six to eight ounce container, preferably a
large-mouth bottle. Prepare this so there are two vents in the cork
of the bottle, which may themselves be corked, so that neither of
these vents extends into the solution. For only the fumes or gases,
which are formed by the combination of that which will be placed in
same, are to be inhaled into the nostril; and the effect is this through
this gas from same to the antrum, throat and the soft tissue of the
face and head. Put, then, into the container first, four ounces of pure
grain alcohol. Then add, in the order named:

Oil of Eucalyptus ....30 minims
Rectified Oil of Turp ....10 minims
Compound Tincture of Benzoin ....20 minims
Oil of Pine Needles ....5 minims
Tolu in Solution ....15 minims

These will be suspended in the alcohol. Shaking together, and then removing both of the small corks, inhale deeply into the nostril. This will
also go into the trachea and bronchi, and it will relieve those tensions,
acting as not only an antiseptic but as an allaying of the inflammation
which tends to affect also the soft tissue and those tendencies towards
the conditions indicated. Do this two or three times each day.

4008-1   M.41   3/28/44

In those areas from the 9th dorsal downward, we find suppressions, subluxations and segments that have become static. Over these areas we would apply, once or twice a week, oil heat—as from toweling dipped in Peanut Oil and applied with heat to the spinal area. Just after these have been applied, have osteopathic adjustments made.

Do this for three to four weeks, then leave off two weeks, and then repeat. Keep this procedure up for quite a long period, some six to eight months and we would find—with these general corrections—there should be brought much better conditions for this body.

This we would do. Don't begin it unless it is to be carried through. Any good osteopath, especially of the Missouri school would be preferable—the Kirksville School, a graduate of that particular school would be preferable . . .

Q-19. What should be done about the sinusitis?

A-19. Do the treatments indicated and the massages that will follow with the osteopathic adjustments for the better circulation through all portions of [the] body, and these will correct [conditions] through the sinus; provided there is the attention given to the keeping of a correct balance in the acidity and alkalinity of the body.

Smoking

3539-1   M.59   1/6/44

Q-3. If smoking is not particularly harmful to the extent that I indulge, is it best that I smoke a pipe or cigarettes?

A-3. Smoking in moderation for this body would be helpful. To excess it's very harmful. The smoking of cigarettes is better than most types.

303-23   F.54   6/10/41

Q-7. Would smoking of cigarettes in any way be beneficial to my body; if so, what brand, and how many a day?

A-7. The nicotine for the body would supply a poison that would counter-balance some of the disturbances in the system. Three to five a day would be correct. This does not necessarily mean that these would be inhaled, but the brand that is of the purer tobacco is the better.

Q-8. Which brands are the pure tobacco?

A-8. Virginia Ovals and [cigarettes] of such natures.

303-32   F.55   4/11/42

Q-7. What is cause and relief for the nervousness, especially after eating or smoking?

A-7. Tiredness, lack of resistance in the body. Take time to be quiet before eating. Take time to be quiet before smoking, or when smoking. Don't smoke and talk or carry on at such a rate that the mind is running away with the body. This does not allow *any* stimulant to come from the relaxation that should come in smoking.

1131-2   M.Adult   10/29/32

Q-8. Is smoking injurious to the body? If not, what brand should be used or would be best for the body?

A-8. Smoking in moderation will be helpful to the body. The best brands, we would find, are those that are of the purer tobacco that are not either toasted or mixed with foreign conditions. Those known as or called Piedmonts are the better [for this body].

462-4   M.49   12/5/33

Q-6. What kind of tobacco, if any, should this body use?

A-6. Pure tobacco is always better than any concoction of the compilation of other things with same. If it's to be used at all, use the natural leaf. Then you won't use so much of it either!

462-6   M.51   8/29/35

Q-5. Is tobacco good?

A-5. Tobacco in moderation, as all stimulants, is not so harmful. However, overacidity or overalkalinity causes same to become detrimental.

Q-6. What brands of tobacco are best?

A-6. Just tobacco, and no brand, is best! In its *natural* state it is preferable to any of the combinations that are ordinarily put on the market in package tobacco!

5545-1   M.41   2/10/30

This we will find [is] well to use as mouthwashes, alternating same; of mornings with one character [of mouthwash], of evenings with another character. Listerine® and *Glyco-Thymoline®—alternating* these, on account of the changes as are to be wrought in [the] system . . .

Q-4. Is smoking aggravating [his] condition?

A-4. He won't want to smoke so much if he washes his mouth out with what we've been giving!

Q-5. Should it be given up entirely?

A-5. No, shouldn't give it up entirely—for there is a relaxation from nicotine for the system that is *not* harmful to anyone, *if* taken moderately. Use these washes, and they will see how moderately it will [make him] smoke—for it will make him sick!

Soul Development

987-4   F.49   11/2/37

For life—or the motivative force of a soul—is eternal . . . For each soul seeks expression. And as it moves through the mental associations and attributes in the surrounding environs, it gives out that which becomes either for selfish reactions of the own ego or—to express—or for the I AM to be at-one with the Great I AM THAT I AM.

What then are the purposes for the activities of an entity in a material plane, surrounded with those environs that make for self-expressions or self-activities in the various ways and manners?

What meaneth these? That self is growing to that which it, the entity, the soul, is to present, as it were, to the Great I AM in those experiences when it is absent from materiality.

These become hard at times for the individual to visualize; that the mental and soul may manifest without a physical vehicle. Yet in the deeper meditations, in those experiences when those influences may arise when the spirit of the Creative Force, the universality of soul, of mind—not as material, not as judgments, not *in* time and space but *of* time and space—may become lost in the Whole, instead of the entity being lost in the maze of confusing influences—then the soul visions arise in the meditations.

And the centers becoming attuned to the vibrations of the bodily force, these give a vision of that as may be to the entity an outlet for the self-expressions, in the beauties and the harmonies and the activities that become, in their last analysis: just being patient, long-suffering, gentle, kind. *These* are the fruits of the spirit of truth; just as hates, malice and the like become in their growths those destructive forces in creating, in making for those things that are as but tares, confusions, dissensions in the experiences of an entity.

Those then are the purposes of the entrance of an entity into a material plane; to choose that which is its ideal.

Then ask thyself the question—gain the answer first in thy physical consciousness:

"What is my ideal of a *spiritual* life?"

Then when the answer has come—for it has been given by Him that is Life, that the kingdom of God, the kingdom of heaven, is within; and we view the kingdom of God without by the application of those things that are of the spirit of truth—these then answered, ye seek again in the inner consciousness: "Am I true to my ideal?"

These become then the answers. This and that and the other; never as pro and con. For the growth in the spirit is as He has given; ye *grow* in grace, in knowledge, in understanding.

How? As ye would have mercy shown thee, ye show mercy to those that even despitefully use thee. If ye would be forgiven for that which is contrary to thy own purposes—yet through the vicissitudes of the experiences about thee, anger and wrath give place to better judgment—ye, too, will forgive those that have despitefully used thee; ye will hold no malice. For ye would that thy Ideal, that Way ye seek, hold no malice—yea, no judgment—against thee. For it is the true law of recompense; yea, the true law of sacrifice.

For not in sacrifice alone has He sought His judgments, but rather in mercy, in grace, in fortitude; yea, in divine love.

The shadows of these are seen in thy inner experience with thy fellow man day by day. For ye have seen a smile, yea a kind word, turn away wrath. Ye have seen a gentleness give hope to those that have lost their hold on purpose, other than the satisfying of an appetite—yea, other than satisfying the desires of the carnal mind.

Hence as ye give, ye receive. For this is mercy, this is grace. This is the beauty of the inner life lived.

Know then it is not that judgment is passed here or there. For know that God looketh upon the heart and He judgeth rather the purposes, the desires, the intents.

For what seekest thou to lord [laud] in thy life? Self-intent? Know ye not that it was selfishness that separated the souls from the spirit of life and light? Then only in the divine love do ye have the opportunity to become to thy fellow man a saving grace, a mercy, yea even a savior.

For until ye have in thy own material associations known thyself to be the saving grace to someone, ye may not know even the whole mercy of the Father with the children of men.

Then it is not of rote; it is not ritual that has made for those influences in thine own experience; but in whom, in what hast thou put thy trust?

He has promised to meet thee within the temple of thine own body. For as has been given, thy body is the temple of the living God; a tabernacle, yea, for thy soul. And in the holy of holies within thine own consciousness He may walk and talk with thee. How? How?

Is it the bringing of sacrifice? Is it the burning of incense? Is it the making of thyself of no estate?

Rather is it that ye *purpose!* For the try, the purpose of thine inner self, to *Him* is the righteousness. For He hath known all the vicissitudes of the earthly experience. He hath walked through the valley of the shadow of death. He hath seen the temptations of man from every phase that may come into thine own experience; and, yea, He hath given thee, "If ye will love me, believing I am able, I will deliver thee from that which so easily besets thee at *any* experience."

And it is thus that He stands; not as a Lord but as thy Brother, as thy Savior; that ye may know indeed the truth that gentleness, kindness, patience, brotherly love, beget—in thy heart of hearts, with him—that peace, that harmony. Not as the world knoweth peace but as He gave: "That peace I give you; that ye may know that thy spirit, yea thy soul, beareth witness with me that ye are mine—I am thine,"even as the Father, the Son, the Holy Spirit.

Even so may thy soul, thy mind, thy body, become aware of that which renews the hope, the faith, the patience within thee.

And until ye show forth in His love that patience, ye cannot become aware of thy relationship with Him. Even as He has given, in patience ye become aware of being that soul—that seeketh the Father's house that is within even thine own consciousness . . .

Q-4. What is holding back my spiritual development?

A-4. Nothing holding [it] back . . . but *self*. For know, as has been given of old, "Though I take the wings of the morning in thought and fly unto the uttermost parts of the earth, Thou art there! Though I fly into the heavenly hosts, Thou art there! Though I make my bed in hell, Thou art there!"

And as He has promised, "When ye cry unto me, I WILL *HEAR*—and answer speedily."

Nothing prevents—only self.

Keep self and the shadow away. Turn thy face to the light and the shadows fall behind.

Stuttering

2015-8   F.2   9/16/41

From outside influences we find that pressures have been caused in the cerebrospinal system; especially in the areas of the 2nd and 3rd dorsal and 3rd cervical; which has caused some deflection to the activity of the stomach, as well as a deflection in the auditory forces—which is indicated in the speaking voice.

This should be corrected, else we may find—while it may be corrected in a manner by the body's own growth—it would leave weaknesses and tendencies to be met later on—in the digestive system as well as in the abilities of enunciation.

Then, in the beginning, we would have first about four osteopathic adjustments; with special reference to those areas in the upper dorsal, through the cervical, *and* at the end of the spine.

With the first of such adjustments we would then begin with massaging the spine, particularly, with Peanut Oil; at least every other day.

To purify the alimentary canal, give every day about three drops of Glyco-Thymoline® or Lavoris®; and keep this up until such may be detected as an odor in the stool.

Do these; and be mindful as to diets; keeping plenty of the vitamins, especially B-1, A and G. These will be found principally in scraped beef or steak, cereals, carrots, yellow yams, yellow peaches and yellow apples. Give the apples only cooked, however, and these in their skins—as roasted, see? Do these for the better conditions for this body.

416-5   M.29   1/3/35

. . . there are many changes in the physical forces of the body in the present from that which we have had here before. Not all of these are for improvements. Rather has there been an upsetting of the system from violent influences from without [auto accident], so that in many portions of the system there is the necessity for a coordinating throughout the cerebrospinal system . . .

From the upper cervical area there is produced the tendency for dizziness, forgetfulness, irritations that cause singing and drumming in the ear, affectations to the speech and even to the vision at times. All of these effects are disturbing factors, not by impingements but rather engorgements in the 3rd, 5th and 2nd cervicals; especially where these make for their associations with the divisions to the vagus nerves.

In the brachial center, or the upper dorsal, we also find an impingement; specifically in the 2nd and 3rd dorsal. This should be coordinated specifically with the cerebrospinal and sympathetic junction in the area, with the specific relationships established in the 2nd and 3rd segment—with the brachial center, you see . . .

These need adjustment, with those stimulations that *have* been given; not given during adjustments but after the adjustments have been made in these particular areas. Not so much the sun ray or the extreme light, but rather the higher vibrations such as found in the sinusoidal for a *general* treatment to the body—stimulating directly through the activities of the upper centers along the 2nd and 3rd dorsal to the sympathetic, and to the gastral centers for the digestive system, and those along the lumbar for the activative forces of the body.

Suffering

3209-2   F.51   12/31/43

For many an individual entity those things that are of sorrow are the greater helps for unfoldment, as the entity has experienced in some of its disappointments.

204-1   M.34   1/10/29

. . . while suffering may bring understanding [to an entity], *causing* [others] to suffer to satisfy one's own self brings reproach . . . Be true to self in such a manner as to not bring reproach from others, and most of all from self.

569-27   F.62   1/12/43

Q-5. Why do I have to suffer so?

A-5. Much might be given as respecting such a question. This would require that all of those activities be reviewed that have brought those disturbances of every nature in the earth.

Know, even as He, though He were the Son, yet learned *He* obedience through the things which He suffered. No servant is above his Master. Ye are one with Him. Know that His strength, His love, His might, will be with thee all the way, if ye trust wholly in Him.

1445-1   F.38   9/22/37

Let the body-mind continue in the attitude of seeking for the *spiritual* awakening. Know that each experience in this material plane is, if used in a constructive manner, *for soul development!* . . . While the trials, the temptations, the sufferings come; and oft may the body ask self "If the Creative Force or God is mindful of man, why does He allow me to suffer so?" Know that though He were the Son, yet learned He obedience through the things suffered in body, in mind, in the material or earthly plane.

5242-1   M.20   6/3/44

Learn, the first primary success which is worthy of emulating is worthy of being suffered for . . . They who would gain the greater will suffer the more. Those who would attain to a more perfect understanding of the true relationships of an individual to creative forces and using of same constructively, recognize the unfoldment of the mind through the experience.

5206-1   M.22   6/10/44

There are, to be sure, pathological disturbances, yet conditions are such here that the greater help may be brought by just being patient, just being kind and loving to the entity . . . For the body is one of those who is meeting its own self in the physical expression in the present. There has been, and is yet to be, a great deal of suffering physically to be experienced by the body . . . do give a great deal of prayer . . . those who are close to the entity.

5194-1   F.52   6/5/44

There should be rather those administrations of the mental and spiritual help . . . to make easier that journey which this entity soon must take. For life is not spent just because changes come about, but the greater opportunity for this soul-entity is to be released from the suffering. For, in the same manner as He, who is the Way, suffered, so must each individual meet that in the flesh; that we may know that the Savior bears with each soul that which will enable life, consciousness, to be a continuous experience.

5265-1   F.57   5/29/44
. . . let thy prayer ever be, "Lord, let me be the channel for supplying that in the experiences of those with whom I come in contact, and for the needs of man at this particular period, that they may know Thee better through the things which they have suffered and do suffer."

Sunbathing

276-7   F.16   4/14/34
Q-10. What is the best formula that will make my skin brown from the sun?
A-10. Sun tan for some is good. But for those that have a certain amount of pigment in the skin, as indicated in this body, to make for variations as to the effect of weather or sun upon exposed portions of the body—made up of the atomic vibrations to which the circulation in various portions of the body is reactive—to get a sun tan would not be well for this body; for it would burn tissue before it would tan. That which would be more effective (if the body is insistent that it desires the tan) would be the use of vinegar and Olive Oil (not vinegar made from acetic acid or synthetic vinegar, but the use of that made from the apples) combined with coffee made from resteaming or re-vaporing used coffee grounds. The tannin in each of these and the acids combined, would become very effective. But it will wear off, of course, in a very short time even—if used.

934-2   F.24   7/11/35
Let there be not too much activity in the middle of the day, or [too much] of the sunshine. The early mornings and the late afternoons are the more preferable times. For the sun during the period between eleven or eleven-thirty and two o'clock carries too *great* a

quantity of the actinic rays that make for destructive forces to the superficial circulation . . .

275-20   F.18   6/29/31

Q-1. What quantity of sunbathing should [the] body take to replace ultraviolet lamp? or should body take both?

A-1. No. We would take the sun bath, but take that that adds to the body; *do not* tan the body *too* much! That that gives the full activity to the capillaries, or to the exterior portions of the system, is fine, but too much sun is worse than too little; for light is penetrating of itself—see?

3051-1   F.45   6/16/43

Any good lotion would be well for the sunburn; such as soda water, or any application that would act as a balm, in the forms of some characters of oils that remove the fire from the affected areas—such as Glyco-Thymoline®.

1709-10   F.24   6/21/43

Q-3. [Please give] Remedy for [the] skin breaking out from [the] sun.

A-3. Use Palmolive soap® baths, followed with a small amount of pure white vaseline rubbed on any rough places.

5126-1   M.42   5/19/44

Q-1. What is the cause of the injury to the eyes?

A-1. Too strong a light when very young, in sunlight.

3172-2   F.1   5/15/44

Keep [the child] in the open often but never with the sun shining directly on the face or eyes. These should ever be shaded. Never during those periods from 11:00 until 2:00. Then the body should not be in the sun, but the early periods and late periods are very well. It is the absorption of the ultraviolet which gives strength and vitality to the nerves and muscular forces, which comes from the effect of the rays of the sun from the activities of the body. It is not so well that there be too much of the tan from the sun on the body. This forms on [the] body to protect the body from same. Thus not so much of the tan but sufficient for the healthy activity of [the] body.

Teeth

3484-1   M.40   12/27/43

Q-3. What is [the] best procedure for care of teeth?

A-3. Have local attention and then take care of the teeth. Use an equal combination of salt and soda for massaging the gums and teeth—don't use a brush [for massaging], use your finger!

3436-1   M.45   11/30/43

Q-5. What can I do to keep my teeth for life?

A-5. You won't. For already these have begun to need local attention. If there is kept the proper balance in the vitamins, it will help—but these precautions should begin—well, during the period of gestation is when they should begin, but for a body should begin at least in the first or second year.

The general care of [teeth] with a good dentifrice as well as a good massage for the gums will aid. Use Ipsab® at least twice a week for the gums. Use Ipana® for brushing the teeth. Massage the gums with Ipsab®, though, and we will have a better chance for keeping the teeth much longer.

365-4   F.38   2/27/35

Q-3. What can I do to prevent the teeth from wearing down?

A-3. Use more of an alkaline-reacting diet; as quantities of orange juice with a little lemon in same, as four parts orange juice to one part lemon; [also] grapefruit, raw vegetables, potato peelings . . .

3051-1   F.45   6/16/43

For local disturbance, use Ipsab® as a massage for the gums; using this just three times a week. Then use any good dentifrice; preferably that of the same combinations [as] of Ipsab®, but without the iodine in same—Ipana®.

3051-3   F.45   10/25/43

Cycles change for the teeth during the second year of each [seven-year life] cycle. During that year take at least 3 to 4 series of Calcios™ [doses] or its equivalent to supply calcium to the system, and it will aid not only the teeth but all the activities of the thyroid glands.

274-5   M.35   11/13/33

Q-5. How often should Ipsab® be used in this case?

A-5. Once or twice a week. Apply a small quantity; or dip the finger into the solution, after it is shaken together, and massage the gums; or apply a small quantity to a tuft of cotton and massage inside and outside the gums; upper and lower. Where specific conditions in the teeth disturb, apply a small quantity on the end of a tooth-pick(with a tuft of cotton around same, to be sure) and rub along the edge of the gums. This will be found most effective. It will destroy those influences known as Rigg's or pyorrhea effects.

257-13   M.33   7/5/26

Use Ipsab® to keep these [teeth] clear from the tartar and from the condition [bleeding gums] as in the mouth, see?

1467-8   M.35   8/2/40

Q-1. Should I continue to use soda and salt, or Ipana® tooth-paste?

A-1. Ipana® at the present time; though there is no better dentifrice than soda and salt ordinarily.

Q-2. Is Ipsab® the acid antiseptic referred to?

A-2. As indicated, one is an acid, one an alkaline. Use the Ipsab® as a massage and a cleanser twice each day. After the use of same rinse the mouth as indicated with Glyco-Thymoline®, full strength.

457-11   F.34   9/3/42

Q-23. What causes the gray film on teeth?

A-23. The chemical balance in the system and the throw-off or discharge from breath in the lungs. This [the breath] is a source from which drosses are relieved from the system, and thus passing through the teeth produce [evidences of] same on the teeth. Keeping such cleansed with an equal combination of soda and salt at least three to four times a week will cleanse these [teeth] of this disturbance. The use of Ipsab® as a wash for mouth and gums will further aid in keeping these conditions cleansed; and [use] any good dentrifrice once or twice a day.

3211-2   M.55   12/26/43

Q-12. Where and under what conditions should ultraviolet ray®

be used in dentistry, and how?

A-12. Ultraviolet rays should be used in dentistry when there are indications of any form of Rigg's [or pyorrhea] disease. It should then be used about half a minute on the back of the neck, and the jaw. And you'll have it!

2981-2   M.33   8/12/43

Q-10. Give care of teeth so I will have less decaying.

A-10. Use as a massage for the gums and teeth an equal combination of common table salt and baking soda; about once a month, add one drop only of chlorine to a pint of water and rinse the mouth with this. Do not swallow it, but rinse the mouth and then brush the teeth. This will preserve them, even aid in filling cavities.

903-21   F.31   1/31/34

Massage gums and teeth with that solution known as Ipsab®, for the thickening of the gums and for the aiding of the general condition.

5313-4   F.40   7/5/44

Q-6. How to prevent tooth decay which I've had an awful lot of the past three years.

A-6. Have them attended to, and add to the system occasionally Atomidine® as a manner of gaining better control of the activity of the glands which formulate the circulation through teeth and structural portion of the body. One drop 5 days at a time and then skip 2 weeks. Then again—do this through a whole year, [and] you'll have your teeth in very good fix if local attention is given to the rest.

903-31   F.36   6/6/38

Q-2. What should be done about her teeth [and] the existing condition of the enamel? Is it due to her diet, or can some correction be made by the dentist?

A-2. As we find, we would include with the diet, twice a day, those properties that are found in Calcios™. This would be most beneficial. About half a teaspoonful, level; taken twice each day, *with* the meal.

325-55   F.62   1/24/35

Q-3. Does gold in the mouth help to cause bitterness?

A-3. It does! No teeth should ever be filled with heavy metals, [such] as gold.

325-54   F.62   1/10/35
Where there is indicated that pus sacs are a portion of the roots of the teeth, remove them! For they only become a storehouse for poisons.

Telepathy

1909-2   M.33   2/5/31
Much may be given to this body as respecting the abilities that may be builded within self, especially as would be related to telepathic influences the entity or body-mind may have upon [its] associates. Beware, or be warned—do not abuse [this ability] and call that upon self that would be called from another! Do not ask another to do that you would *not* do your own self.

1135-4   M.35   4/9/36
[Suggestion:] You will have before you [Mr. 1135], his intent and desire to conduct specific experiments with the view of enlarging our understanding of thought transference (mental telepathy). You will advise him regarding the best procedure to follow, including basic principles and suggestions for properly conducting the individual experiments.

Mr. Cayce: . . . In considering conditions conducive to such an experience in the activities of individuals, there are three phases or three elements that go to make up the basic ideas or basic conditions that become relative or correlated to such experience.

First, the Physical; then the Spiritual; and then the Processive Manners.

In the first process there are from the pathological standpoint of view those elements in the first cause, or in the eugenics of that cause, that produce in the plasm the vibratory rates that go to make for the urge that produces itself through its relative activity to itself in its process—or the very nature physically or pathologically of the man, or portion of the animal in its activity.

These are basic forces that make for the process of the activity of relative thought, or primary interest, or a receptivity, or the ability to become—as it were—subject to those very influences that go to produce same.

Just as may be seen in certain necessary influences or forces that go to make for conductors of energies used for transmissions of this or that influence that may become active. Some are good conductors, some are bad. Hence the physical force—these processes, these conditions are to be considered in making the study of, or in producing the ideal setting for such an activity.

Then the spiritual, or the intent, the purpose, the influence that possesses such a house, such a body; not merely from the physical, the tangible intelligencer of the activity, but the purpose and intent and desire of that manifesting through same; whether it, that activity, of the spirit, is in that process of its own ego or that merely as the channel for those expressions that may be an activity in such a process.

If these are of the nature that they are for, or have as their keynotes, the exploitation or self-indulgence or self aggrandizement of the man's activity, then they must eventually become as those influences that would destroy the very influence that would be activative through such a channel.

Then the process, as indicated, in knowing, in realizing or classifying those that are from their very natures those subjects for such an activity. And those influences as indicated should be the basis for such attempts for the creative force or activity of that which is indeed the psychic force. For here, as indicated by the very term itself, the spirit or soul of the entity or individual (not the personality but the individuality of those that are in accord or may be attuned) is active. Not all elements may be attuned to a vibratory influence sufficient for sending or receiving. Some may send while others may receive. There may be those that are able to do both. And such activities make for, then, a unison that becomes coordinant in its every relationship.

1135-6   M.36   11/11/36

There may be specific tests in mind reading, telepathy, thought transference, moving of objects even; yet these when presented out of their realm of activity, dealing with the individual for a helpful experience in the seeking, become channels that are of an entirely different nature—and partake, as we have given, either of subconscious impressions or the activities of consciousnesses in the realm of the interbetween that would become detrimental to the value of such information in the experience of consecrated seeking individuals for their aid and help to an understanding of their relationships to Creative Forces in this particular experience . . .

For, as we have given, there are almost as many types of psychic phenomena or psychic experience as there are individuals.

For *psychic* is of the soul, if in its true constructive sense. And as the soul is an individual, intricate portion of the whole, then the experience of each soul in its reaction with, upon or from experiences in that field of activity presents a study within itself.

This then, as we find, should be [the suggestion] to any group or any university:

There be presented what been the experience of individuals taken in every way and manner that have been recorded by the Association and those interested in same. If these [records] do not present sufficient truth, sufficient confidence of there being, not only the unusual, but that which the individuals applying—not merely knowing of but applying in their experience day by day—will make them as individuals better citizens, better neighbors, better parents, better friends, then forget it!

For unless such experiences create such in the lives of individuals that interest or apply themselves in the study of such, then it is indeed of little thought; nor has it any place in man's experience, and is not worthy of a name or consideration of *any* sort—or of any soul.

Then, these are the manners we would give for consideration:

If experiments are sought, these then must be weighed in the light of that given.

Many an individual, many a personage has given his all for the demonstrating of a truth.

As it has been indicated from the first through *this* channel, there should ever be that ideal, "What does such information as may come through such a channel produce in the experience of individuals, as to not their thoughts, nor their relations other than does such make them better parents, better children, better husbands, better wives, better neighbors, better friends, better citizens?"

And if and when it does *not*, LEAVE IT ALONE!

3343-1   M.36   11/1/43

... there is the great tendency for the entity to judge according to material standards and to depend mentally upon physical manifestations. These are well, but—with such standards and with such a measuring stick—one may easily deceive self. For we are warned that there is a way that seemeth right to a man but the end thereof is death. Death is separation, lost opportunity—in some sphere of activity in which there is a consciousness, either spiritual or material. Mind is ever the builder, for it is the companion of soul and body, and is the way that is demonstrated and manifested in the earth in the Christ.

Varicose Veins

243-38   F.63   4/10/43

... the acute conditions that are the more disturbing in the present are those of the varicose veins ... aggravating and tiring to the body. Thus the great distress that is caused when the body is on the feet for any great length of time; causing not only the disorders through the lower limbs and thighs but in the feet also.

And this general pressure, with the body attempting to go, causes the nerve pressures that become reflexly aggravating throughout the body.

Parts of this, of course, have a reflex in the general condition which has existed—where superacidity has caused distress. And this has caused undue activity to the kidneys as well.

As we find in the present, those pressures that exist in the lumbar and sacral axis, as well as in the lower portion—or coccyx end of the spine—are the areas that need the more adjustment to alleviate those tendencies for the circulation that carries blood away from the heart, and yet is so slow in the return of same; thus causing the enlarging of the veins in the lower limbs.

We would also take Mullein tea. This should be made of the fresh, green tender leaves. Pour a pint of boiling water over an ounce of the Mullein leaves and let steep for about 20 to 30 minutes. Then strain and keep in the ice box, so that it may be kept fresh. Take about an ounce to an ounce and a half of this each day. Make this fresh at least every 2 or 3 days. Keep this up, and it will aid in the circulation, in the elimination of the character of acid in the system, and aid in the circulation through the veins—that are disturbing.

When there is the ability to rest, apply the Mullein stupes to the areas in knee and along the thigh, and just below the knee where the veins are the more severe. But the tea taken internally will be more effective.

Do keep up eliminations.

Massage the feet and lower limbs daily in a tannic acid solution, or that preferably obtained from using old coffee grounds—which carries a mild tannic acid as well as other properties that would be beneficial—that is, the coffee made from the same, see? Boil these and use these, as well as the liquid, to bathe feet in—of evenings.

Do have the corrections osteopathically made in lumbar sacral axis, *and* the coccyx area; and coordinate the rest of the body, for the tiredness and for the relaxing of the nerves, when these are done.

243-39   F.64   2/17/44

Q-4. What are those terrible pains from, in toes next small one on each foot, particularly the left one?

A-4. Poor circulation through the lower limbs. The varicose veins, of course, fail to carry the circulation, thus causing the swelling of limbs and the disturbance of the body.

Vocational Guidance

165-24   M.60   6/28/37

. . . there may be a variation in suggestions or outlines, [but] to gain that which is a basic truth or law one must *commence.* For there should be, and if there is the proper basic understanding there must be, the basis upon spiritual laws that deal with the individual and the application of spiritual and mental law and truth in their association.

And this, as development, is as a first law. Do first things first, and then—as there is the understanding—the application comes; and day by day it grows not only in import but in purpose and in activity.

Do not let the vastness or the shadow of what may be the outcome topple the basis or the purposes; for if the basic principles are the correct ones in the foundation, no matter to what heights nor to what extent nor in what great scope of activity it may advance, basic principles being first correct, it would not be over top-heavy.

. . . Commence with the associations first in those lines that are in keeping with the abilities of the body, by its own initiative, its own purposes, its own desires . . .

2940-1   M.26   3/21/43

Q-1. Which of these three would I preferably do—teach, write, or lecture?

A-1. Each will lead into the other. Teach first, then lecture, and write as you do both.

For, in teaching—as will be indicated in self—you will learn to apply. For, you cannot teach—to any success—that you do not practice in thine own self.

1599-1   F.54   5/29/38

Q-1. Just what should be my life work, according to my abilities?

A-1. First, find *self;* and then be led by that as was first given—let thy prayer be, "Here am I, O Lord; send me, *use* me!"

1575-1   M.32   4/21/38

The greater abilities, as we shall see, lie in two *definite* directions. Either in that direction as a writer or lecturer (or both), or in that field as an actor. But these have been *so* latent, and require so much effort, they have been overlooked in the experience of the entity. And the analyses in those directions in which the entity has engaged in past experiences become rather as a matter of *convenience,* rather than choice—or exertion.

It would behoove the entity, then, to look deeply within self; analyze the abilities, analyze the faults as well as the virtues; and make the efforts to correct the faults and magnify the virtues. And do these in a way that self is not attempting to take shortcuts, nor to do the easy things—because these are the natural tendencies . . .

Q-2. Just what should be the first step to get into a work of this kind?

A-2. Analyzing of self, and—as has been indicated—why, and what for, and whether these would be constructive or in keeping with the best within self.

2329-3   F.42   5/1/41

Thus the entity in the present is endowed with those abilities for teaching, admonishing, ministering to those who would prepare themselves—either in the mental or the physical state—for certain particular activities individually. For example, the entity may aid those who are preparing for motherhood, or for the particular office of teaching; because of the combination of the entity's abilities to enter within, to the psychic or the inner self.

These should be the channels, the means of expression, if the entity would gain the more in the present in fulfilling those purposes, those abilities in which the entity may excel—or exceed many of those who partake of certain ritualistic activities, or ritualistic performances.

1901-1   M.38   5/30/39

Q-1. In order that the work may be done properly, please give me advice as to how to combine vocational guidance and psychology, etc., with our ordinary every day routine to make it most effective for the individual.

A-1. As has just been indicated. As ye will study in that way and manner to show thyself approved unto God, a workman not ashamed, He—with the promises and with those applications ye have made—will *open* thy mind, thy heart, to the opportunities before thee.

Q-2. Please give me the advice and guidance needed as to the plan on which I have been working the past 14 years, which would revolutionize this entire industry. I need this guidance before taking the final step.

A-2. Take that which has been given—and *do not* with that plan become the dictator at heart, but rather the big brother to thy fellowman—as also to thy home, thy child . . .

For he that makes material gains at the expense of home or of opportunities and obligations with his own family does so to his own undoing.

487-25   M.21   1/19/40

Q-3. What suggestions may I make to Mr. [257], who has tried to help me with this connection, that will aid him in being of the greatest assistance to me?

A-3. Not to overdo it! For, to be in the position where there is so much the going over heads as to cause an individual to be placed, it would mean rather—after a little—the putting of the individual himself "on the spot"; and unless exceptional indications were made as to abilities, it would blacklist the entity . . .

Q-13. *Considering all situations existent in the present, how long before the entity may expect a connection with General Electric?*

A-13. How long is it before tomorrow, or next month, or next week? According to the activities! This depends entirely upon circumstances and conditions which may arise, and depends greatly upon the practical application of the entity in the direction of making practical application of knowledge attained or gained! Within six months or two years, three years, or ten years—what's the difference, just so it's attained and carried on!

487-29   M.23   9/20/41

Q-15. *Is there anything that I can do to better follow the suggestions given in my reading?*

A-15. Be upright, straightforward, doing the duty ever; relying on the Right to carry through.

487-19   M.17   1/13/35

Q-6. *In preparation for my work in Duke in technology, would you suggest any specific books that would be of help to me to read before entering school?*

A-6. The New Testament will be the best one, and then those of the kindred subjects that are the choice of the body. These are the better, as to any specifics. These would be rather along on *any* of the lines in which the body chooses. Some good subjects on physics—that is, elementary physics. Some of those on the chemical reactions, and then the activities of same. And when you work this—it's four years from now, but work on this: Electrify, through the chemical change, that of sodium and calcium combinations for its *radial* effect.

Will

5023-2   M.45   7/18/44

. . . there is no urge in the astrological, in the vocational, in the hereditary or the environmental which surpasses the will or determination of an entity . . . it is true [that] there is nothing in heaven or hell that may separate the entity from the knowledge or from the love of the Creative Force called God, but self.

2448-2   F.25   5/31/41

Know that there is only one Spirit, and that thou possessest thy measure of same. Thy *will* is given thee to use or abuse that Spirit. For, the Spirit is of the Creator, and thy body is the temple of that Spirit manifested in the earth to defend or to use in thine own ego, or thine own self-indulgence, or to thine own glory, *or* unto the glory of Him who gave thee life and immortality—if ye preserve that life, that spirit in Him.

416-2   M.28   4/29/34

For, when the will to do is ever present and not faltered by doubts and fears that may arise in the experience of all, then does it build, then does it attract that which builds and builds and *is* the constructive force in the experience of all.

590-1   F.52   6/19/34

While will is the ruling factor and is beyond any environmental, hereditary or innate experience, the entity or individual may allow self to be so governed by mental urges as to become subject to them. For, there is not the same application by the entity in this direction as to its own qualifications and its own abilities in relationships to that which it might have accomplished, as is felt innate in the mental abilities of the self. For *here* the entity comes to depend upon, or is inclined to blame circumstance for the very things that come into the experience; yet if the entity would declare itself as respecting those things that are as innate qualifications or abilities in these directions, *much* might be accomplished.

As to whether circumstance or environ is to rule an entity's being or experience, or *will*, depends then—the most—upon what the entity or soul sets as its standard of qualifications to meet or measure up to, within its *own* self; or as to how well self may be guided by its standard in making decisions in those directions.

For, would that all souls could know that He, the Giver of good and perfect gifts, is ever ready and willing to assist, even in the minutest details of a human experience, or in those things that deal with the activities of a soul with its fellow man, if the trust will but be put in Him . . .

2072-14   F.34   4/17/44

Q-6. How can one be sure that a decision is in accordance with God's will?

A-6. As indicated here before. Ask self in the own conscious self, "Shall I do this or not?" The voice will answer within. Then meditate, ask the same, Yes or No. You may be very sure if thine own conscious self and the divine self is in accord, you are truly in that activity indicated, "My spirit beareth witness with thy spirit." You can't get far wrong in following the Word, as ye call the word of God.

262-81   5/12/35

What, then, is *will?* That which makes for the dividing line between the finite and the infinite, the divine and the wholly human, the carnal and the spiritual. For the *will* may be made one *with* HIM, or for self alone. With the Will, then, does man destine in the activities of a material experience how he shall make for the relationships with Truth.

Yoga

2475-1   M.44   3/27/41

Hugh Lynn Cayce: You will have before you the body and enquiring mind of [2475] . . . in special reference to the yoga exercises with which he has been experimenting, in breathing. You will indicate just what has taken place in the body and what should be done from this point, considering the best physical, mental and spiritual development of the entity .. .

Mr. Cayce: Yes, we have the body, the enquiring mind . . . those experiences . . .

To give that as would be helpful to the body at this time, there might be indicated for the body something of that which takes place when such exercises are used—and the experiences had by one so doing.

These exercises are excellent, yet it is necessary that special preparation be made—or that a perfect understanding be had by the body as to what takes place when such exercises are used.

For, *breath* is the basis of the living organism's activity. Thus, such exercises may be beneficial or detrimental in their effect upon a body.

Hence it is necessary that an understanding be had as to how, as to when, or in what manner such may be used.

It would be very well for the body to study very carefully the information which we have given through these sources as respecting meditation. Then this information as may be given here may prove of beneficial effect in the experiences of the body.

Each soul, individual or entity, finds these facts existent:

There is the body-physical—with all its attributes for the functioning of the body in a three-dimensional or a manifested earth plane.

Also there is the body-mental—which is that directing influence of the physical, the mental and the spiritual emotions and manifestations of the body; or the way, the manner in which conduct is related to self, to individuals, as well as to things, conditions and circumstances. While the mind may not be seen by the physical senses, it can be sensed by others; that is, others may sense the conclusions that have been drawn by the body-mind of an individual, by the manner in which such an individual conducts himself in relationship to things, conditions or people.

Then there is the body-spiritual, or soul-body—that eternal something that is invisible. It is only visible to that consciousness in which the individual entity in patience becomes aware of its relationship to the mental and the physical being.

All of these then are one—in an entity; just as it is considered, realized or acknowledged that the body, mind and soul are one—that God, the Son and the Holy Spirit are one.

Then in the physical body there *are* those influences, then, through which each of these phases of an entity may or does become an active influence.

There may be brought about an awareness of this by the exercising of the mind, through the manner of directing the breathing.

For, in the body there is that center in which the soul is expressive, creative, in its nature—the Leydig center.

By this breathing, this may be made to expand—as it moves along the path that is taken in its first inception, at conception, and opens the seven centers of the body that radiate or are active upon the organisms of the body.

This in its direction may be held or made to be a helpful influence for specific conditions, at times—by those who have taught, or who through experience have found as it were the key, or that which one may do and yet must not do; owing to whatever preparation has been made or may be made by the body for the use of this ability, this expression through the body-forces.

As this life-force is expanded, it moves first from the Leydig center through the adrenals, in what may be termed an upward trend, to the pineal and to the centers in control of the emotions—or reflexes through the nerve forces of the body.

Thus an entity puts itself, through such an activity, into association or in conjunction with all it has *ever* been or may be. For, it loosens the physical consciousness to the universal consciousness.

To allow self in a universal state to be controlled, or to be dominated, may become harmful

But to know, to feel, to comprehend as to *who* or as to *what* is the directing influence when the self-consciousness has been released and the real ego allowed to rise to expression is to be in that state of the universal consciousness—which is indicated in this body here, Edgar Cayce, through which there is given this interpretation for [2475].

So, in analyzing all this—first study the variations of what has been the body-temperament, in thought, in food. For, the body-physical becomes that which it assimilates from material nature. The body-mental becomes that it assimilates from both the physical-mental and the spiritual mental. The soul is *all* of that the entity is, has been or may be.

Then, *who* and *what* would the entity have to direct self in such experiences?

To be loosed without a governor, or a director, may easily become harmful.

But, as we would give from here, let not such a director be that of an entity. Rather so surround self with the universal consciousness of the *Christ* as to be directed by that influence as may be committed to thee.

Thus the entity may use constructively that which has been attained.

But to prevent physical harm, mental harm—attune self in body, in mind, with that influence by which the entity seeks to be directed; not haphazardly, not by chance—but as of old—choose thou this day *whom* ye will serve; the living God within thee, by thee, through thee? or those influences of knowledge without wisdom, that would enslave or empower thee with the material things which only gratify for the moment?

Rather choose thou as he of old—let others do as they may, but as for thee, serve thou the living God.

Thus ye may constructively use that ability of spiritual attunement, which is the birthright of each soul; ye may use it as a helpful influence in thy experiences in the earth.

But make haste *slowly!* Prepare the body. Prepare the mind, before ye attempt to loosen it in such measures [or] manners that it may be taken hold upon by those influences which constantly seek expressions of self rather than of a living, constructive influence of a *crucified* Savior.

Then, crucify desire in self; that ye may be awakened to the real abilities of helpfulness that lie within thy grasp.

Zoroastrianism

1211-1   M.36   7/03/36

Before that we find the entity was in the land now known as the Persian and Arabian, or in the 'city in the hills and in the plains,' when there were those peoples from the Grecian land who came first as those to take advantage of the situation.

The entity then was among those that persuaded those of its own people that there was power, there was might, not only the answering for the turmoils from within but for the material aids and the material help to the bodily afflictions of those that had come under the influence of the teacher.

And there again the entity gained and became as a leader; and was among those that were in power, being—as would be termed in the present—the second mayor of the 'city in the hills and the plains,' during those periods of Uhjltd's activity, during those periods of the rise of the city's activities as a commercial center, as a spiritual center, with the moral laws that became as a part of the Zoroastrian influences later in the experience of many peoples.

Then in the name Philossan, the entity gained much. For the position of the entity rose then to what might be said to be in the present as a high priest, or one commanding the people not only of the city but of many nations. For the influence of the entity went abroad to those that came to seek, and the activities then surpassed those of many that in the experience became as a portion of those activities in the 'city in the hills' that came from other nations.

For the experience of those activities there became as the melting pot, as it were; the Cosmopolitan of the many places, the democratic influence as was expressed or manifested—to use those terms that express such activities of the peoples as led so much by the entity during that particular expression or sojourn.

1219-1   F.40   7/13/36

Before that we find the entity was in what is now known as the Mongoloid or the Gobi land, when there were those interpretations by the Carpathians, those of the land of On [?], those by Saneid, those by Ra Ta; and those studies first from the earlier portions of the Zoroasters, as termed today.

The entity then was a princess in the Golden Temple of those peoples, aiding—after much persuasion—in the correlating of truths.

Hence we may find the entity's interests in many of the various thoughts that have grown to seed in the varied groups and the varied traditions of groups in their activity or a social order, or a worshipfulness order. Yet to the entity they all lead from the one, the source, the sun—with its *inner* meaning.

The name then, as would be termed now, was Um-Cmu.

1297-1   M.42   11/25/36

The entity then was among those of the Jewish race, yet had withdrawn as it were from those teachings of tradition—or the mere service in the temple—and had joined rather with those who had become of the understanding as handed down by the old Persian teacher, Zoroaster.

And that understanding the entity finds in its studies, in its application must be held to; as has ever been the experience of each soul; that the Law is *one*, the Source is *one!* and those that seek other than that find tribulation, turmoils, confusion.

Though there may be many approaches, cooperation in the activities—as in the Universe—brings the harmony of the universal activity; as does cooperation in human experience bring harmony and peace; while egotism and self-assertion and self-exaltation and self-indulgence bring inharmonious experiences, and the activity of turmoils, wars, strifes.

The name then was Armad-Heliel.

263-4   F.23   3/06/35

Then in the name Vashten, the entity brought to those of the Persian land that of the leader later associated with the Zoroasterian reactions, or a companion with that teacher in the land. Hence we will find those things of an oriental nature, whether they be of the dance, the rug, the dress, the manner of service or of rote, that were of an innate activity in the experience of that period, the entity finds a harkening within self to those things. These would be *well* to develop in the experience, for they will make for that awakening to the abilities within self to use not only the mental and innate faculties of the mind and soul in spiritual imports and truths, but making for a strength of purpose in the experiences in the earth.

364-8   4/15/32

(Q) In the Persian experience as San (or Zend) did Jesus give the basic teachings of what became Zoroastrianism?

(A) In all those periods that the basic principle was the Oneness of the Father, He has walked with men.

3685-1   F.29   2/20/44

For the entity then was the keeper of the records for what became the Zoroastrian religious purposes.

The entity gained, and the entity should use those religious purposes as comparative experiences in the present—but know that these also from that same one who gave, "I am the way, the truth and the light."

The name then was Elclara.

INDIVIDUAL
REFERENCE
FILE

INDEX

Aaron, daughters of: 49
abdominal area: 11, 66, 67, 166, 172, 222, 234, 235-236, 290
abilities: 5-6, 21, 29, 33, 37, 48, 50, 64-65, 68, 78-79, 94-95, 104, 154, 167, 169, 177, 180, 200, 210, 213, 220, 225, 229, 231, 237, 253, 259-260, 271-274, 286, 296, 304, 309, 310-311, 312, 316, 318
acclimatization: 108
acid: 24, 85, 122, 124, 125, 131, 134, 143, 156, 161, 162, 185, 195,196
   acetic: 120, 122, 299
   boracic: 174, 176
   fruit: 108, 125
   hydrochloric: 157, 239
   picric: 268
   tannic: 61, 184-185, 308
   uric: 117, 127
acid-forming foods: 121, 122, 135
acidity: 24, 74, 83, 122-124, 131, 258, 291, 294, 308
   superacidity: 307
acne: 283
Aconite: 235, 236
Adam: 179
adenoids: 70, 71
adjustments, spinal
   cervical area: 91
   1st cervical: 14, 22, 105, 106, 238
   2nd cervical: 14, 105, 175, 238, 297
   3rd cervical: 11, 14, 44, 100-102, 105, 238, 258, 296, 297
   4th cervical: 14
   5th cervical: 14, 297
   dorsal and cervical areas: 26, 91, 103, 198, 200, 212, 252, 296
   2nd dorsal: 296, 297
   3rd dorsal: 105, 175, 296, 297
   4th dorsal: 13, 105
   5th dorsal: 13, 101, 202
   6th dorsal: 12, 25, 101-102, 238, 250
   7th dorsal: 25, 250
   9th dorsal:11, 22, 24-26, 100-101, 105, 198, 250, 291
   10th dorsal: 281
   11th dorsal: 281
   lumbar axis: 44, 101, 238
   3rd lumbar: 44
   4th lumbar: 11, 44, 100, 105
   See lumbar
adolescence: 3-6
   See family; child care
adoption: 207

affection: 27
aging: 88, 94, 153, 155, 175
   See longevity
airplanes: 18
   (lighter than air machines)
Akashic records: 6-7
Alcaroid: 67, 128-129, 197
alcohol: 7, 9-10, 45, 87, 127, 143, 151, 187, 194-195, 198, 204, 252, 264, 268, 269, 290
   grain: 23, 45, 69, 91, 187, 194, 198, 290
   rubbing: 184
alcoholic beverages: 7-10
alcoholism: 268-269
ales: 8
   ginger ale: 9
alimentary canal: 13, 24-25, 46, 67, 69, 103, 146, 160-163, 165-166, 196, 204, 233-234, 236-237, 261, 264, 290, 296
Alka-Seltzer: 129
alkaline foods: 60, 123-125, 132, 142, 301
   alkaline properties: 165
alkalinity: 83, 85, 123-126, 165, 291
   alkaline reacting: 123, 125-126, 142, 192, 195, 301
alkalizer: 86, 129, 132, 160
allergy: 10-13, 238
almond: 108, 141
alum: 268
aluminum: 127, 128
America: 20
American Revolution: 21, 177
amnesia: 13-15
anaesthesia, counter effects from: 113
angels and archangels: 15-17, 190, 255
anger: 29-31, 242, 294
   See attitude and emotions
animals, prehistoric: 17-19
   animal-man: 201, 253
antiseptic: 43, 60, 67, 123, 160, 175-176, 191-192, 196, 198, 267, 290, 302
antiseptic solution: 60, 67, 123, 160, 176, 192, 196, 198, 267
anxiety: 28, 33, 45, 193, 199, 280
appendicitis: 166
apple: 108-109, 117, 121-122, 125-126, 132, 147,167, 194, 296, 299
   skins of cooked: 194
appliances: 19
   bulb applicator: 89, 156
   fountain syringe: 193
   hand machine: 89, 156, 176
   mechanical: 19, 97-98, 103,105, 261

radio-active appliance: 14, 237
sponge applicator: 234
violet ray (hand applicator): 89, 156,
   176, 193, 234, 281, 302-303
wet cell appliance: 99, 199
application: 5-7, 12-13, 19, 25-26, 33-34,
   37, 43, 48, 53, 55, 57, 59-60, 64, 79,
   82, 91, 93, 98, 128, 151, 157, 167, 174,
   175, 176, 178, 179, 180, 187, 189, 201,
   204, 212, 225, 226, 229, 232, 235, 236,
   245, 258, 259, 261, 270, 271, 272, 273,
   282, 283, 288, 294, 300, 308, 310, 311,
   312, 317
applications (medical): 12-13, 26, 43,
   59-60, 71, 89, 101, 103
Arabian: 19
archaeology, personal: 19-22
arches: 172
Arizona: 19
Armad-Heliel: 318
Arrowroot: 130
art: 241
   drawing: 22
artichoke, Jerusalem: 109-111, 135, 221-
   222, 250
   cooking instructions: 250
   growing instructions: 110
   indications for use: 221-222
ash, medicated: 157
aspirin: 62
assimilate: 8, 13, 57, 67, 72, 85, 86-87,
   112, 121, 130-131, 139, 141, 142, 145,
   147, 221, 315
associations: 13, 29, 31, 32, 47, 48, 56, 65,
   76, 78, 81, 93, 95, 150, 151, 178, 208,
   209, 226, 227, 231, 233, 248, 250, 252,
   255, 276, 288, 293, 295, 297, 309
asthma: 22-26
   asthmatic attacks: 13, 22
   asthmatic reactions: 22, 24
astringent: 88
astrological subjects: 41
   See also: sojourn, influences, urge
astrology: 5, 219, 312
atom: 33, 94, 96, 98, 154, 201
   See structure(s)
Atomic Iodine: 90
Atomidine: 43-44, 72, 90, 233, 246, 265,
   266, 267, 268, 303
   information and cautions: 43
attitude: 15, 30, 32-34, 37, 53, 63, 65, 96,
   124, 157, 202, 216, 228, 241, 242, 247,
   287, 298

and emotions: 27-29
healing: 200-203
spiritual: 23
See specific one
attune: 100, 104, 154, 201, 249, 257, 258,
   293, 305, 316
attunement of body: 258
automatic writing: 38-41, 260
awakening: 5, 18, 35, 82, 287, 298, 318
awareness: 53, 78, 154, 182, 201, 218,
   227, 229, 247, 270, 273-275, 288-289,
   314

bacillus: 264
balance:
   body: 83, 84, 85, 86, 90, 103, 114, 160,
     267, 280, 284, 285, 291
   life: 41-43
   medical: 25
   of foods: 60, 70,72
   precautions against colds: 83
baldness: 43-47
Balsam of Peru: 106
Balsam of Tolu In solution: 92
Balsam of White Pine: 23
   See Oil of White Pine
banjo: 243
Barak: 47-48, 178
baths: 89, 251-252, 268
   Epsom salts: 152
   for poison ivy: 265
   fume: 89
     See Physiotherapy
   Palmolive soap for breaking out: 300
   sweats: 251
B.C. Powders: 155
beans
   green: 174
   wax: 79
beauty: 7, 27, 34, 53, 169, 182, 188-189,
   190, 220, 227-228, 241, 244, 248, 249,
   294
beef juice: 111-113, 138
beets: 69, 116, 124, 147, 174
   tops: 135
beer: 8, 10
believe: 27, 36, 52, 96, 97, 149, 151, 184,
   218, 227, 254
Belladonna: 176
Belial: 52
   See devil
Benzosol: 23, 198
Benzoin (tincture of): 23, 70, 91, 184,

cure: 86-87
  precautions: 83-85
  susceptibility: 83
colitis (colon distress): 62
colon: 46, 62, 66-67, 103, 114, 152, 160, 162, 166, 216, 234, 237, 238, 261
  colonic: 62, 67, 68, 69, 70, 152-153, 160, 192, 237, 252, 262
color: 79-82
complexion: 87-90
conception: 124, 168, 240, 241, 243, 248, 315
congestion: 24, 71, 92, 104, 123-124, 126, 152, 166, 199, 236, 237, 261
conscience: 37, 151, 177, 180, 199
consciousness: 4, 7, 17, 31, 38, 39, 49, 64, 71, 78, 94, 95, 96, 157, 158, 167, 202, 218, 219, 225, 226, 227, 229, 232, 247, 249, 257, 260, 270, 273, 274, 275, 288, 289, 294, 295, 299, 305, 307, 314
  Christ: 4, 224, 315
  conscious activity: 84
  God: 273, 275
  mental: 232, 274 (Mind Is the Builder)
  physical: 95, 226, 232, 273, 274, 294, 315
  self-consciousness 184, 315
  superconscious: 100, 278
  unconsciousness: 95, 278
  universal: 7, 28, 82, 94, 95, 190, 217, 273, 315
consistency: 34, 150, 151, 229
constipation: 205, 252
  See colon: colonic; eliminations
control: 12, 29, 30, 42, 64, 68, 69, 70, 71, 73, 145, 149, 178, 182, 201, 206, 218, 244, 268, 280, 286, 303, 315
cooperation: 65, 84, 181, 211, 318
corn: 125, 133, 147
  bread: 110
  cakes: 263
  drink: 9
  starch: 143
cornmeal: 110, 120, 147
corns: 185
corn starch: 143
coughs and hiccoughs: 90-93
counseling: 272
cramps (at menstruation): 236
creation: 16, 93-95, 168, 180, 199, 242, 270
creativity: 272
  See Forces: creative

cremation: 95-96
  See burial
Creosote, rectified: 198
criticism: 31-32
cross: 17, 29, 49, 272
crude oil: 43, 194
Cuticura ointment: 245
cycles: 96-99, 301
cysts: 238-240

dandruff: 195
danger(s): 59, 72, 80, 272
David: 50, 53, 247
deafness: 100-105
  deaf-mutism: 99-100, 211
death: 256, 271, 295, 307
Deborah: 47-48
decisions: 11, 313
dentistry: 303
deodorant and powder: 105-106
devil: 52, 228, 259
diabetes (diabetic): 109, 110, 221
diaphragm area: 88, 92, 172, 200
diathermy: 12, 268
diet: 9, 25, 44, 46, 60, 62, 69, 73, 85-87, 89, 90, 102, 106-149, 159, 167, 171, 174, 180-181, 198, 201, 221, 235, 250-252, 262-264 266, 281, 296, 301, 303
  apple (cleansing): 108-109, 167
  balanced: 60, 70, 85, 109, 117, 120, 121, 125, 137, 144, 263
  blood poisoning (recovery): 58-61
  colds (prevention of): 83
  colon distress: 62
  convalescence (during): 147
  corrections in general elimination: 251
  diabetic: 109-110, 221
  easily assimilated for recovery period: 86, 112, 130-131
  gall duct draining (during): 101-102
  hemorrhoids: 203-205
  infants: 73-75, 242
  menopause (during): 235
  mental activity (in relation to): 148
  nasal catarrh: 69-70
  nursing mother: 114, 242
  pinworms: 262-264
  pregnancy: 135, 141, 242
digestive system: 13, 24, 33, 73, 108, 125, 162, 263, 296
  digestion: 8, 57-58, 72, 113, 115-117, 128-130, 135, 156

gall duct: 12, 66, 92, 101-102, 164
  stones: 66
ganglia: 101, 257
gargling: 191
gas: 112, 115, 129, 135, 290
  nature of: 255
gastric flow: 24, 112, 119, 125, 144, 196
  gastral centers: 297
gelatin: 102, 118, 136-137, 144, 174
genealogy: 167-168
genital system: 269
Gerber: 73-74, 131
germ: 83, 267, 268
  germicidal condition: 195
gestation: 24, 124, 301
glands: 11-12, 43-45, 47, 72, 90, 105, 109,
  119, 136, 145, 194, 225, 251, 267, 269,
  281, 301, 303
  organs of generation: 104
  Peyers glands: 281
  prostate: 152
  purifier: 44
  "the seven centers": 100, 270, 315
glasses
  bi-focals: 173
glycerin: 87, 90-91
Glyco-Thymoline: 13, 67, 123, 153, 161-
  162, 173-174, 191-192, 195-196, 237,
  290, 293, 296, 300, 302
Gobi land: 317
God's book of remembrance: 6
gold: 16, 19, 21, 99, 303, 304
  chloride of: 99
good: 6, 15, 28, 30-32, 39, 44, 51, 54, 64,
  80-82, 101, 150, 170, 183-184, 190,
  201-202, 205, 213, 218, 220, 224-225,
  228, 244, 254, 271, 275, 278, 313
gossip(er): 32, 36, 81
grace: 9, 31-32, 79, 97, 148, 214, 218, 226-
  227, 241, 255, 294
grape juice: 130, 251
  sugar: 143, 251
green peppers: 135
guardian angel(s): 15
gynecologist: 242

habits: 70-71, 203, 246
hair: 3, 43-45, 47, 74, 192-195
  color: 90, 193-195
  stimulate growth: 194
  superfluous: 89-90
halitosis: 195-197
Hannah: 241

harmony: 30-31, 53-54, 64, 78, 158, 169-
  170, 177, 189, 206-207, 210, 227, 244,
  285-286, 295, 318
hate: 32-34, 64, 188, 228, 231, 271, 294
hay fever (shots): 156, 197-198
headaches: 33, 92, 113, 236
  migraine: 237-238
head noises: 100, 102, 199-200
healing: 33, 47, 51, 55, 82, 91, 97, 106,
  149, 154, 180, 200-203, 213, 216, 258,
  271-272, 287
  magnetic healing: 180, 213
  through attitude: 200-203
health(y): 9, 46, 141, 156, 159, 171, 196,
  200-201, 214, 251, 258, 282, 287, 300
hearing: 100, 102-105, 218
  noises: 100, 102, 199-200
heart: 11, 30, 33, 59-60, 145-146, 233, 235,
  250-251, 307
  disorder: 33
  regularity: 44
  stimulant: 59-60
  stroke: 157
heaven: 42, 151, 202, 244, 294, 312
hell: 5, 54, 182, 244, 296, 312
hemorrhoids: 203-205
hepatic circulation: 24, 93, 127, 163,
  234, 281
  disturbed hepatic: 127
heredity: 167-170
hiccoughs: 90-92, 212
  cause of: 92
high blood pressure: 150-151
hired mourner: 47
hobbies: 205-206
hog lard: 44, 46
Holy Land: 49-50
holy women (the): 4, 47
home and marriage: 206-211
  See family
honey: 90-91, 110, 118-119, 144, 252,
  263, 280
Honey Charcoal Tablet: 282
hope: 6, 30, 36, 42, 50, 53, 63, 65, 93,
  151, 159, 170, 177, 189, 202, 216-217,
  227-228, 230, 241-242, 247, 270-271,
  275, 294-295
hot flushes: 11
humility: 34-35, 51
hydrophobia: 156
hydrotherapy: 88, 152-154, 237, 258,
  260-262, 278
hydrotherapist: 192

A.R.E. PRESS

Edgar Cayce (1877–1945) founded the non-profit Association for Research and Enlightenment (A.R.E.) in 1931, to explore spirituality, holistic health, intuition, dream interpretation, psychic development, reincarnation, and ancient mysteries—all subjects that frequently came up in the more than 14,000 documented psychic readings given by Cayce.

Edgar Cayce's A.R.E. provides individuals from all walks of life and a variety of religious backgrounds with tools for personal transformation and healing at all levels—body, mind, and spirit.

A.R.E. Press has been publishing since 1931 as well, with the mission of furthering the work of A.R.E. by publishing books, DVDs, and CDs to support the organization's goal of helping people to change their lives for the better physically, mentally, and spiritually.

In 2009, A.R.E. Press launched its second imprint, 4th Dimension Press. While A.R.E. Press features topics directly related to the work of Edgar Cayce and often includes excerpts from the Cayce readings, 4th Dimension Press allows us to take our publishing efforts further with like-minded and expansive explorations into the mysteries and spirituality of our existence without direct reference to Cayce specific content.

A.R.E. Press/4th Dimension Press
215 67th Street
Virginia Beach, VA 23451

Learn more at EdgarCayce.org. Visit ARECatalog.com to browse and purchase additional titles.

ARE PRESS.COM